WHITE LIBERALS IN TRANSITION

WHITE LIBERALS IN TRANSITION

Current Dilemmas of Ethnic Integration

Judith Caditz, Ph.D.
Immaculate Heart College
Los Angeles, California

S P Books Division of
SPECTRUM PUBLICATIONS, INC.
New York

Distributed by Halsted Press
A Division of John Wiley & Sons

New York   Toronto   London   Sydney

SPECTRUM PUBLICATIONS, INC.
86-19 Sancho Street, Holliswood, N.Y. 11423

Distributed solely by the Halsted Press division of John Wiley & Sons, Inc., New York

Library of Congress Cataloging in Publication Data

Caditz, Judith.
White liberals in transition.

   Bibliography: p.
   Includes index.
   1. Afro-Americans--Segregation. 2. School
integration--United States. 3. Afro-Americans--
Employment. 4. Afro-Americans--History. 5. U-
nited States--Race question. I. Title.
E185.615.C23   301.45'1'0973   76-21339
ISBN 0-470-15182-X

Preface

In this book I challenge the commonly held view that the source of opposition to the principles of the American Creed and racial integration lies primarily within the working class, lower class, or only among the poorly educated. Much social science literature rests on the assumption that the social location of opposition to social justice and equality of opportunity rests in the lower status rungs of society. Working class authoritarians are the opponents of civil liberties and civil rights, while the well-to-do are supporters of humanitarian causes. I found that many, though not all, well educated white liberals are consistent with their lower-class and working-class counterparts insofar as status threats—including job security, threats to prestige and style of life, and threats to their children's class of destination—affect their attitudes regarding racial integration.

First, I begin my analysis with an examination of some major current issues concerning racial integration as a means of attaining equal opportunity in education, employment, and housing. Many of these issues obstruct or make unclear the application of the principles embodied in the American Creed. In Chapter I, I explore city-surburban mergers of school districts designed to make integration possible where minorities reside in inner city areas and whites reside in the outlying suburbs. Do metropolitan area plans strip away power from various ethnic communities desirous of maintaining community control, developing their own educational programs which include their own history and culture, and employing their own administrative personnel in locally controlled programs? A look at "white flight" is important where resegregation occurs and effectively sidesteps integration plans, such as those created by school busing. The benefits derived from ethnic integration and its underlying rationale are explored. Will minority students achievement be raised by attendance at white middle-class schools? What benefits accrue to white students in integrated settings? The current debate surrounding student school assignments, special admissions, quotas, and affirmative action programs is discussed. Do they implement equality of opportunity by affording assurance of racial balance where a proportionate representation of minorities and women are included in educational and employment settings *on the basis of* race, color, creed, and sex? Or, alternately, are opportunities better guaranteed where assignments to schools and jobs are made *irrespective of* race, color, creed, and sex? Do antiintegration attitudes in specific settings cloak prejudices by the use of statements seemingly consistent with the American Creed?

Second, I direct attention to my study of a random sample of white liberals who were interviewed about their attitudes toward six interracial situations: (1) busing in schools for the purpose of ending de facto segregation; (2) the entrance of blacks into occupational fields filled mainly by whites; (3) blacks moving into predominantly white neighborhoods; (4) the quota system as the basis for college admission to obtain a proportionate representation of minorities; (5) rentals to blacks in white-occupied apartment buildings; and (6) hiring of blacks. In this study, white liberals are defined by their general belief in racial integration and by their membership in an organization supportive of civil rights. They believe in nondiscrimination, fair housing, fair employment, quality education for all, and diffusion of voting rights. They believe in eradication of prejudicial attitudes, discriminatory behavior, and institutionalized racism. In Chapter II, the social basis of Jewish liberalism and of Protestant liberalism is traced.

In Chapter III, a descriptive analysis of current dilemmas of the white liberal is presented. The focus is primarily on discrepancies between general principles and specific beliefs. Attitudes versus attitudes are scrutinized, rather than attitudes versus behavior. Generally, four types of attitudes emerge. First, favorable attitudes indicate support of school busing, quotas in college admissions, rentals to blacks in white-occupied apartment buildings, blacks moving into a predominantly white neighborhood, and blacks entering various occupational fields. Second, conditional attitudes demonstrate support of an integration procedure, as long as certain limits are met. One may affirm support for neighborhood integration, as long as the minorities moving in are middle-class persons. One may endorse school busing, as long as only the smartest minority students are bused to predominantly white school districts. One may contend that hiring minorities is acceptable, only if all job requirements and professional standards are satisfied. Third, ambivalent attitudes often take the form of role conflicts. Parents are caught between the role of liberal integrationists, where they support all forms of desegregation, and the role of parents, where they do not want to send their children to ghetto areas because of fears of physical danger or of an inferior education. Fourth, unfavorable attitudes indicate opposition to school busing, apartment rentals to blacks, or minorities in one's occupational field. These unfavorable attitudes exist side-by-side a general belief in the principles of equality of opportunity for all.

Chapters IV and V bring us to some reasons that a segment of white liberals is ambivalent, affirms role conflicts, or endorses a decidedly anti-integration viewpoint. Those who are status threatened, who perceive status dimensions as important, who are generally status conscious, or who have been very mobile, stationary, or downwardly mobile in occupational status find themselves in ambivalent positions regarding quotas in the colleges, school busing, apartment rentals to blacks, and blacks in their neighborhoods or occupational settings. Furthermore, there is an examination of the relationship between ethnic involvement and attitudes toward the six interracial situations. Interethnic conflicts, such as those between blacks and chicanos, Jews and blacks, and Chinese and others in the San Francisco community will be discussed. Ethnic groups are status groups striving for prestige and a certain style of life which is unique and distinct. Protection of group boundaries is generated not only by membership in organizations representative of the ethnic group, but also by interacting primarily within the ethnic group. Ethnic identifiers engaging in communal relationships are more ambivalent about the situations than nonidentifiers.

In Chapter VI, I present a microsociological analysis of the experience of dissonance and role conflicts, and the mechanisms of dissonance reduction. Typically, people who express attitudes inconsistent with their general principles will experience dissonance and will be compelled to reduce its effects by adopting certain modes of reduction, such as "differentiation," "denial," "avoidance," "categorization," and "reaffirmation" of a belief in the general principles.

Finally, the issue of integration in light of ideological commitments of those in the black power movement as well as white liberals is reviewed. I suggest new definitions of liberalism regarding interethnic relations and ethnic integration. Hopefully, a realistic appraisal of the attitudinal dilemmas of white liberals will help lift the screens which shield the issues surrounding college quotas, school busing, and neighborhood and occupational integration

Parts of the study I report here are in print in sociological journals: "Ambivalence Toward Integration: The Sequence of Response to Six Interracial Situations," *The Sociological Quarterly*, Winter, 1975; "Jewish Liberals in Transition," *Sociology and Social Research*, April, 1975; "Dilemmas Over Racial Integration: Status Consciousness vs. Direct Threat," *Sociological Inquiry*, Winter, 1975; "Ethnic Identification, Interethnic Contact, and Belief in Integration Among White Liberals," *Social Forces*, Spring, 1976; and "Coping With the American Dilemma; Dissonance Reduction Among White Liberals," *Pacific Sociological Review*, 1977.

I wish to thank Ralph H. Turner and Leo Kuper for their helpful suggestions on an earlier version of the portion of the book based on the study of white liberals.

Judith Caditz
Los Angeles, California
November, 1975

Contents

CHAPTER 1

Is There an American Dilemma?

White liberal supporters of racial and ethnic integration are increasingly finding themselves in attitudinal dilemmas or retreating from their general principles when confronted by interracial situations. This book examines this social phenomenon and its underlying conditions. Why do white liberals usually endorsing fair housing legislation and members of Fair Housing Councils experience attitudinal and behavioral dilemmas when confronted with blacks moving into their neighborhoods? Why are they in conflict when posed with the threat of the economic loss they might encounter if blacks move into an apartment house they own? Why do white liberals affirming general principles of integration in the schools retreat when there is implementation of a busing program in their school districts? Why do those desiring to make up for inequities in educational and occupational opportunities react negatively to affirmative action programs and perceive them as affording unfair preferential treatment for minorities and women? Why do believers in equal employment opportunities become ambivalent about their basic ideology when blacks enter their occupational fields or places of work?

Many cite Gunnar Myrdal's thesis of the "American Dilemma" when they perceive gaps between *ideal* principles and *real* attitudes and behaviors. Essentially, Myrdal states that the American Creed is a pervasive ideology within American culture and calls for equality, social justice, freedom and opportunity for all, and racial tolerance. Yet, there are many deviations from these principles in everyday life. This inconsistency between the principles of the American Creed and the everyday, real discrepancies produces the American Dilemma.

Frank R. Westie's empirical test shows that most of his sample of residents of Indianapolis in 1957 do, indeed, support the American Creed and the consequent Dilemma. People hold general valuations which state the major premises of the American Creed and also hold specific valuations about interracial interactions. Valuation-inconsistencies are created and are resolved by enlisting rationalizations existing in culturally shared beliefs. Westie suggests that a general valuation may be the goal that all Americans should have equality of opportunity. A specific valuation may be that blacks and whites should not attend the same school. Rationalization of this inconsistency may be the culturally defined belief that "Negroes are inherently less capable intellectually than whites."

Certainly, favorable attitudes toward racial integration are consistent with the American Creed, since they rest upon the assumption that integration will lead to equality of opportunity and social justice. In 1966, Paul B. Sheatsley reported that endorsement of racial integration was the majority view among whites in the North, upheld by about half the white population nationwide, and favored in areas where it was practiced in the South. More recently, a 1975 Gallup Poll revealed that school integration was accepted in the 70s more than in the 60s. In 1963, 78 percent of Southern white parents and 33 percent of Northern white parents opposed sending their children to schools in which half the enrollment was black. By 1975, 38 percent in the South and 24 percent in the North objected to such schooling arrangements. In contrast, however was the negative view toward school busing for purposes of achieving racially balanced schools. Nationally, only 4 percent of the population endorsed school busing for integration goals.[1]

Recent nationwide events indicate that the American Creed is not a reality in all segments of American society. Twenty years after the 1954 *Brown v. Board of Education* decision, communities across the country persist in resisting efforts to integrate the schools. In the *Brown* decision, the United States Supreme Court—under the equal protection clause of the Fourteenth Amendment to the U.S. Constitution—held that the principle of "separate but equal" is invalid, that racially separate schools are inherently unequal, and that black children receive education in inferior schools.

Indeed, equality in education by school integration seemed workable in the example set by the Berkeley school district. In the fall of 1968, Berkeley became the first city in the United States with a population of over 100,000 to achieve racial integration in the schools by busing. Zones were created which cut across socio-economic and racial areas. For each zone, black and other minority pupils from the flatlands were bused from kindergarten through the third grade to schools at the city's upper elevations which were predominantly white. From the fourth grade through the sixth grades, white students were transported to the predominantly minority areas. Thus, a two-way busing plan integrated the community which included 50 percent white, 40 percent black, and 10 percent Oriental students.

In 1970, Superior Court Judge Alfred Gitelson in *Crawford v. Board of Education of the City of Los Angeles* ruled that the Los Angeles City school system must create racial and ethnic integration. He used a 15 percent formula in setting guidelines for desegregation, endorsing the rule that when its minority enrollment is 15 percent above or below the minority enrollment of the entire school district, a school is considered racially imbalanced. Gitelson affirmed that "The segregation. . .in Board's schools was not, is not, de facto. It is de jure." Because the school board had not made a good faith effort to integrate and had selected school sites and set attendance zones knowing that desegregation would not be facilitated, segregation was de jure. Gitelson's decision reasons that segregation restricts the aspirations of children and creates lack of confidence so that as adults they will be less likely to participate in the mainstream of American society. In segregated schools, black and Mexican-American children do not achieve as well as black, Mexican-American, or Anglo children in integrated schools. Although Gitelson did not order massive busing to desegregate the schools, citizens perceived that transporting students would be the only method by which the court decision could be carried out. Shortly after Gitelson handed down his decision, his opponents for reelection to Superior Court Judgeship mustered votes for William P. Kennedy, using the busing issue and indicating that Kennedy was not in favor of busing for achieving racial balance. Gitelson lost the election. The Gitelson decision was overturned by the California Court of Appeals in 1975. In January of 1976, the California Supreme Court took the case under submission after hearing arguments concerning segregation intent and the remedy, the role of the Court in school desegregation, and the importance of percentages in determining racial imbalance.

Although school bus transportation has been used for many years for children attending private and parochial schools, its use for integration engenders adamant protests. In 1972, it was estimated that 40 percent of the students in public schools in the United States were transported at public cost, but only a small fraction rode buses for purposes of integrating the schools.[2] Yet in Selma, as well as in Boston, black children have been bused to and from school to maintain racially segregated schools, oftentimes riding as much as 50 miles away from their local neighborhood schools which limited attendance to white students.

In contrast, busing as a means of desegregating schools is being obstructed in the South, East, North, and West. Violence in Pontiac in 1971, Boston in 1974 and 1975, and in Louisville in 1975 shows the intensity of resistance to busing. In Pontiac, angry whites—including the former grand dragon of the Michigan Ku Klux Klan—participated in the destruction of ten buses. A school boycott ensued, and picketing and other disturbances forced the General Motors manufacturing complex to shut down.

U.S. District Judge W. Arthur Garrity, Jr.'s Boston busing plan was challenged, as national guardsmen, police and federal marshals were called to ward off violence at the beginning of the school year. Parents opposing busing peacefully and prayerfully marched in South Boston, Charlestown, and Hyde Park. Councilwoman Louise Day Hicks spoke before many citizens affirming opposition to busing. Parents were concerned about their children's safety and whites demanded their civil rights. ROAR (Restore Our Alienated Rights) organized white disapproval of busing, while the West Roxbury Information Center was one of several neighborhood groups permitting freedom of speech against busing. President Ford made public statements against forced busing, while, at the same time, he opposed the use of violence to protest school busing. A court order prevented the gathering of groups of more than three persons near schools. Enrollments dropped between 1974 and 1975, as whites sent their children to private and parochial schools. "Look at the nigger" was shouted as teenagers and parents watched a burning effigy. One parent said,

> We raise our children right. I feel sorry for these black kids, because they're not raised right. They're brought up in lower classes and some of them are fifteen years old and they are still in the fifth grade—or they ought to be. I'm sorry, but I don't want my kids going to school with them. I'm afraid, and I've got to look out for my children.[3]

In response to a NAACP suit to close South Boston High School, Judge Garrity placed the school in receivership in December of 1975. Assessing that the Boston School Committee had failed to promote peaceful desegregation, he set into motion a plan by which the school administration would report directly to the Court.

The Irish were accused of having a "Belfast mentality," and busing created friction between poor Irish and poor blacks, while middle-class white liberals looked on.

In Louisville, the opening of the 1975 school year showed community opposition to a court-ordered busing plan drawn by U.S. Judge James F. Gordon in compliance with the 6th Circuit Court of Appeals request for a city-county desegregation unit. The city, known as a "model city" in 1956 because of its voluntary student transfer plan, has become resegregated since whites used the transfers to avoid attendance at predominantly black schools. The merger of Louisville and Jefferson County schools provided the basis for desegregating 165 schools. To control disorderly conduct and public unrest, national guardsmen, state, county, and city officers were enlisted to insure community safety as schools opened. Antibusing rallies, antiintegration signs, and burning school buses were indicators of vehement protest against busing. Some gas station owners, fearing loss of business from regular customers, refused to sell to school bus drivers. The Ku Klux Klan organized antibusing demonstrations. As in Boston, a court order prohibited protests near public schools and prevented gathering and assembling.

In the fall of 1975, President Ford cancelled his planned trip to Louisville because of local disturbances related to school busing. He affirmed, "There has been some turmoil as a result of court-ordered forced busing to achieve racial balance in the public schools and I think you all know that I have consistently and vigorously opposed court-ordered, forced busing to achieve racial balance. I think there's a better answer to quality education."[4]

Reportedly, blue-collar workers were the major opponents of school busing in Louisville, and they engaged in friction with lower-class blacks, while middle- and upper middle-class whites remained silent, though ambivalent.

Working-class resistance to busing is not only reported in Louisville and Boston, but also in Richmond, California and Gary, Indiana. Although questioning the analysis of working-class authoritarianism, Lillian B. Rubin indicates the unity among conservatives and their ultimate defeat of an integration plan using busing endorsed by a coalition of indecisive white liberals with black leaders Schools in Richmond had become more segregated after the 1968 decision of the liberal school board to bus some black children out of overcrowded schools. The absolute numbers of children decreased, and the proportion of black students rose as whites moved out of the area. Unification of the school district, including the districts of Pinole-Hercules, Richmond, San Pablo, and Sheldon, presented new barriers to desegregating elementary schools. During World War II large numbers of Southern whites and blacks came to work in the Richmond shipyards. Friction between blacks and whites had always been sharply antagonistic. Craft unions prohibited the entrance of blacks who suffered from severe job discrimination. After the war, many whites moved to the suburban developments outside the city. Unification brought together three primary groups with different political philosophies, including blacks, working-class and lower middle-class whites, and upper middle-class whites. Conservatives mustered full support among their working-class and lower middle-class ranks, and in finally gaining control of the school board, prevented school desegregation. No issue was felt as sharply as that of busing in the schools, and support for George C. Wallace in the 1968 presidential election was highest where sentiment against busing was the strongest. Also, opposition to open housing as indicated by a favorable vote on Proposition 14 in the 1964 election was highest in the San Pablo district, a stronghold of conservative working-class people.

Blue-collar workers in Gary, Indiana, showed substantial support for George C. Wallace in the 1968 presidential election. According to a study conducted by Thomas F. Pettigrew and Robert T. Riley, Wallace supporters were typically blue-collar workers having high school educations and an annual family income between $7,500 and $10,000. Wallace made clear anti-busing statements during his campaign, capturing the vote of those threatened by school integration—especially by the means of busing. In the Florida primary, Wallace received 41.5 percent of the vote, and in the Michigan primary 56 percent of the total vote.

The thesis of "working-class authoritarianism" has been extensively applied in the study of prejudice, discrimination, and racism. Through cross cultural techniques and a synthesis of many psychological, political, and sociological studies, Seymour Martin Lipset points to a stratum of society not upholding civil liberties:

> The poorer strata everywhere are more liberal or leftist on economic issues; they favor more welfare state measures, higher wages, graduated income taxes, support of trade-unions, and so forth. But when liberalism is defined in non-economic terms—as support of civil liberties, internationalism, etc.—the correlation is reversed. The more well-to-do are more liberal, the poorer are more intolerant.[5]

Documentation of working-class authoritarianism rests on the studies of Theodore W. Adorno, et al. who measured deeply rooted personality factors associated with ethnocentrism, anti-Semitism, and tendencies to adopt fascistic beliefs. Rigid personality structure, power orientation in interpersonal relationships, lack of love in early childhood, and concern with family status surface in ethnic prejudice. Attributed to the working class are traits of suggestibility, antiintellectualism, belief in the concrete and immediate, and inability to take a complex world view. Such traits result in participation in extremist political movements and opposition to civil liberties and civil rights.

In a critique that challenges these findings, Herbert H. Hyman and Paul B. Sheatsley demonstrate that prejudice is related to the degree of formal education rather than to an authoritarian personality emerging in the family milieu. Certainly, the thesis that the lower the formal education, the greater the prejudice and the less the support for desegregation is well documented in empirical studies. However, since the degree of formal education is generally highly correlated with occupational and socio-economic status, the working class or lower class will be most likely to oppose desegregation.

At least tentatively, these observations and social science studies lead to the conclusion that middle-class and upper middle-class persons with high formal education and high socio-economic status will be likely to favor racial integration and busing as a means of desegregating the schools.

METROPOLITAN AREA MERGERS vs. COMMUNITY CONTROL

City-suburban merger of school districts as a strategy for eliminating racial imbalance is being tested in the courts. The first test case came before the U.S. Supreme Court in 1973, after the 1972 court order by U.S. District Judge Robert H. Herhigh, Jr. to merge the Richmond, Virginia school district, totalling 65 percent black students, and neighboring Chesterfield and Henrico Counties, with 90 percent white students. Plans were being designed for busing 78,000 students, when the U.S. Supreme Court found itself in a stalemate. Due to Justice Powell's disqualification because he had been a member of the Richmond and Virginia school boards before he was a Supreme Court Justice, the Court was divided, with four justices upholding the legality of the merger and four finding no legal or constitutional basis to uphold such a decision.

The second test case centered on Detroit. In contrast to a merger approval by both a District Court in 1972, and an Appellate Court in 1973, the U.S. Supreme Court, in July of 1974, rejected plans for the merger of the Detroit city schools with 53 independent suburban school districts creating a new metropolitan area unit. The majority ruled that there was no precedent or constitutional principle for the Court to uphold city-suburban consolidation. Further, it held that the Court did not find any racially discriminatory acts on the part of the suburban or state school districts. De jure segregation existed only in the Detroit city schools. Therefore, the majority opinion in *Milliken v. Bradley* stated,

> Thus, an inter-district remedy might be in order where the racially dis-
> criminatory acts of one or more school districts caused racial segregation
> in an adjacent district, or where district lines have been deliberately drawn
> on the basis of race. In such circumstances an inter-district remedy would
> be appropriate to eliminate the inter-district segregation directly caused by
> the constitutional violation. Conversely, without an inter-district effect,
> there is no constitutional wrong calling for an inter-district remedy.

The reasoning of the Court included the concepts that local community
leadership in the operation of schools is a primary historical tradition in
public education in the United States, and that federal judges could not step
into school district matters by disregarding established school boundaries.
The Court also held that changing the base to "super school" districts inter-
rupts quality educational processes. Furthermore, massive transportation and
financial problems would be the outcome of setting up multi-district units.

The U.S. Supreme Court's judgement is a challenge to civil rights leaders
who advocate the metropolitan area technique as the only way of attaining
and maintaining racial balance in schools. Also, it is counter to the 1972
District Court's argument that "school district lines are simply matters of
political convenience and may not be used to deny constitutional rights"
and the 1973 Appellate Court's concurrence that only by crossing existent
political boundaries can desegregation be a reality in Detroit's schools.

In a dissenting view, Justice Thurgood Marshall asserted that the black
children of Detroit will continue to receive a "separate and inherently unequal education," and, "In the short run, it may seem to be the easier course
to allow our great metropolitan areas to be divided up each into two cities,
one white, the other black. But it is a course, I predict, our people will ulti-
mately regret."

The pace of desegregation in the city of Detroit has been slowed by U.S.
District Judge Robert E. Demascio's 1975 ruling that prevented massive city-
wide busing, except as a last resort, in a school system which has 71.5 percent
black students and 26.4 percent white students.

A contrasting opinion emerged in a third test case. On November 17,
1975, the U.S. Supreme Court, in a one-line opinion, upheld the three judge
federal district court decision calling for the black school district in Wilming-
ton, Delaware, to integrate with white schools in suburban New Castle
County.

Counter to the strategy of city-suburban mergers is that of community
control, where decentralization of large school district units into small units
takes place. At issue in the teacher strikes during 1967 and 1968 in Ocean
Hill-Brownsville was community control of public schools as opposed to
district centralization. The policy of local control rests on the ideology that

the public has the democratic right to determine educational programs, curricula, hiring, and allocating the use of funds for education in its school district. Moreover, community control rests upon the tenet that quality education is rooted in the people having the right to determination of the values and ideals, as well as the specific subjects taught to their own children. Rooted in these beliefs are the minority communities' concerns that the history, struggles, and contributions of their people to American society, so long neglected in courses and textbooks, are included in educational programs. The rationale for community control argues that minorities must have the right for self-respect, dignity, and active participation in school policies. Only through ethnic groups' involvement in their schools can their children be guaranteed quality education.

The Ocean Hill-Brownsville confrontation polarized the community into two main groups. Ironically, a strange alliance emerged that pitted the radical left, black poor, and antiintegrationist conservatives against white liberal professionals. The certified professionals were largely New Deal liberals holding a general belief in racial integration, compensatory education programs, and a dedicated desire to help minorities catch up in their low educational achievements as compared with white middle- and upper middle-class students.

When the Ocean Hill-Brownsville community school board, in May, 1968, ordered the transfer of 13 teachers, 5 assistant principals and 1 principal to the central district headquarters for reassignment, the United Federation of Teachers (the largest teachers' union in the United States) charged violation of due process, based on the Fourteenth Amendment to the U.S. Constitution. Teachers, well-rooted in the system before the creation of local community control, were threatened in their job security and their civil liberties. Furthermore, these teachers believed in the principle that "separate schools are inherently inferior" and reiterated their belief in racial integration. The UFT charged,

> Breaking the school system up into 20 to 100 districts is a segregationist move. It leads to ethnic and racial domination of particular districts. This is apartheid education for living in an apartheid world. This is the kind of education that leads to Watts and Newark, to hate and violence, to crime and chaos. . .

> *Decentralization* is both necessary and inevitable. But it should not mean destructive fragmentation of the City. The number of local school districts should be kept under 15 in order to reduce administrative costs and to insure the possibility of *Integration*. . .The Coleman Report and the Civil Rights Commission Report show that what children learn from each other and their social interaction in the classroom setting is a more important variable in academic success than textbooks (or teachers). . .[6]

A major feature of the Ocean Hill-Brownsville conflict over local control and decentralization was the charge of black anti-Semitism and Jewish racism. Although 70 percent of the teachers were white, and 50 percent of those were Jewish, a composite group of white, black, Jewish and non-Jewish leaders advertized in the *New York Times* protesting focus on Jewish-black friction as the cause of the problems in Ocean Hill-Brownsville.[7] Indeed, the New York Civil Liberties Union argued that "The UFT is trying to pin responsibility for the anti-white and anti-Semitic sentiments in these leaflets on the OHB decentralization program. This is a smear tactic reminiscent of the days of Senator Joseph McCarthy."[8]

In contrast, in 1970, Louis Harris and Bert E. Swanson found that a common solidarity existed among Jews and blacks after the disturbances in Ocean Hill-Brownsville. Each perceived the other as being objects of discrimination in American society. Blacks in Manhattan, the Bronx, Queens, and Brooklyn perceived discrimination against Jews more than their white Catholic, Puerto Rican or white Protestant counterparts. Similarly, Jews, especially the college educated, perceived discrimination against blacks more than their non-Jewish counterparts.

The ideology of the black power movement—as elaborated by Stokely Carmichael and Charles V. Hamilton—is consistent with the efforts for community control among blacks in Ocean Hill-Brownsville. Asserting an ideology of self-identification and self-determination, they contend that blacks should seek an "effective share in the total power of the society," rather than being the victims of domination and exploitation. Addressing themselves to the question of racial integration in the schools, they affirm,

> The goal is not to take black children out of the black community and expose them to white middle-class values; the goal is to build and strengthen the black community.

> "Integration" also means that black people must give up their identity, deny their heritage. . .The fact is that integration, as traditionally articulated, would abolish the black community. The fact is that what must be abolished is not the black community, but the dependent colonial status that has been inflicted upon it.[9]

Although black power advocates and outspoken white segregationists appear to be similar in their opposition to racial integration, they diverge in that they represent two distinct ideologies. The ideology of black power affirms separateness as the means of attaining economic, social, and political equality, and of instilling positive self-concepts in the identities of black people. In contrast, the ideology of white segregationists affirms separateness as a method of "keeping blacks in their place" and of keeping races apart because of the alleged inferiority of blacks and other minorities.

Resistance rooted in ethnic enclaves and their adherence to the maintenance of cultural pluralism rather than integration became visible in the implementation of a court-ordered integration plan requiring busing of students throughout the city of San Francisco. In the fall of 1971, U.S. District Judge Stanley A. Weigel's order for integration was set into motion. The ethnic breakdown of the city at that time included 35 percent Anglo, 28 percent Negro, 15 percent Chinese and 13.6 percent Spanish surnamed children. Not only did resistance to busing emerge among those forming the Concerned Parents Association, but also among the Chinese community of San Francisco, the largest Oriental community outside the Orient. The Chinese engaged in a large boycott of public schools when desegregation and busing started in 1971.

Large numbers of Chinese parents established Freedom Schools, in which their children could continue to be educated in their own neighborhood schools, and in which Chinese customs, language, arts, and history would be perpetuated. Oftentimes these schools were staffed by uncredentialed part-time teachers, and a small fee was charged because many Chinese could not afford large financial resources to support such schools. The Chinese Six Companies, a federation of family associations traditionally having great influence in Chinatown, gave financial assistance to the schools.

The Chinese feared the breakdown of family ties and weakening of respon- .sibilities fundamental to Chinese culture. Many charged the Chinese with racism, since they also feared their shy children's being hurt by physically stronger and aggressive black children in schools near the Chinese community. Reportedly, some Chinese feared that blacks and Latins were inferior intellectually.

Ironically, many in the Chinese community had been victims of forced segregation since the early days of Chinese immigration to California. As late as 1947, (when it was repealed) there was a California law instituting the segregation of the Chinese people. The schools to be desegregated included the Commodore Stockton School, originally called Oriental School, which was at one time the only public school to which Chinese students were permitted attendance.

Several non-English speaking Chinese students brought suit against the San Francisco Unified School District for its failure to establish a program to teach English to some 1800 Chinese students who could not read textbooks, understand the teachers and the classroom discussions, and were therefore denied equal educational opportunities. They argued that the district's failure to establish special English instruction classes for these students was in violation of the equal protection clause of the Fourteenth Amendment to the U.S. Constitution and Section 601 of the Civil Rights Act of 1964. The class action suit, entitled *Lau v. Nichols,* was initially heard in the Federal District Court and appealed to the U.S. Ninth Circuit Court of Appeals. Both courts held that the constitutional rights of Chinese-speaking students had not been violated. However, in reversing the Court of Appeals, the U.S. Supreme Court decided on January 21, 1974, that the school district had violated Section 601 of the Civil Rights Act which bans discrimination based on race, color, or national origin in any program receiving federal financial assistance.

"WHITE FLIGHT"

Resegregated schools often result from "en masse flight of the whites," where white families move out of a community with racially integrated schools, or where whites send their children to private or parochial schools. The Inglewood, California, school district stopped crosstown busing for school integration in 1975 and returned to the neighborhood school arrangement. Superior Judge Max F. Deutz, who first ordered busing for integration in 1970, said "as a practical matter we are now busing black children from predominantly black schools to other predominantly black schools." When busing was first ordered, the city of Inglewood had a school composition of 62 percent white and 38 percent minority students. Since the original integration of 17 schools, the student population has become 80 percent black, Mexican-American, and Asian American. Reportedly, the city of Inglewood is still predominantly white, but the schools contain primarily minority students, since some whites send their children to private schools and others are older people without school age children.

The uneasiness of "white flight" in Pasadena is a constant issue among opponents of busing on the Board of Education and among citizens protesting busing. Anglo student enrollments had steadily dropped from 61 percent of the district's total student body in 1968 to 54 percent in 1970, 47 percent in 1972, and 40 percent in 1975.[10] Headlines such as "Pasadena Tells Plan to Alter Integration Ordered by Court: Elimination of 'Forced' Busing Would Be Accomplished by Returning District to Neighborhood School Concept" appeared in the *Los Angeles Times.*[11] Claiming that forced busing would not work, Henry Marcheschi, Pasadena Board of Education president, confirmed that the busing program does not always bring school racial balance—five schools in 1973 had enrollments of over 50 percent black.[12]

In the 1963 case of *Jackson v. Pasadena School District,* the California

Supreme Court ruled that the Pasadena School District must alleviate racial imbalance caused by de facto segregation from housing patterns. The court held that if it could be shown that the schools were racially segregated, the plaintiff could compel the Pasadena School District to permit him to transfer to another school. This rule is valid even if segregation were not an overt act of the school board. In 1970, U.S. District Judge Manuel L. Real ordered desegregation of 32 schools at all grade levels declaring that no single school could have a majority of students who were members of a racial minority group. Moreover, desegregation must cover teacher assignments, planned school construction, and hiring and promotional practices. Judge Real affirmed that the issue was not de facto segregation, and that in the 1954 Supreme Court ruling, it was only opponents of the decision that applied the "de facto" and "de jure" segregation labels. At the time of the 1970 court order, the composition of the student body was 58 percent white, 30 percent black, and 11.7 percent Mexican-American, Oriental and other minorities.[13] Of the district's 30,600 students, half were to be bused to achieve desegregation. The maximum distance any students would be bused was eight and a half miles from home. Children were assigned to a school within walking distance of their homes for one-half of their elementary school career.

Many times since Judge Real's integration order there were attempts to alter it in some way. Although all efforts have failed, there are strong antibusing sentiments in Pasadena. The initial effort in 1970 to recall prointegration and probusing school board members failed. Later, new school board members were elected on the basis of their clear antibusing stands. In October of 1975, Judge Real opposed enrollments in "fundamental schools," set up to stress the three Rs, patriotism and discipline, until studies showed whether these schools placed a burden on minority students to be bused to achieve racial balance. However, in December of 1975, U.S. Supreme Court Justice William Rehnquist granted the Pasadena Board of Education a stay from Judge Real's order to restore Audubon Primary School, a fundamental school, to a regular educational program.

On November 11, 1975, the U.S. Supreme Court granted the petition of the Pasadena Board of Education for hearing on the Pasadena desegregation situation. The school board will have a chance to indicate its reasons that busing to eliminate school segregation does not work. Dr. Henry Myers, 1975 school board president says, "It has been completely counterproductive and we have far more polarization between races than before."[14] With whites representing 40.9 percent, blacks 41.6 percent, and other minorities 18 percent of the school population in 1975, the issue of whether Judge Real's order that no school in the district have a "majority of any minority students" is at stake. The question raised is whether school boards must continuously shift student assignments around in order to comply with percentages to attain racial balance. *Pasadena City Board v. Spangler and United States* will have implications throughout the nation for communities showing "white flight," for school boards, for desegregation plans, and for the role of the courts in issues concerning school desegregation.

"White flight" coupled with court rejection of city-suburban mergers in favor of the neighborhood school concept and community control paint a bleak picture for supporters of racial balance in the schools. Nationwide, by the mid 1960s, 80 percent of white children were attending public schools which were at least 90 percent white, while 65 percent of all black students attended schools in which at least 90 percent of the pupils were black.[15]

According to the 1967 U.S. Commission on Civil Rights report, *Racial Isolation in the Public Schools,* some of the cities showing 100 percent of white students attending predominantly white schools are Mobile, Tuscaloosa, Tallahassee, Augusta, Atlanta, and cities in Mississippi, North Carolina, and South Carolina. Some cities showing over 80 percent of white students attending predominantly white schools include Los Angeles, Richmond (California), East St. Louis, Springfield, Omaha, Buffalo, Cleveland, Portland, Houston, and Seattle. In seventy-five school systems across the country, blacks attended majority black schools.

In the 1970s, urban concentration of minority school children is revealed in New York City where 70 percent of the school children were nonwhite or Puerto Rican,[16] and in Baltimore, New Orleans, Atlanta, Newark and Chicago, where over 50 percent of the school children were black. In Washington, D.C., 95 percent of the public school children were black.[17] In cities such as Detroit, it is predicted that by 1992, as the white exodus to the suburbs increasingly continues, the city population will be all black.

BENEFITS DERIVED FROM ETHNIC INTEGRATION

The philosophical rationale favoring school desegregation rests upon certain assumptions, some of which have been tested by studies of the quality of educational processes, teacher dedication and attitudes, and children's achievement in desegregated compared with segregated school settings. The 1954 *Brown* decision rests upon the belief that children in inferior schools had feelings of inferiority which impaired their motivation to learn. The Court affirmed that segregated public schools result in a "a tendency to retard the educational and mental development of Negro children and to deprive them of some of the benefits they would receive in a racially integrated school system."

A major study in 1967 by James S. Coleman et al., *Equality of Educational Opportunity in the Public Schools,* substantiated these early court findings. Where the greatest educational disadvantage exists, such as in the South and the Southwest, school effects on student achievements and desires to learn are negligible. The report concludes,

> Taking all these results together, one implication stands out above all: That schools bring little influence to bear on a child's achievement that is independent of his background and general social context; and that this very lack of an independent effect means that the inequalities imposed on children by their home, neighborhood, and peer environment are carried along to become the inequalities with which they confront adult life at the end of school. For equality of educational opportunity through the schools must imply a strong effect of schools that is independent of the child's immediate social environment, and that strong independent effect is not present in American schools.[18]

Another investigation of student motivation and achievement, and their relationship to integrated schools was the 1967 documentation entitled *Racial Isolation in the Public Schools.* In many ways it corroborated the findings of the report by Coleman and his colleagues. It showed different backgrounds affect students' aspirations for college, and disadvantaged students are unlikely to find encouragement or examples among their peer groups for academic achievement. It affirms that "Where the majority of students have low achievement, others will be likely to follow suit."[19] Furthermore, it found that racial composition of the classroom, by itself, affected learning, in that "disadvantaged Negro students perform better when they are in a class with a majority of similarly disadvantaged white students than when they are in a class with a majority of disadvantaged Negores."[20] Thus, controlling for socioeconomic status, the racial factor alone affects children's academic achievement in public schools.

The results of these studies lend support to the policy that school integration is the only route to increasing achievement among disadvantaged children, and since more blacks and other minorities are in low socio-economic strata in American society, achieving racial balance in schools will facilitate an increase in achievement, morale, dedication to learning, and college attendance.

One finding of the survey of Coleman and his colleagues was that integrated schools may have a *negative* effect on the racial self-concept of minority students. An early study by Kenneth B. Clark and Mamie Phipps Clark indicated that black children attending Northern integrated schools held fewer positive images of themselves and exhibited more self-hatred than black children attending segregated Southern schools. Certainly, the black power movement emphasizes positive self-concepts, in that "black is beautiful," and focuses on pride in the self as well as the black group. The same holds true for members of other ethnic groups, where in the 1960s and 1970s there are positive stresses on ethnic groups and their cultures, rather than on total assimilation to white middle-class norms. The basis of ethnic movements in recent years is an examination of the unique histories, values, and cultures of various peoples, evidenced by their striving to include this information in history textbooks, news media, and other communication facilities where it had previously been excluded.

Related to the low motivational levels of students in segregated schools and communities is the finding that teachers in these areas also have low motivational career levels. Oftentimes, they feel the schools in which they teach are inferior and have low social prestige. Sometimes, they believe the students cannot attain high achievement levels, and this is conveyed to the students. Thus, teacher aspirations for the students emerge in students' low levels of motivation as well as achievement.

Kenneth B. Clark in *Dark Ghetto* points out that ghetto children experiencing defeatism, ". . .by and large, do not learn because they are not being taught effectively and they are not being taught because those who are charged with the responsibility of teaching them do not believe that they can learn, and do not act toward them in ways which help them to learn."[21]

Within the white liberal community of teachers, these findings sometimes facilitate teachers' attempts to instill motivation in minority students by positive reinforcement, by praise, by complimenting the student when work is progressing. Reacting to negative reinforcements which hinder student progress and, in turn create anger and negative self-concepts, teachers reason they must provide a positive atmosphere in the school.

One negative consequence of the philosophy surrounding a simple strategy of positive reinforcement has been reported by G.C. Massey, M.V. Scott, and S.M. Dornbusch in their 1974 study of San Francisco high schools. San Francisco's integration plan went into effect by 1971, and by 1974, high school teachers were 77 percent white, 7 percent black, 5 percent brown, and 4 percent Chinese, while the high school student body was comprised of 27 percent white, 27 percent black, 19 percent Chinese, and 14 percent Spanish surname pupils. Teachers showed friendliness, concern for academic progress, and the happiness of students, but in their concern they substituted warmth and friendliness for realistic assessment of the minority students' work. Thus, the students were overly praised if they performed a little better than they had previously. Their praise was negatively correlated with achievement, so that the poorer the performance of the students, the more they reported getting praised. There was a discrepancy between student achievement as measured by grades and test scores and what efforts the students themselves thought they were making, based on a self-assessment scale. Dornbusch concluded that for an integrated school system to work, students need encouragement as well as realistic standards.

How about the white students' benefits from integrated school settings? There is no question that most reports stress that whites *will not suffer* from integrated schools in terms of their academic achievements, particularly if no more than one-half of the student body is comprised of minority students. However, what about the *positive consequences* for white students of having a learning environment more representative of what exists in American society with its multi-ethnic make up? What do white students gain from interethnic social settings within the schools? The social climate of an integrated environment not only increases achievement but also increases human understanding and appreciation of the values, history, and culture among the many ethnic groups in American society.

It is wise to point out that the findings of Coleman and his colleagues as well as the U.S. Commission on Civil Rights appear to contain negative assumptions about the home, neighborhood, and peers along with the ethnic group culture of the "disadvantaged." The assertion of ethnic pride along with the maintenance of ethnics' unique cultural heritage should not be stripped away in processes of school integration and abolition of socioeconomic inequality.

"ON THE BASIS OF RACE, COLOR, OR CREED" OR "IRRESPECTIVE OF RACE, COLOR, OR CREED"?

School Assignments

A major value in the ideology of the American Creed is that all people should be given the same opportunities, regardless of race, color, or creed. However, certain current issues strike at the very heart of the ideology, especially when they use the rationale of the Creed for upholding antiintegration measures. The California legislative, initiative, and court confrontations involved in the "Wakefield Parental Consent Initiative," entitled "Schools: Busing for Integration" and later the furor over Proposition 21 on the November, 1972 ballot provide illustrations of such issues.

Initially, when Floyd L. Wakefield was first elected to the California State Assembly from the 52nd District in 1966, he tried to enact a law barring compulsory school busing for purposes of racial integration, but for three years, the bill failed to pass the Assembly Education Committee. Then, he decided to take the issue directly to the voters by initiative procedure; finally he was successful in obtaining approval by the Assembly and Senate, and the signature of Governor Ronald Reagan. Of importance is that before final passage of the bill, the phrase "busing for the purpose of integration" was deleted, due to fear of the bill's being declared unconstitutional. Wakefield was encouraged by State Superintendent of Public Instruction Max Rafferty, who endorsed the idea that mandatory busing causes hatred between the schools and parents. Rafferty also advocated the rights of parents to decide whether their children should be bused to schools.

Opponents of the Wakefield bill said that passage would certainly be challenged in the courts, in light of the 1954 Supreme Court decision making it clear that the Fourteenth Amendment to the U.S. Constitution prevents the states from maintaining racially segregated schools and also in light of the precedent set by the 1963 *Jackson v. Pasadena School District* decision where the equal protection clause substantiated a prointegration policy for the school district.

In a letter to the editor in the *Los Angeles Times* on July 14, 1970, Wakefield stated,

> AB 551 does not say you can or cannot bus. All it says is that before you bus you must first get permission from the parent or guardian of the child. The child belongs to the parent, not the school board, and it is the parents' prerogative to decide the issue.

> It should be pointed out that local school boards throughout the State of California have been operating at a deficit for some time and their lobbyist in Sacramento has been pleading with the Legislature for additional funds. It is ironic that these same school boards who are pleading for additional funds have squandered millions to implement bussing programs to achieve a racial balance against the wishes of the parent who wants to maintain the neighborhood school concept. . .

> Let's get down to the hard facts: The opponents of AB 551 are trying to force integration upon everyone except themselves. These are the people who have created hatred and animosity among the races. Integration will . never be successful unless it is on an individual basis.

Meanwhile, in October of 1970, the New York State Antibusing Law was held unconstitutional by a three judge Federal Court ruling, because it violated the Fourteenth Amendment to the Constitution which guarantees equal protection under the law.

Upon adoption of the Wakefield Act, it was added to the California Education Code and provided that "no governing board of a school district shall require any student or pupils to be transported for any purpose or for any reason without the written permission of the parent or guardian."

A suit filed by a group of San Francisco parents, whose children were directly affected by San Francisco's integration plan, was heard before the California Supreme Court. The Court upheld the constitutionality of the law and affirmed that school districts may not bus children outside their neighborhoods without parental consent. However, it ruled that school districts may assign pupils and parents do not have the right to prevent their children from going to the assigned school; they merely have the right to refuse using buses provided by the school districts! The Court affirmed that obstruction of the right of school districts to assign pupils "would beget a parental right to discriminate, and do so in a context of racial strife that would enable many to exploit that right to inflict racial prejudice." Further, "it would empower these private persons to inject the venom of racial discrimination into the veins of government. Such a statute would be unconstitutional on its face."

In April of 1971, the U.S. Supreme Court refused to review the case and thus concurred in the California Supreme Court decision to permit assignments of pupils to schools outside their neighborhoods for purposes of racial integration.

Determined not to accept a watered-down version of his efforts, Wakefield rallied support for Proposition 21 appearing on the November 7, 1972, California ballot. Proposition 21 was designed to erase that portion of the Education Code which made it state policy to prevent and eliminate racial and ethnic imbalance in public schools, and further, it was designed to forbid the assignment of students to particular schools because of their race, creed, or color. Wakefield expected the proposition to receive 75 percent of the vote and claimed that "65% of the blacks, 95% of all Mexican-Americans and 99% of the Chinese-Americans are against forced integration and busing."[22]

The proposition was approved by 63 percent of the voters and became part of the State Education Code in a provision that "no public school student shall, because of his race, creed, or color, be assigned to or be required to attend a particular school." Though not specifically referring to school busing, the statement was generally understood by proponents and opponents of busing to constitute a ban on school busing for racial integration.

In the meantime, Assemblyman William T. Bagley won passage of a bill establishing state policy for the prevention and elimination of racial and ethnic imbalance in pupil enrollments. The Bagley Act became part of the Education Code. Thus, both Wakefield's and Bagley's efforts were incorporated in the Education Code, though neither mentioned school busing.

The National Association for the Advancement of Colored People filed suit in Sacramento County and San Bernardino County Superior Courts, charging that Proposition 21 was unconstitutional since it violated the Fourteenth Amendment to the Constitution, and a similar suit was filed by the American Civil Liberties Union in the California courts. Underlying an integrationist viewpoint was the position that school districts must calculate and report the racial and ethnic composition of their student bodies.

In January, 1975, the California Supreme Court overturned part of Proposition 21 and it supported the principle that race must be considered a factor in assigning pupils for eliminating school segregation. However, the court did not rule out that portion of the proposition invalidating the Bagley Act which included standards and procedures to improve racial balance in the schools and set percentage guidelines.

The U.S. Supreme Court did not uphold a similar law in North Carolina, and the majority opinion reasoned,

> Just as the race of students must be considered in determining whether a constitutional violation has occurred, so also must race be considered in formulating a remedy...to forbid all assignments made on the basis of race would deprive school authorities of the one tool absolutely essential to fulfillment of their constitutional obligation to eliminate dual school systems.

In contrast, the California Republican Party in September of 1975 underpinned its stand against forced busing by the statement that "the right of students to attend the public school nearest their place of residency shall not be denied or abridged for reasons of race, color, national origin, creed, religion or sex."[23]

Similarly, the Senate exerted its influence to oppose implementation of busing programs by adopting the Biden and Byrd amendments to a 1975 HEW money bill. Opposition to forced busing and endorsement of the neighborhood school concept rest on the principle that assignments of students or teachers on the basis of race is unjust.

In October of 1975, Senator John G. Tower proposed an amendment to the U.S. Constitution which would read,

> The right of students to attend the public school nearest to their place of residence shall not be denied or abridged on account of race, religion, sex, or national origin.

Does assignment to schools on the basis of race help eradicate institutionalized inequities in American society? Does assignment to schools irrespective of race concur with the principles imbedded in the American Creed? Do stands taken in the words of the American Creed justify antiintegration practices and conceal prejudice, discrimination, and racism? The answers are unresolved in the courts, in the legislatures, and in the mind of the white liberal.

Affirmative Action and Special Admissions

Affirmative action programs, including special admissions for college, also strike at the very center of meaning of the American Creed and the ways the Creed is used to justify either liberal or conservative programs and procedures. Affirmative action programs and special admissions in colleges, graduate schools, law schools, medical schools and other schools are either being implemented or sidestepped across the country. Many are based on Executive Order 11246, signed by President Johnson on September 24, 1965. Two key concepts are embodied in the Executive Order. First is nondiscrimination which means that "*no* person may be denied employment or related benefits on grounds of his or her race, color, religion, sex, or national origin."[24] Second is affirmative action which means,

> *Affirmative action* requires the contractor to do more than ensure employment neutrality with regard to race, color, religion, sex, and national origin. As the phrase implies, affirmative action requires the employer to make additional efforts to recruit, employ and promote qualified members of groups formerly excluded, even if that exclusion cannot be traced to particular discriminatory actions on the part of the employer. The premise of the affirmative action concept of the Executive Order is that unless positive action is undertaken to overcome the effects of systemic institutional forms of exclusion and discrimination, a benign neutrality in employment practices will tend to perpetuate the *status quo ante* indefinitely.[25]

One basic cause of opposition to affirmative action is the fear it produces. Prevalent are fears that standards will be lowered and unqualified doctors, lawyers, professors, nurses, social workers, teachers, computer programmers and accountants will pervade primarily middle and upper status occupational positions. These programs pose threats to the educational and employment security of those engaging in a middle class standard of living.

A second basic cause of opposition to affirmative action and special admissions programs is that they constitute "reverse discrimination." If a minority or woman is chosen over a white male in employment or admission to universities, law schools, or medical schools, is this practice not "preferential treatment," and unconstitutional? If a "less qualified" minority or woman is selected over a "more qualified" white male, does this not constitute infringement on the equal protection of the white male?

Highlighting these issues was the case of *DeFunis v. Odegaard.* Marco

DeFunis, a Phi Beta Kappa graduate of the University of Washington, applied for admission to the University's law school and was denied entrance while, at the same time, the law school admitted thirty-six black, Mexican-American, and other minority group members with lower grades and test scores. Forty-eight nonminority students with lower averages than DeFunis were also admitted. For minorities other bases of judgement, such as personal recommendations and their ethnic identities, were used and, accordingly, DeFunis filed suit. He charged that the law school, in classifying applicants by their race or ethnicity, violated the U.S. Constitution.

The Washington State trial judge rejected the law school's rationale in support of special admissions and ordered DeFunis' admission to the law school. Subsequently, the university appealed the case, and the ruling was reversed by the Washington Supreme Court. But upon appeal to the U.S. Supreme Court, DeFunis obtained an order by Supreme Court Justice William O. Douglas allowing him to continue his studies until his case came before the Supreme Court. When it was considered by the U.S. Supreme Court in April of 1974, the majority ruled the case moot, because DeFunis had been accepted to the law school by court order and was near completion of the requirements for his law degree. The Court said, "federal courts are without power to decide questions that cannot affect the rights of the litigants before them." The dissenting view, however, held that the case was not moot and that the majority view declaring its mootness sidestepped resolution of a difficult case.

Supporting the position of DeFunis were Alexander M. Bickel of Yale University and Philip B. Kurland of the University of Chicago, who wrote a brief for the Anti-Defamation League of B'nai B'rith opposing special preferences for minorities. They demonstrated that the University of Washington law school had an enrollment of 2 percent black students and since this represented the proportion in the population in the state, there was no wrong which needed to be corrected. Only when there was evidence that past racial discrimination had occurred could special admissions policies on the basis of race be instituted.

Opposing the position of DeFunis were Archibald Cox, filing a brief for Harvard College, and former U.S. Solicitor General Ervin N. Griswold for the Association of American Law Schools. Both favored preferences or special admissions policies to halt discrimination against certain minorities.

Invoking the principle of merit when not employing minorities or women, or not admitting them to universities, many persons forget that for years there have been other bases than job or school related qualifications. Examining university admissions policies, Joan Abramson in *The Invisible Woman: Discrimination in the Academic Profession,* contends,

Indeed, these kinds of factors [students' extracurricular activities, personal recommendations, and place of origin] have been an accepted part of admission policies at most universities for decades. Some schools seek geographical balance, while others grant first preference to residents of the home state. Some grant preference to sons and daughters of alumni or to individuals who will bolster the athletic teams. Such special considerations have long been a part of the American college and regardless of their merit as a means of selecting students, it is unlikely that the backers of DeFunis really had in mind their destruction. Yet it was just such special considerations that were the heart of the legal case.[26]

Showing the intrinsic difficulties in such cases, Justice Douglas' own dissenting opinion, claiming that the underlying issues had not been discussed by the court, revealed a major dilemma. On the one hand, he stressed that the equal protection clause does not require that law schools admit students only on the basis of test results and grades. The recognition of differences in cultural and racial backgrounds is an important factor in considering minority applicants separately. On the other hand, he maintained that the goal is for applicants to be judged on the basis of individual merits in a racially neutral way. In his opinion, Justice Douglas urged that the case be remanded for a new trial to determine whether DeFunis had been discriminated against because of his race.

Encapsulating the problematical contradictions in special admissions, Justice William J. Brennan, Jr., writing with the dissenting opinion, said the constitutional issues were avoided and will not disappear. He predicted that interested parties will be forced to further litigations and affirmed that "Few constitutional questions in recent history have stirred as much debate."[27]

Other cases testing the constitutionality of "reverse discrimination" are in the courts. Among them is a suit filed by Allan Bakke where he contends a special admissions policy at the University of California Davis Medical School allowed minority students entrance even though they had lower grades and test scores than other applicants. He claims special admissions violate the equal protection clause of the Fourteenth Amendment to the Constitution, Title VI of the Civil Rights Act of 1964, and the "privileges and immunities" clause of the California Constitution. University officials and others supporting special admissions reason that there are so many applicants that minority students would not achieve places if test scores and grades were the only means of selection. For example, in the first year UC Davis Medical School class for fall, 1974, there were 4,000 applicants for 100 places. Policies of reserving a percentage of places for minority students are followed across the country in law schools, medical, dental, nursing, social welfare, and other graduate and professional schools.

A "backlash effect" also exists against compensatory programs, special tutoring facilities, and extra classes held for minority students already enrolled in colleges. Often, "high potential" minority students in high schools are given special classes and training in medical laboratories to facilitate their motivation and interest in embarking on medical careers. White students often feel these programs discriminate against them.

At the University of California, Los Angeles, there was constant debate among those responsible for administering the Undergraduate Recruitment and Development program, which tutored and academically assisted students admitted under special procedures for minority students.[28] The program included blacks, Mexican-Americans, American Indians, Asian-Americans, and a few poor white students. Controversies existed about whether regular students could attend the special "back-up" study sessions designed to assist learning among URD students. Tutors differed in their beliefs and practices, some desiring to include all students who wanted to attend the sessions and others refusing the attendance of regular students. Some felt the minority students were helped by the interchange of ideas in discussions with a cross section of students in the class. Others contended that minority students were intimidated by "bright students who seem to know it all," since minority students feared failure and had negative academic self-concepts. These tutors also stated they were exploited by overwork when regular students attended the special classes. Furthermore, when regular students attended sessions with URD students, there were often charges that white students could not possibly understand the material covered because of "white middle-class bias." In large undergraduate courses on ethnic relations, many URD students contended that white students could never understand the "gut level" of experiences, and many expressed the view that sociological theories on prejudice, discrimination, and racism were useless. Because of these confrontations, all students showed the positive consequences of experiencing a microcosm of society-at-large, with interpretations and re-interpretations of current interracial problems by persons with different socio-cultural identities.

Controversies over affirmative action programs are evidenced not only in higher education, but also in hiring programs, in businesses and in labor unions. In February, 1975, Superior Court Judge Lyle Cook in Alameda County ruled that Berkeley's equal opportunity hiring program was unconstitutional. Violation of the equal protection clause of the Constitution and the Civil Rights Act had occurred, and he said, "Those portions of the program that provide for racial quotas, noncompetitive examinations and preferential hiring based on race or sex to the exclusion of merit, experience and record must be deemed arbitrary and discriminatory."[29] The program was instituted in 1972 and required the city to hire persons according to the percentage of each race and sex residing in the community.

The well-known Philadelphia Plan, setting an example for similar plans across the country, sought to hire minority workers in the skilled construction trades. By 1970, federally funded construction projects were to begin a plan of showing good faith efforts to hire a certain percentage of minority workers. The Plan was strongly opposed by many employers and unions who denounced it because it set "goals" which are really quotas, and in so doing, violated the Civil Rights Act of 1964. The Chicago Plan was designed to include all construction industries, not only those with government contracts. Five-year goals were established during which time minorities were to make up 30 percent of the work force. This percentage represented the percent of minorities in the population. In the early 1970s similar plans were designed in Los Angeles, San Francisco, St. Louis, New Orleans, New York, Buffalo, Cincinatti, Denver, Houston, Indianapolis, Chicago, Atlanta, Kansas City, Miami, Milwaukee, and Pittsburgh. Many plans included on-the-job training and classroom instruction.

While these plans were being drawn, minority leaders charged that certain ethnic groups were underrepresented in county libraries, in the film industry, in the fire departments, and in state government offices. The Equal Employment Opportunity Commission found the nation's trucking industry and American Telephone and Telegraph discriminating in hiring practices and in the treatment of women, blacks, and Spanish surnamed Americans.

Obstruction of affirmative action plans takes familiar forms in restricting the inclusion of minorities and women. The contention that unions and organized labor excluded nonwhites in many nationwide industries is upheld by Assistant Secretary of Labor Arthur A. Fletcher. Moreover, columnist Joseph Alsop affirmed that the Philadelphia Plan and other similar plans never were really enforced, and he wrote, "Nonenforcement was almost total, in particular, in the construction industry, with its many powerful craft unions, many of them rigidly lily-white."[30] Outlining a picketing protest in twenty-five states, Herbert Hill, labor director for the NAACP, argued that public officials have failed in enforcing federally ordered increases in the percentage of minority workers where public funds for construction projects operate. This is in violation of equal hiring standards. Furthermore, he targets much of his criticism at the Nixon Administration's irresponsibility and destruction of the Philadelphia Plan, and the fact that many black workers on federal construction projects throughout the country result from the lily-white monopoly of building trade unions.

Other methods of impeding the enactment of hiring more minorities and women include "checkerboarding," where an employer moves minority employees from one project to another during a month and then counts them as more persons; or hires minorities part time and reports them in statistical summaries showing a higher proportion than are really employed.

The use of tests to determine job eligibility is another practice which has restricted the inclusion of minority workers and women in all levels of employment. This practice is reminiscent of the days of the poll tax and demonstration of blacks' ability to read or recite portions of the Constitution before voting was permitted. It is also reminiscent of the necessity to be male or to own property to be a voter. These practices served to screen "undesirables" from democratic rights granting the same privileges to every individual in a free society.

An important U.S. Supreme Court decision challenging the use of eligibility tests was made in the case of *Griggs v. Duke Power* in 1971. The debate centered on whether the company had the right to require standardized general intelligence tests as a condition of employment or promotion. Black applicants argued before the Court that they did not perform as well on the tests as their white counterparts since they had received poor educations. Further, they argued that scores on intelligence tests were not related to the performance on the jobs for which they were applying. Ruling in favor of the employees, the Court wrote:

> What is required by Congress is the removal of artificial, arbitrary, and unnecessary barriers to employment when the barriers operate invidiously to discriminate on the basis of racial or other impermissible classification. . . . If an employment practice which operates to exclude Negroes cannot be shown to be related to job performance, the practice is prohibited.

This decision affirms that employers must show the relationship between job qualifications and job performance when they hire or promote employees. When their work force is not representative of minorities and women in the community, employers will be on the defensive in demonstrating the types of qualifications they require for hiring.

In its first decision regarding "reverse discrimination," the U.S. Supreme Court, on March 24, 1976, in the case of *Franks v. Bowman Transportation Co.,* ruled that black job applicants denied employment must be granted the full seniority they would have obtained if the employers had not illegally discriminated against them. Seniority must be retroactive to the time they would have been hired, had there not been discrimination; it includes full rights, such as pension benefits, vacation privileges, and protection from layoffs. Indicating that seniority systems are important in the economic employment system of the United States, the Court reasoned that seniority could serve as a perpetuator of inequality by allocating privileges to non-victims. The Court's decision strengthens the interpretation of affirmative action as a remedy under Title VII of the Civil Rights Act of 1964, which prohibits discrimination in employment because of race, religion, sex, or national origin. Bringing attention to the controversial nature of the issues,, Chief Justice Warren E. Burger, in a separate opinion, stated, "I cannot join in judicial approval of 'robbing Peter to pay Paul.' "

The civil liberties issues surrounding "quotas," "percentage goals," and "affirmative action programs" remain acute. Examination of opposite stands, both pro and anti, with respect to these plans and practices reveals that both positions are oftentimes couched in the same terms, bringing forth the principle that all people should have equal opportunity and that social justice should prevail.

Quotas: Inclusion or Exclusion?

The use of quotas to limit the percentage of Jewish students in American universities occurred by the 1920s. At first, when university enrollments were expanding and there were plenty of places for students, Jews were not limited by any entrance restrictions. However, by the time a great number of Jews from Southeast Europe immigrated to the United States, Jews, seeking a way out of the lower class and having faith in education per se, often were represented far greater than their percentage in the population in Eastern universities. Both City College of New York and Hunter College had enrollments of between 80 and 90 percent Jews.[31] Prior to World War I, before quotas were designed to limit the percentage of Jewish students, Columbia had a Jewish enrollment of 40 percent and Harvard was 20 percent Jewish.[32]

Before the 1924 immigration quotas were imposed, several million Jews were heavily concentrated in Northeastern urban areas after immigrating to the United States. Thus, even though Jews were a small minority of 3 percent, they constituted 30 percent of the population of New York by 1920.[33]

Stephen Steinberg in his analysis of Jewish quotas acknowledges that there were three primary reasons for the restriction of Jewish enrollments in universities. First, there was violation of "frivolous habits" and, quoting Thorstein Veblen, "the canons of genteel intercourse" where "scholarship is. . . made subordinate to genteel dissipation, to a grounding in those methods of conspicuous consumption that should engage the thought and energies of a well-to-do man of the world."[34] Jewish students, because they were lower class and visibly exhibited ethnic characteristics, did not fit in with this upper-class style of life. Second, Jewish students showed excellent academic performance not only providing competition for other students, but also challenging their social style as well as their lack of interest in intellectuality. Third, there was fear that Jewish visibility would lower the reputational standing of the college and the other students' degrees. Jews were less respectable than others, and Steinberg reports, "No one suggested that Jewish students threatened academic standards. Rather it was argued that the college stood for other things, and that social standards were as important and valid as intellectual ones."[35]

Jews, a small minority but highly represented in institutions of higher education, either as students or as faculty members, are clearly insecure about the negative effects of proportional representation. Furthermore, they know that in America the first higher education quotas were designed specifically to restrict them.

Recent cases of Jewish women attempting to obtain faculty positions reveal the obstructive effect of those who point to the high proportion of faculty members who are Jews, forgetting that they are Jewish males. "You know that Jews are overrepresented here. Being a woman won't help you." Jewish women highly qualified on the basis of merit in teaching, excellent scholarship, and research abilities, are told they are "pushy" when they try to enter the "mainstream of academia."

The use of quotas in the Soviet Union to limit the number of Jews has come to the attention of the American Jewish community. For more than twenty years, ethnic quotas based on population proportions have been the guidelines for admission to universities, according to William Korey. Although the percentage of Jews in the population is .9, the percent of Jews in higher education is 1.9 percent. However, previously, it had been 13 percent in 1935 and 3.2 percent in 1961.[36] Increasingly, limits on Jews as "scientific workers" restricts opportunities for Jews entering fields of science and promotions for those already in the scientific fields. Korey writes, "These restrictions have not ordinarily struck at older Jews already occupying senior or administrative positions. It is the middle and younger generations of scientists and academics that have been affected most."[37]

To prevent resegregation and to maintain a stable racially integrated neighborhood, the community of Oak Park, Illinois, early in 1974 circulated a proposed ordinance to limit the percentage of blacks who could live there to 30 percent. A suburban community within ten miles of the center of Chicago, it had passed a fair housing law in 1968 when hardly any blacks resided in the community. The area was comprised of liberal, open-minded egalitarian people who opposed the overt hostility and violent actions against minorities trying to settle in places like Cicero. The residents were concerned with one border area where whites might flee "en masse" if sizable numbers of blacks were to move in. Thus, they reasoned a limitation placed on residential mobility of blacks into the area would preserve integrationist principles.

In contrast, Charles Silberman in *Crisis in Black and White* calls for the use of quotas to increase the number of blacks in all segments of life. Looking at the history of employment for blacks in the United States, he urges that blacks should be in positions at all levels of responsibility. There must be strong resistance to white employers' statements that they are not prejudiced, but their clients are; that they are willing to hire blacks, but none apply; that they are seeking blacks for positions, but none qualify. He suggests recruiting of blacks wherever they are, in high schools, in lower-class jobs, in black radio stations and newspapers, since blacks are outside the "web of job gossip" and informal relationships which usually generate jobs for whites. Silberman objects to the rationale of some white liberals who state there must be an increase in job opportunities for blacks due to past inequities. He states,

> Most of the discussions of Negro demands for preferential treatment and for "reverse quotas" have missed the point. The object is not compensation, in the sense of making up to the Negro for past injustices; it is to overcome the tendencies to exclude the Negro which are built into the very marrow of American society. There are, indeed, an incredible number of factors which will operate to prevent any rapid increase in employment of Negroes unless a concerted and special effort is made. A formal policy of non-discrimination, of employing people "regardless of race, color, or creed," however estimable, usually works out in practice to be a policy of employing whites only.[38]

He writes that all kinds of subjective elements enter into the selection of employees, but employers still sanctify the principle of merit. However, overtly retreating from the merit principle is another thing, and Silberman predicts there will be hostilities on the part of qualified whites.

Do quotas encourage preferential treatment and thereby violate civil liberties? Long a leader in civil liberties fighting (since its founding in 1913) against racial, ethnic, and religious discrimination in employment, housing, and education, the Anti-Defamation League of B'nai B'rith has established its position regarding "preferential treatment." It reasons that racial quotas are in violation of the Fourteenth Amendment to the Constitution and the Civil Rights Act of 1964. This position directly stems from the history of Jewish exclusion on the basis of ethnic or religious quotas, not only in the United States, but in the European countries from which most Jews emigrated.

In letters to the Regents of the University of California and the Trustees of the California State University and Colleges in 1972, Zad Leavy, Chairman of the Pacific Southwest Regional Office, stated ADL's opposition to preferential treatment and racial quotas,

> Our opposition to preferential treatment and racial quotas is based on our conviction that they substitute one form of injustice for another, that they are immoral and undemocratic, and that they are violative of the

California Constitution, of the Civil Rights Act of 1964, and of the public policy of the United States. . . . There is no question that Blacks and Mexican Americans, for example, have been greatly disadvantaged in the past due to a long and historical application of such bias and its continuing after-effects. But past discrimination does not justify, as a remedial measure, a new and equally deliberate and arbitrary discrimination against others.[39]

More specifically, ADL's position opposes special admissions programs, using the terms "preferential treatment" and "quotas," in effect at the University of California, both at the undergraduate and the graduate level— including schools of law, medicine, public health, and social welfare, and at the California state universities. It endorses adding to pools of available and qualified applicants for admission and for employment by the universities, but cites as discriminatory the selection of one individual over another on the basis of race, ethnic origin, or religion. It affirms compensatory training, counseling and scholarships, as long as the same opportunities are available to all applicants, irrespective of race, ethnicity, or religious identification.

Policies in Affirmative Action for Equal Opportunities in Employment call for a minimum number of minority employees at all levels which is no less than the total proportion of minorities in the community. ADL sees that hiring on a proportionate basis inevitably establishes quotas. They are interpreted as violating Fair Employment Practices Acts, State and Federal constitutional provisions concerning the privileges and immunities of citizens, and the equal protection clause of the Fourteenth Amendment. Title VII of the Civil Rights Act requires that employers, labor unions, and employment agencies treat all persons fairly without regard to their race, color, religion, sex, or national origins. Section 703 (j) of Title VII of the Civil Rights Act of 1964 states,

Nothing contained in this title shall be interpreted to require any employer. . .to grant preferential treatment to any individual or to any group because of the race, color, religion, sex. or national origin of such individual or group on account of an imbalance which may exist with respect to the total number or percentage of persons of any race, color, religion, sex, or national origin employed by an employer. . .in comparison with the total number or percentage of persons of such race, color, religion, sex, or national origin in any community, State, section, or other area, or in the available work force in any community, State, section, or other area.

The Anti-Defamation League believes affirmative action programs can be instituted without relying on preferential treatment. It endorses recruiting at the undergraduate level by counselors and recruiters at high schools with substantial proportions of minority students. Counselors are encouraged to refer students to particular colleges, but it opposes inclusion of questions on racial background on students' records or on standard entrance examinations for colleges, medical and law schools. It approves compensatory training, as long as all students needing such training are eligible. It is "wrongful preferential treatment" to choose a lesser qualified person over a better qualified person because of the racial factor.

At a House Committee meeting in May of 1975 where special admissions to medical schools were examined, Democratic Representative Henry A. Waxman publically addressed the question of quotas, affirming the basic position of ADL. Affirmative action to increase the number of "disadvantaged" persons to qualify for admission to schools was supported, but granting preference on the basis of race, color, national origin, religion or sex was defined as "reverse discrimination." Waxman pointed out that "under the old quota system, the despised minority applicant had to have substantially better grades and scores than his WASP counterpart to gain admissions. Under the new quota system, the desirable minority applicant qualifies for special consideration only by virtue of his or her presence in the pool." Waxman continued by indicating that Jews comprise only 3 percent of the population of the United States. However, "they are overrepresented in law, medicine, accounting and the academic professions." he stressed that this attainment rests on the American Jewish culture and unique experience and was not gained "illegitimately."[40]

At the same House meeting, Representative Ralph H. Metcalfe favored special admissions declaring that they prevent the perpetuation of the exclusion of racial minority groups and women from the health profession.

In February, 1975, San Jose State University President John H. Bunzel endorsed the view that the use of race and sex quotas in politics, employment, and education was not only the "worst form of condescension" but it also defined equality such that "in order to make some people equal, we must use the authority of the state to make others unequal."[41] Bunzel has a record of being a liberal Democrat with a personal commitment to equal opportunity and civil rights.

Although "goals" and "timetables" do not reveal this conflict, affirmative action programs are perceived by both those engaging in hiring and those desiring employment as pitting one minority against another and minorities against women. If a black person is hired, will this mean that a Chicano will not be hired? Is a black person more "visible" than an Asian indicating to on-lookers that affirmative action has been implemented in a specific employment institution? Where is the white women? Is ethnicity pitted against sex?

Where is the ethnic woman? Does the black woman suffer double oppression, or is she an especially favorable candidate for affirmative action? Are more qualified white women unemployed when less qualified black males are hired? Must today's white males, long "overrepresented," suffer the consequences of unemployment so that more minorities and women will fill occupational positions? Do affirmative action plans set up a "divide and conquer" technique, where the white male domination of many occupations will be maintained? And what is "due process" for the white male?

The issues at the heart of quotas, affirmative action, preferential treatment and special admissions remain unresolved and will be addressed in the future by the courts. On the one hand, there is the principle that nondiscrimination and equality be effectuated *irrespective of* race, national origin, creed, or sex. On the other, is the principle that nondiscrimination and equality be established only *on the basis of* race, national origin, creed, or sex.

Both are general principles inherent in the American Creed. Both are designed to affirm positive efforts for attaining justness in American society. However, both can be used to legitimize expressions of prejudicial attitudes and discriminatory behavior. And both can be used to maintain institutionalized racism and sexism in the American educational, political, and social sectors. It is when prejudices are maintained through cloaking fears of unqualified, lower class, ethnic persons or women entering the "mainstream of American life" that one sees illegitimacy in the use of principles in the American Creed. To legitimate prejudicial attitudes or discriminatory behavior in particular inter-ethnic situations by use of the concept of equality irrespective of race, color, creed, or sex is to camouflage the real intent of egalitarian principles. Likewise, to prevent minorities and women entrance into the mainstream of American life on the basis of race, color, or creed is an obstruction of the real intent of egalitarian principles. Invoking the American Creed, either by use of "irrespective of race, color, creed, or sex," or by use of "on the basis of race, color, creed, or sex," in order to engage in prejudicial attitudes and discriminatory behavior is the focus of concern in this analysis.

With these complex issues in mind, a crucial question arises: to which social groupings within American society does Myrdal's thesis apply? Do his ideas of the American Creed and the consequent American Dilemma exist at all? Are there any Americans holding the values of social justice and equal opportunity central to their ideology? Is the manifestation of these values in the form of law—in the Bill of Rights, the Fourteenth Amendment to the Constitution, and the Civil Rights Acts of 1964 and 1968—entirely disparate from what Americans advocate?

Although it is not possible to fully answer these questions, certain organizations of liberals in American society articulate the values of equal opportunity and social justice and actively fight for these values in the courts. If, indeed, there is an American Dilemma, members of these groups will be particularly affected by interracial situations generating direct conflicts between the basic tenet of equality, irrespeetive of race, color, creed, or sex, and other values central to their life-styles. Moreover, among members of groups whose prime goal is racial and ethnic integration, there will be a magnification of dilemmas when specific social situations become imminent. For these liberals, Myrdal's thesis will be especially prnounced.

Examination of a representative sample of white liberals who are members of an organization supportive of civil rights and civil liberties will clarify the issue of whether the American Dilemma appears in their beliefs and experiences.

METHODOLOGY[42]

Personal interviews averaging an hour and a half in duration were completed with a random sample of 204 white liberals (97 women and 107 men) selected from the Los Angeles County portion of a national organization. The interviews were conducted between October 9, 1969, and December 15, 1969, with a response rate of 89 percent.

The respondents were presented with open-ended and probing questions concerning six interracial situations: (1) busing in the schools for the purpose of ending de facto segregation; (2) the entrance of blacks into the respondents' occupational fields; (3) blacks moving into the respondents' neighborhoods; (4) the quota system as the basis for college admission to obtain a proportionate representation of minority students; (5) rentals to blacks in white-occupied apartment buildings (hypothetically) owned by the respondents; and (6) hiring of blacks. The respondents' attitudes toward these six situations formed the basic *dependent variables* of this study.

The major *independent variables* explored in this analysis include status consciousness, the degree and direction of occupational and educational mobility, and the degree of ethnic identification and interethnic contact. A final exploration examines the area of cognitive dissonance and role conflicts and the methods of dissonance reduction employed by the respondents.

It is hoped that this study will lead to clarification and a better understanding of the issues raised here.

REFERENCES

1. *Los Angeles Times,* October 12, 1975.
2. George E. Simpson and J. Milton Yinger, *Racial and Cultural Minorities,* 1972, p. 562.

3. Charles T. Powers, "Troops, Police Ready for Violence: Boston Uneasy on Eve of School Year," *Los Angeles Times,* September 8, 1975.

4. Rudy Abramson, "Ford Won't Visit Louisville Due to Busing Threat," *Los Angeles Times,* October 10, 1975.

5. Seymour Martin Lipset, "Working-Class Authoritarianism," *Political Man, the Social Bases of Politics,* 1963, p. 92.

6. Maurice J. Goldbloom, "The New York School Crisis," *Commentary* (January, 1969), pp. 54-55.

7. *The New York Times,* November 11, 1968.

8. Maurice R. Berube and Marilyn Gittell, editors, *Confrontation at Ocean Hill-Brownsville,* 1969, p. 171.

9. Stokely Carmichael and Charles V. Hamilton, *Black Power: The Politics of Liberation in America,* 1967, p. 47.

10. U.S. Department of Health, Education and Welfare. Office for Civil Rights. *Directory of Public Elementary and Secondary Schools in Selected Districts. Enrollment and Staff by Racial/Ethnic Group,* 1968, p. 115; U.S. Department of Health, Education and Welfare. Office for Civil Rights. *Directory of Public Elementary and Secondary Schools in Selected Districts. Enrollment and Staff by Racial/Ethnic Group,* 1970, p. 154; U.S. Department of Health, Education and Welfare. Office for Civil Rights. *Directory of Public Elementary and Secondary Schools in Selected Districts. Enrollment and Staff by Racial/Ethnic Group,* 1972. p. 140; Pasadena Unified School District, Department of Planning, Research and Development, "Racial and Ethnic Distribution of Enrollments," Research Report No. 75/76-02, November 6, 1975.

11. *Los Angeles Times,* December 19, 1973.

12. Lee Austin, "Pasadena Tells Plan to Alter Integration Ordered by Court: Elimination of 'Forced' Busing Would Be Accomplished by Returning District to Neighborhood School Concept," *Los Angeles Times,* December 19, 1973.

13. Gene Blake, "Pasadena Schools Told to Integrate: Judge Rules That Racial Balance Must Be Achieved by September," *Los Angeles Times,* January 21, 1970.

14. Robert Rawitch and Lee Austin, "Pasadena Board Enthusiastic: Officials See Chance to 'Expose' Busing," *Los Angeles Times,* November 12, 1975.

15. James S. Coleman, et al., *Equality of Educational Opportunity,* 1966, p. 3.

16. George F. Will, "Busing and the Frightening Prospect for '76," *Los Angeles Times,* June 4, 1974 (70 percent of New York City school population is black or Puerto Rican); New York City Board of Education, "City-Wide Ethnic Census N.Y.C. Schools," October 31, 1973 (65 percent of the school population is minority); U.S. Department of Health, Education and Welfare. Office for Civil Rights. *Directory of Public Elementary and Secondary Schools in Selected Districts. Enrollment and Staff by Racial/Ethnic Group,* 1972, p. 936 (65 percent of the school population is minority).

17. U.S. Department of Health, Education and Welfare. Office for Civil Rights. *Directory of Public Elementary and Secondary Schools in Selected Districts. Enrollment and Staff by Racial/Ethnic Group,* 1972, p. 551 (69 percent of the school population in Baltimore is minority), p. 527 (76 percent of the school population in New Orleans is minority), p. 254 (77 percent of the school population in Atlanta is minority), p. 854 (87 percent of the school population in Newark is minority), p. 311 (69 percent of the school population in Chicago is minority), and p. 228 (96 percent of the school population in Washington, D.C. is minority with 95 percent Negro).

18. James S. Coleman, et al., *Equality of Educational Opportunity*, p. 325.
19. U.S. Commission on Civil Rights. *Racial Isolation in the Public Schools*, Vol. 1, 1967, p. 89.
20. Ibid.
21. Kenneth B. Clark, *Dark Ghetto: Dilemmas of Social Power*, 1958, p. 131.
22. *Los Angeles Times*, September 29, 1972.
23. Richard Bergholz, "State GOP Calls for End to Forced Busing: Central Committee Urges Congress to Pass Amendment," *Los Angeles Times*, September 22, 1975.
24. U.S. Department of Health, Education, and Welfare, *Higher Education Guidelines— Executive Order 11246*, October 1, 1972, p. 3.
25. Ibid., p. 3.
26. Joan Abramson, *The Invisible Woman: Discrimination in the Academic Profession*, 1975, pp. 100-101.
27. Linda Mathews, "Supreme Court Declines to Rule on Reverse Discrimination Case," *Los Angeles Times*, April 24, 1974.
28. Based on my personal experience as a professor.
29. *Los Angeles Times*, February 15, 1975.
30. Joseph Alsop, Editorial in *Los Angeles Times*, January 6, 1970.
31. Stephen Steinberg, "How Jewish Quotas Began," *Commentary*, September, 1971, p. 72.
32. Ibid., p. 72.
33. Ibid., p. 68.
34. Ibid., p. 70.
35. Ibid., p. 71.
36. William Korey, "Quotas and Soviet Jewry," *Commentary* (May, 1974), p. 55.
37. Ibid., p. 56.
38. Charles E. Silberman, *Crisis in Black and White*, 1964, p. 241.
39. Zad Leavy, letter to the Regents of the University of California, July 12, 1972.
40. Paul Houston, "Rights Advocates Clash on Quotas Ban," *Los Angeles Times*, May 1, 1975.
41. Philip Hager, " 'Quota Mentality' in Seeking Equality Rapped by Educator: Merit Still Should Be Determining Factor, San Jose State President Declares in Speech," *Los Angeles Times*, February 15, 1975.
42. Judith Caditz, "Dilemmas of the White Liberal: A Study in the Application of Anti-Discriminatory Principles to Current Situations," 1972. Detailed documentation of the methodology, including sampling procedure, ordinal ranks, and statistical tests, is found in this work.

CHAPTER II
A Profile of
the White Liberal

Individuals who are liberals in the areas of race, ethnic, and human relations are the focus of this analysis. The American Creed is central to the ideology of the white liberal. Intrinsic in the ideology are values of social justice, equal opportunity—irrespective of race, religion, or color—and respect for all persons as human beings worthy of development to their fullest potential. An integral part of the ideology is the belief in nondiscrimination, implemented by support for fair housing, fair employment, quality education for all, and egalitarian diffusion of voting privileges. The American Creed calls for eradication of prejudicial attitudes, discriminatory behavior, and institutionalized racism.

BELIEF IN THE AMERICAN CREED AND RACIAL INTEGRATION

Manifestations of such beliefs are endorsement and active support of racial integration as a means of attaining nondiscrimination and reduction of prejudice. Even though the organization affirms this policy, the sample was asked, "Do you believe in racial integration in housing education, and jobs, separatism, or some other arrangement?" Of those answering, 94 percent (186) believe in integration, a few believe in "whatever people want, integration or separatism," and a few believe in "equality, fair treatment for minorities, not integration, not separatism, but one human race." Probing the strength of commitment to belief in integration, separatism, or other arrangements, another question reveals that 96 percent (183) hold a strong dedication to integration. Of those believing in integration, 88 percent (164) reply they had always believed in integration, while a few integrationists say they had "never thought about it until recently, since the question never came up because no blacks lived where I grew up." Only 1 percent (2) report a prior belief in separatism, saying they used to feel "safer with my own group."

In response to a question asking the reasons they originally joined the organization, a preponderant group confirms this position,

> I believe in the ideals and purposes of the organization. It fights for civil rights and constitutional law. I believe in justice for minorities and the organization's opposition to Joe McCarthy in the '50s. Civil liberties must be defended and the organization is one of the most active fighters for equal protection under constitutional law. The Fourteenth Amendment is the basis of many legal decisions. Ethnic integration in schools, housing, employment and all areas must be the goal of American society, and my membership in this organization shows my belief in my ideals.

A small group of 6 percent (13) joined because of the membership of their friends or other admired persons.

When asked if they contribute money to organizations supportive of civil rights, 91 percent (181) state they do. However, when asked if they engage in any civil rights activities within their communities, 36 percent (73) say they are active, while 64 percent (131) are not.

A study of some respondents' replies to the six interracial situations captures the values and beliefs incorporated in the ideology of white liberals and their adherence to the principles of the American Creed.

THE BUSING SITUATION

Question: How do you personally feel about busing as a solution to de facto segregation in the schools?

Answer: I'm in favor of busing, because actual contact between people reduces prejudice. Busing would make up for the disparities in the education of blacks and whites. It will provide for equal educational opportunities for all. It will show that "separate is not equal" as ruled in the 1954 Supreme Court decision.

Question: Do you feel only the smarter black children, or those with the highest academic potential, should be bused into predominantly white schools?

Answer: No, because all children ought to have the same opportunity. We should not separate the smart from the not smart, and a cross section is best anyway. We do not know the potential of children, and we can't test at this age. Besides, tests are geared to white middle-class children, and we really don't know the potential of the black child.

In these favorable responses toward the busing situation, the respondents stress the principles of equal educational opportunities for all children and the application of egalitarian rules in the procedures employed for the implementation of any busing program.

THE OCCUPATION SITUATION

Question: How do you feel about blacks starting to work in *(the respondent's occupational field)?*

Answer: It's fine. The color of one's skin makes no difference. I don't draw racial lines. I'm in favor. We need to make positive efforts to see that blacks are in more and better occupations.

Question: Do you feel only those blacks who are middle-class people should enter your occupational field?

Answer: No, because color doesn't make any difference. There should be equal opportunities for all. Class status would make another barrier for blacks trying to get into this field. Race and class are irrelevant to the occupational position.

Once again, the white liberal's dedication to the principle of equal opportunity is reflected. The racial factor is considered unimportant to the issues involved in the occupational sector of American society.

THE RESIDENCE SITUATION

Question: What would you do if blacks began to move into your neighborhood?

Answer: Nothing. It wouldn't bother me, and I'd accept it. It won't affect anything. Color makes no difference. Negroes have a right to live where they want as well as I do. It is *the* answer to the race problem.

Question: Do you feel you might suffer an economic loss if blacks were to move in?

Answer: Color makes no difference. It's a myth. Evidence shows this doesn't happen. There is no relationship between race and economics. But if there were a loss, I'd be willing to take it.

These attitudes indicate the white liberal's devotion to open housing and dedication to the belief that the color of one's skin is not related to economic factors.

THE QUOTA SITUATION

Question: What do you think about colleges using a quota system so that minorities will be represented according to their proportion in the population?

Answer: It's a good idea. It will overcome present discrepancies between blacks and whites in educational opportunities. They should be overrepresented. They should be represented more than their proportion in the population. It's the only way to make up for past injustices. And it s the only way to advance minorities in the economic and occupational system of the country. It's the means to create equality of opportunity in jobs. Their qualifications will be on par with whites.

Question: Do you feel that quotas should be used only if the qualifications of the black students matched those of the white students?

Answer: No, it's unrealistic to expect minorities to meet the same standards. The fact is that they are from poor schools and don't have a chance. There are not enough qualified. We should lower the standards to compensate for years of discrimination. And besides qualifications are based on white middle-class standards.

Replies such as these reflect the white liberal's belief in combatting the preferential treatment which has existed for whites since the beginning of American slavery. Quotas are the basis for increasing educational opportunities for all minorities and will be the means by which occupational and economic status can be increased for all Americans, irrespective of race, color, or creed.

THE APARTMENT SITUATION

Question: What would you do if a black family wanted to rent one of your apartments and you personally didn't mind renting to blacks but your tenants threatened to move out?

Answer: I'd stand on my principles and rent. Color makes no difference. Let the white tenants move out. Let them move out because I'm in favor of breaking down segregation. I'm for fair housing. I would rent and stand by my principles. I believe in open housing, and I'm not prejudiced.

Question: Do you think the reputation of your property would go down if blacks began to move in?

Answer: No, because people are people. We need total integration. That s a stereotype. Studies refute this. There is no relationship between property value and color. Human beings are more important than reputation or money.

These positive attitudes express the white liberal's devotion to open housing, integration, and adherence to the principles of the ideology in the face of a possible confrontation between the ideology and an interracial situation. In addition, these statements reflect the white liberal's firm belief in the value of human beings and their rights as being higher than monetary values.

THE HIRING SITUATION

Question: How do you feel about hiring blacks?

Answer: I will not discriminate because of color. It's fine. I'm for it. They should have every opportunity to work. They should be hired on the same levels as whites. I'm indifferent to color, and I hire on the same basis as I would hire anyone. I hire people on an individual basis. I hire people.

Question: Do you think there would be danger in hiring many blacks within a short period of time?

Answer: No, color is not a criterion of danger! What a question! Blacks are called for in this area. There are not enough. There must be equal opportunity for all, and it's good to experience all types of people. All Americans should get to know different classes of people.

These attitudes toward hiring blacks exemplify the white liberal's support for fair employment, the belief that people's color shall not work against them, and the endorsement for positive efforts to include more blacks in jobs in all existent occupational categories.

VOTING PATTERNS, EDUCATION, OCCUPATION, AND INCOME

Voting behavior provides another indicator of commitment to the Civil Rights Movement. It is presumed that in recent years endorsement of Democratic rather than Republican candidates is associated with a commitment to racial integration in housing, schools, and employment. Observation of Table I shows that in the sample of white liberals, voting is predominantly Democratic, with most supporting Kennedy in the 1960 presidential election, Johnson, 1964, and Humphrey in 1968. Further, in the Los Angeles City mayoralty election in 1969, most rallied behind Thomas Bradley, who became the first black mayor in Los Angeles.

Another indicator of commitment to civil liberties is afforded by analysis of the vote on Proposition 14 in the 1964 California election. By their "no on 14" vote, the majority of respondents were decidedly in favor of keeping

TABLE I

Voting Behavior

	%	N
Voted for Kennedy in 1960	87.3	178
Voted for Johnson in 1964	93.1	190
Voted for Humphrey in 1968	77.5	158
Voted for McCarthy in 1968	6.4	13
Voted for Cleaver, Gregory in 1968	3.9	8
Voted for Bradley in Los Angeles City in 1969	86.9	127*
Voted against Proposition 14 in 1964	88.2	180**

Note—These percentages are based on the total of 204 respondents. Some categories are different than those indicated above, including "don't know" and "no answer."

*This question was asked only of those living in the city of Los Angeles at the time of the election.
**A vote against Proposition 14 was a vote in favor of keeping the Rumford Act which was supportive of open housing.

TABLE II

Education

	Jews		Non-Jews	
	%	f	%	f
0. no formal education	0.0	(0)	0.0	(0)
1. grades 1-8	0.0	(0)	1.1	(1)
2. grades 9-11	1.8	(2)	1.1	(1)
3. high school graduate	8.9	(10)	6.5	(6)
4. some college	21.4	(24)	13.1	(12)
5. college graduate	12.5	(14)	15.2	(14)
6. some post graduate	17.9	(20)	9.8	(9)
7. M.A., M.S.	11.6	(13)	30.4	(28)
8. M.D., Ph.D., L.L.B.,				
other higher degree	24.1	(27)	18.5	(17)
no answers	1.8	(2)	4.3	(4)
	100.0%	(112)	100.0%	(92)

to the Rumford Act, evidenced by a "yes on 14" vote, existed in the area of in the California Richmond Unified School District, the strongest opposition to the Rumford Act, evidenced by a "yes on 14" vote, existed in the area of San Pablo, a stronghold of anti-busing sentiments.

A study of Table II indicates the high educational level of the respondents. Their mean education is "some post graduate," while their parents' mean education is "high school graduate," and the national United States mean education in 1969 was between "two years high school" and "high school graduation."

The high occupational level of the sample is shown in Table III. The mean occupational rank is the fifth highest rank on Duncan's Index of Occupational Status which differentiates nineteen prestige categories.[1] The fifth rank includes elementary, junior and senior high school teachers, designers, and proprietors in wholesale trade. The respondents' fathers' occupational ranks fall in the ninth category, in which bookkeepers, clergy, musicians, and officials and administrators in local public administration are listed. The national United States population mean in 1962 was the thirteenth rank, where building managers, machinists, plumbers, sheriffs, and self-employed persons in food and dairy products are classified.

Placing in the fourth highest rank, the occupations of Jews as a group are

TABLE III

Occupation

Rank	Jews		Non-Jews	
	%	f	%	f
1.	21.4	(24)	8.7	(8)
2.	5.4	(6)	2.2	(2)
3.	12.5	(14)	23.9	(22)
4.	11.6	(13)	2.2	(2)
5.	9.8	(11)	5.4	(5)
6.	14.3	(16)	19.5	(18)
7.	10.7	(12)	15.2	(14)
8.	1.8	(2)	4.3	(4)
9.	1.8	(2)	8.7	(8)
10.	6.2	(7)	3.3	(3)
11.	2.7	(3)	1.1	(1)
12.	0.0	(0)	3.3	(3)
13.	1.8	(2)	0.0	(0)
14.			0.0	(0)
15.			1.1	(1)
16.			1.1	(1)
17.				
18.				
19.				
	100.0%	(112)	100.0%	(92)

somewhat higher in prestige than non-Jews, who place in the sixth rank.

With respect to intergenerational occupational mobility, 44 percent of the Jewish respondents are highly mobile compared with 34 percent of the non-Jewish respondents. Educational mobility shows even greater differences between Jews and non-Jews, with 36 percent of the Jewish respondents and 16 percent of the non-Jewish respondents very mobile when compared with the educational levels attained by their parents.

Consistent with their high educational and occupational status are the high income levels of the respondents. In 1968, total family income before taxes was between $20,000 and $24,999, while the national United States population mean in 1969 was between $8,000 and $8,999. Related to their somewhat higher occupational status, those from Jewish origins average a higher income than those from non-Jewish origins, with the first group averaging in the $20,000-$24,999 category and the latter group averaging in the $15,000-$19,999 category.

The majority of respondents, 78 percent (158), are between 35 and 65 years in age, while 12 percent (25) are under 35 and 10 percent (21) are over 65. There are 97 women and 107 men in the sample.

With respect to religious and ethnic origins, the sample is essentially bifurcated. Slightly over half (55 percent, 112) stem from Jewish origins, 44 percent (90) are from white Protestant origins, and only 1 percent (2) are from Catholic origins. Of those stating their religious affiliation as "atheist," 61 percent (49) are from Protestant origins and 40 percent (32) are from Jewish origins.

Analysis of national origins shows that 79 percent of the Jews are first and second generation Americans, while 72 percent of the non-Jews are third or fourth generation Americans.

SOCIAL ORIGINS OF THE WHITE LIBERAL

The values and beliefs crystallized in the ideology of white liberals are understandable in terms of the socio-cultural fabric within which they live. Utilizing the method of the sociology of knowledge, Karl Mannheim writes,

> The principal thesis of the sociology of knowledge is that there are modes of thought which cannot be adequately understood as long as their social origins are obscured. . .it would be false to deduce. . .that all the ideas and sentiments which motivate an individual have their origin in him alone, and can be adequately explained solely on the basis of his own life-experience. . .[2]

> . . .the sociology of knowledge seeks to comprehend thought in the concrete setting of an historical-social situation out of which individually differentiated thought only very gradually emerges. Thus, it is not men in general who think, or even isolated individuals who do the thinking, but men in certain groups who have developed a particular style of thought in an endless series of responses to certain typical situations characterizing their common plight.[3]

Taking into consideration immigration patterns, occupational and educational mobility, social status, voting behavior, exposure to values, and sources from which social friction and prejudice derive, one can understand the rationale underlying white liberals' adherence to the ideological commitments embedded in the American Creed.

Basis of Jewish Liberalism

According to Lawrence Fuchs in *The Political Behavior of American Jews,* Jewish liberalism is attributable to three central values of Jewish culture: learning (Torah), charity or social justice (Zedakeh), and nonascetism. Some writers trace Jewish humanitarian values to religious tradition, while others associate them with Jewish reactions to anti-Semitism, social discrimination, persecution and genocide during the Hitler era.

Marshall Sklare in *America's Jews* suggests that humanitarian values result from Jewish emphasis on learning, at first centering on religious objects and issues, and later on a more general dedication to learning which generated the "educational explosion that occurred among Jews in the United States." Nathan Glazer in *American Judaism* contends that Jewish commitment to social justice is universal and remains strong in spite of a decline among some Jews of interest in traditional religious sources. He indicates that concern for social justice engenders Jewish leadership and support for civil liberties, civil rights, desegregation, and extension of free speech rights.

In his work *Crisis in Black and White,* Charles E. Silberman documents the religious origins of Jewish antipathy toward slavery,

> ...the Jews, far from trying to erase the memory of slavery, have made it central to their religion: every Jew is enjoined to recall the fact that "we were slaves to Pharoah in Egypt." The pronoun "we" is used because each individual is to imagine that he himself, not just his ancestors, had been enslaved.[4]

In his analysis of Max Weber's writings, Reinhard Bendix shows that Weber viewed the Jewish prophets as fighting against social injustice, advocating protection of the debtor and the stranger, and stressing the Talmudic moral legal basis which guided the everyday lives of people. Since they were structurally independent of any particular political institution, the Jewish prophets spoke against various regimes, and thus practiced and advocated the rights of free speech.

Examining the social conditions under which Jews lived in many countries, Gerhard Lenski concludes that learning and scholarship as well as emphasis on social justice result from Jews being "cut off from opportunities to rise in the major institutional systems of the larger society." This view is consistent with the thesis that social, legal, and political barriers relegated Jews to the status of "second class" citizenship which resulted in the flourishing of learning among Jews and Jewish empathy for all minority group people.

In this study, most Jewish respondents are first or second generation

Americans, while fewer are third or fourth generation. Most of their parents came to this country in the great wave of Jewish immigration from Southeast Europe between 1870 and 1924, when approximately two and a half million Jews arrived in the United States. Many of their parents were subjected to discrimination and anti-Semitism in Southeast Europe. Those from Czarist Russia had lived much of their lives in fear of pogroms. The children of these immigrants grew up in an atmosphere where these life experiences of their parents were vividly remembered and clearly expressed. Even if particular Jews did not witness these life events personally or through the eyes of their parents, they are well aware of them, since they form part of the common knowledge of Jewish people and provoke common feelings among them. Although individual Jews may have chosen to assimilate, shed the immigrant past of their parents, and detach themselves from the Jewish community, they, nevertheless, hold a common feeling and understanding of this period in their social history. Central values within the context of this experience are social justice, nondiscrimination, civil rights, human rights, human dignity, and egalitarianism.

Another specific event which occurred during the lifetimes of the respondents was Hitler's destruction of six million Jews during World War II. Jews were deeply affected by the holocaust and were tragically reminded of the extreme degree to which genocide may be practiced. This event is a major factor in the life experiences of Jews and provides a compelling impetus for adherence to antidiscriminatory principles and an ideological commitment to social justice.

These experiences and values sensitize Jews to the discrimination to which others are subjected. Jewish support for the Civil Rights Movement is well documented. Lenski found that when compared with Protestants and Catholics, Jews are the least likely to advocate segregated school systems. In fact, when investigating four areas of liberalism-conservatism—including freedom of speech, foreign aid, welfare state, and racial integration—he discovered that Jews were most liberal, especially on the issue of school segregation.

The Berelson, Lazarsfeld, and McPhee study of voting behavior in the 1948 presidential election revealed that Jews vote Democratic even when there are controls for social class level. The highest income Jewish voters voted for Truman rather than Dewey in a ratio of about three to one. The researchers attribute the Democratic Jewish vote to the matching of political party with voters' values of support for civil rights legislation.

Even though they have been very upwardly mobile in American society, Jews have maintained their consistency in voting Democratic. Lawrence Fuchs documents this observation with analysis of presidential elections, based on small precinct and historical materials, and shows that adherence to

Jewish values hold together political beliefs of American Jews from Portugal, Spain, Russia, Lithuania, France and Germany.

In a more recent summary of nationwide surveys between 1964 and 1970 of fifteen major cities across the United States, Angus Campbell confirmed that Jews are consistently positive toward racial equality. They favor interracial contact, perceive discrimination toward blacks, are sympathetic to black protest, favor civil rights legislation, federal aid to cities, and improvement of black living and working conditions. Campbell suggests this positive orientation toward civil rights is not necessarily related to Jewish participation in organized religion, since many unaffiliated Jews hold these views. However, he does suggest that the Jewish experience of discrimination emanates in Jewish leadership in civil rights programs and policies combating racial prejudice.

Andrew M. Greeley reported in 1975 that on four measures of racial attitudes Jews were most favorable compared with other ethnic groups, including Poles who were least favorable. The attitudes analyzed were support for the election of a black mayor, civil rights legislation, interracial contact, and disapproval of repressive riot control. Favorableness toward racial integration for non-Southerners was higher among Jews than any other ethnic group studied, and Jewish support for integration was higher than all Northerners combined.

The McCarthy attacks during the 1950s were readily opposed by Jews, whose life experiences lead them to identify with liberal Democratic leadership. Further, Jews are leaders in the Civil Rights Movement disproportionately to their numbers in the general population. Particular Jews have been outspoken leaders in the struggle for equal rights: Julius Rosenwald in the education of blacks; Joel Spingarn in the founding of the National Association for the Advancement of Colored People; Morris Milgram in racially integrated housing. After the passing of the 1964 Civil Rights Act, many Jewish college students volunteered to encourage black voter registration in Mississippi, to set up community centers and establish "Freedom Schools" where black children were taught courses in remedial reading and political science. In peacefully protesting the exclusion of blacks from a motor lodge in Florida, sixteen rabbis were placed in jail. In telling of their reasons for participation in the protest they said, "We came because we could not stand silently by our brother's blood. . .We came as Jews who remember the millions of faceless people who stood quietly watching the smoke rise from Hitler's crematoria."[5]

In sum, the modal respondent in the sample from Jewish origins is primarily a first or second generation American, high in educational, occupational and income status, is very mobile in social status when compared with parents, is a Democrat in political voting, opposes radical right movements, and has a value orientation rooted in both religious tradition and experiences of discrimination which underpin commitment to social justice and civil rights.

Basis of Protestant Liberalism

Half of the sample derives from white Anglo-Saxon Protestant social origins, and 72 percent are at least third or fourth generation Americans. Many of the respondents' grandparents and great-grandparents came to the United States as immigrants from Northern and Western Europe before 1880, and many were in the country during the Civil War and its aftermath.

These generations were nurtured in democratic principles and values anchored in the Bill of Rights, which found practical expression in Jeffersonian and Jacksonian political philosophy. Although these basic civil liberties and civil rights did not originally apply to blacks, their extension to blacks has steadily increased. The application of the "due process" and "equal protection of the law" clauses of the Fourteenth Amendment is the basis upon which many court battles have been fought and civil rights legislation has been passed.

Based on his study of socio-religious groups in Detroit, Gerhard Lenski demonstrates that Protestants, particularly those involved in their formal religious organizations, tend to hold commitment to liberal interpretations of the Bill of Rights. Further, he found that the higher the Protestants' social status, the more they will support desegregation of schools, freedom of speech, and minority rights. Moreover, the higher their formal education, the more likely Protestants will affirm attitudes consistent with civil liberties and civil rights.

The findings of Seymour Martin Lipset's analyses concur, insofar as many Protestants, particularly those with the highest socio-economic status, have been opponents of radical right movements. In the United States, they oppose McCarthyites, Coughlinites, and Birchers.

The effect of regional socio-political climate on civil liberties attitudes is stressed in the work of Samuel A. Stouffer in *Communism, Conformity, and Civil Liberties*. Both Southern Protestants and their Catholic counterparts are less tolerant toward nonconformity and freedom of speech than Northern Protestants. However, Protestants living in the South are less tolerant than Catholics living in the North, whether or not either group members attend church. Of all the groups compared, Stouffer's data show that Northern Protestants who do not attend church are most supportive of civil liberties.

Protestants committed to democratic values, the Bill of Rights, and the

Fourteenth Amendment to the Constitution, are often the targets of attack by radical right wing movements. Joseph McCarthy and his followers specified State Department officials as being sympathetic to Communism. Characteristics singled out by the right wing extremists were the upper class backgrounds and high educational training of those in the State Department who received their education at Princeton, Yale, or Harvard. Alan F. Westin, likewise, in his discussion of Birchers, explains that "the Birchers impugn the integrity and patriotism of those at the head of the major social and economic groups of the nation. . . . The leadership of our universities, corporations, foundations, communications media—all are riddled with Communists."[6]

A segment of those from the Protestant socio-religious group do not support civil rights, but rather endorse movements of the radical right. Daniel Bell describes "the dispossessed," those likely to adopt the ideology of radical right movements. He says,

> . . .one can say that the social group most threatened by the structural changes in society is the "old" middle class—the independent physician, farm owner, small-town lawyer, real estate promoter, home builder, automobile dealer, gasoline-station owner, small businessman, and the like—and that, regionally, its greatest political concentration is in the South and the Southwest, and in California. But a much more telltale indicator of the group that feels most anxious—since life-styles and values provide the emotional fuel of beliefs and actions—is the strain of Protestant fundamentalism, of nativist nationalism, of good-and-evil moralism which is the organizing basis for the "world view" of such people.[7]

Consistent with this view is the analysis of Richard Hofstadter, who singles out two types of people likely to become involved in the radical right. First are "some types of old-family, Anglo Saxon Protestants," and second are "many types of immigrant families, most notably among the Germans and Irish, who are very frequently Catholic." He explains that Anglo Saxons are most likely to adopt radical right ideologies when they are *losing* status, and the immigrants are likely to adopt such ideologies when they are *gaining* status.

In conclusion, analysis of sociological and political studies demonstrates that those traditionally committed to the American Creed include old-time Americans from white Anglo-Saxon Protestant origins, relatively high in socio-economic status, and not living in the South. Although they are anchored in a secure status position within American society, they are the objects of attack by radical right wing extremist movements. Their social experiences, rooted in the basic tenets of democratic values, seal their support of civil liberties and civil rights.

The modal respondent in the sample from white Anglo-Saxon Protestant origins is at least a third or fourth generation American, linked with high educational, occupational and income status rungs in American society, is a Democrat in political preference, and as likely to state "atheist" as "Protestant" in religious affiliation. Further, this white liberal opposes socio-political movements of the radical right, espouses the values and beliefs of the American Creed, and believes in racial integration as the means of attaining social justice within the American democracy.

REFERENCES

1. The nineteen categories are based on grouped score intervals in Peter M. Blau and Otis Dudley Duncan, *The American Occupational Structure*, 1967, pp. 122-123.
2. Karl Mannheim, *Ideology and Utopia*, 1936, p. 2.
3. Ibid., p. 3.
4. Charles E. Silberman, *Crisis in Black and White*, p. 78.
5. Rabbi Henry Cohen, *Justice, Justice*, 1968, p. 18.
6. Alan F. Westin, "The John Birch Society (1962)," in Bell, ed., *The Radical Right*, 1964, pp. 245-246.
7. Daniel Bell, "The Dispossessed," in Bell, ed., *The Radical Right*, p. 24.

CHAPTER III

Dilemmas of the White Liberal

An exploration of attitudinal dilemmas of white liberals requires interpretation of their reactions to the current interracial scene. During the respondents' interviews, they discussed their views, concerns, and the issues surrounding six situations: (1) busing in schools for purposes of racial integration; (2) the entrance of blacks into the respondents' occupational fields; (3) blacks moving into the respondents' neighborhoods; (4) the quota system in the colleges; (5) rentals to blacks in white-occupied apartment buildings (hypothetically) owned by the respondents; and (6) hiring of blacks.

For each situation, the respondents first expressed their attitudes in reply to an initial open-ended question. Next, they responded to a series of probing questions designed to elicit attitudes on the potential conditions and consequences of each situation. Finally, toward the end of the series of questions for each situation, they informed the interviewer what their actions would be if they were involved in the interracial situation in real life. If the methodology required filling in questionnaires by a simple "yes," "no," or "don't know" answer to each interracial situation, the subleties of meaning in. beliefs and sensitivities of feelings would not have been revealed and extensively elaborated.

The respondents' replies exhibit four attitudinal forms. First, there are decidedly favorable attitudes. Second, there are conditional attitudes, which specify the limitations to a favorable position. Third, there are ambivalent attitudes or role conflicts. Fourth, there are clearly unfavorable attitudes.[1]

Typically, respondents show a differing extent of favorableness or un-favorableness toward each situation. They also demonstrate differing degrees of attitudinal complexity. Although some state simple, clear, and ideologically consistent answers, most demonstrate complexity as they delve deeper into the relevant issues of each situation. Examination of the sequences of expressed attitudes captures white liberals' dilemmas as the conditions, attitudinal ambivalences, role conflicts, and fears about the consequences of each situation are disclosed.

In kaleidoscopic fashion, most respondents change the attitudes they express during their interviews. They may state a favorable attitude, then elaborate various conditions under which a situation is acceptable to them, and finally express attitudes unfavorable toward the situation. Some affirm conditional views, discuss further negative consequences of the situation, and then state they will favor an integrationist position if they were confronted with the situation in their everyday lives. For example, in the busing situation, some white liberals state a probusing attitude, then move to expressions of fears about their being involved, and finally say they will cooperate with the implementation of busing in their school districts. In the apartment situation, respondents may initially assert positive attitudes toward renting to a black family, then proceed to discuss ambivalent feelings due to the potential economic loss involved, and finally say they will not rent to blacks.

The respondents knew they were being interviewed because of their membership in an organization which is a major reference group for them. Since the organization supports civil rights and racial integration, the respondents felt that at some point during their interviews, they should favor school busing, college quotas, the entrance of blacks into various occupational fields, and blacks moving into predominantly white residential areas.

It is important to point out that the interviews were conducted from October, 1969, through December, 1969, before the February 11, 1970, decision by Judge Alfred Gitelson of the Los Angeles Superior Court. He ruled that the Los Angeles City School system *must* integrate its schools. Although the suit charged that the Los Angeles City schools had deliberately maintained a segregated school system, the Gitelson decision did not order busing as the means of obliterating racial imbalance. However, many residents perceived that, in effect, massive busing would be the only means of carrying out the court order.

A content analysis of articles appearing in the *Los Angeles Times* reveals that before the Gitelson decision, there were very few articles about school busing. In contrast, after the decision, there were many articles reporting events relating to busing in the South, Boston, Pontiac, Riverside, Pasadena, Oxnard, San Francisco, Denver, and elsewhere across the nation. In addition, there have been many events reported in the newspapers, television and radio, including the controversial Wakefield Act in California, the U.S. Supreme Court decisions upholding cross-city busing to break down segregation, the antibusing statements of Governor George C. Wallace and his belief in a "freedom of choice plan," the proposal by Senator Ribicoff to bus inner-city blacks to white suburbs in 245 metropolitan areas, and statements by former President Nixon on the maintenance of the neighborhood school concept and his proposed moratorium which would prevent any new busing orders by federal courts.

Since the Gitelson decision, there has been some clarification of the "definition of the situation" regarding school busing. Busing has become a symbol: those taking a probusing position fall into the desegregationist camp; those taking an antibusing position fall into the segregationist camp, endorsing the preservation of the status quo with respect to the degree of racial integration in the schools.

Various inconsistencies and lack of attitudinal crystallization offer evidence that these six interracial situations pose many dilemmas for white liberals ideally supportive of efforts to attain the goal of racial integration in American society.

THE BUSING SITUATION

How do you personally feel about busing as a solution to de facto segregation in the schools?

Favorable Attitudes.

Busing affords an excellent means of breaking up patterns of segregation, whether defined as *de facto segregation* or *de jure segregation*. School busing institutes a method of making up for disparities in the education of blacks, Mexican-Americans, other minorities and whites. It is a catalyst providing the necessary stimulus for various boards of education, and other local, state, and federal authorities to improve schools in ghetto areas, primarily because white parents do not want their children to attend inferior schools.

Underlying these probusing attitudes is the thesis that busing facilitates reduction in prejudice. School busing makes possible interpersonal contact between people of different racial and ethnic groups, which, in turn, reduces prejudicial attitudes, intergroup hostility, and discriminatory behavior.

Any limits on busing, such as a percentage limitation, a limitation based on the potential of black children, or one based on the class status of black children, set up other forms of discrimination. All children should have the opportunity for an equally sound education, and a "democratic basis of selection should be implemented, not an elitist one."

Because people experience racial integration during the young, formative years of their lives, the primary impact of busing is in facilitating a constructive method of attaining the long range, positively valued goal of integration in American society.

Conditional Attitudes

The view that busing is feasible, only if it is limited to a certain percent of black children bused into predominantly white schools, was endorsed by 33 percent (68) of the respondents.

Some expressing this condition affirm that a percentage limitation of black students is the only way to eradicate racial imbalance. One respondent says,

> That's the only way to obtain a mixture. It is not good to have whites in a minority situation either. If the percent of blacks bused is too high, whites will feel encroached upon and will run, and then what would you have accomplished?

Others maintain that a percentage limitation on the number of black students bused into predominantly white schools is necessary because "it takes time for assimilation." In the words of one person,

> If there were too many blacks, they would ban together and defeat the purpose of busing. You can only absorb so many at one time. It's so difficult for those bused to be accepted and to adjust.

Two-thirds of the sample denied the importance of a percentage limitation on the black or white students bused. This denial is related to the feeling that any percentage limitation will be similar to a quota, which can operate as an exclusive factor rather than an inclusive factor.

The opinion that busing is a favorable plan, only if black children with the greatest academic potential, or with the highest IQs are bused into schools composed primarily of white students was affirmed by 24 percent (48) of the sample. Two primary stances are taken by those expressing this view. Some take the *standpoint of the white students,* and state that "it will be less disruptive for the white children already in the schools to be in classes with the brighter black children." Some conclude that prejudice will be reduced only if "whites see blacks who are excellent academically."

Others take the *standpoint of the black students.* Black children with the highest potential will gain most from the experiences to which they are exposed in better schools. As expressed by one interviewee,

> Smart blacks can cope best with new situations. Duller ones will feel frustrated. They would feel defeated among white students who have had better academic facilities. The smart ones would be better able to mix and keep up with the work.

The viewpoint that busing is an acceptable procedure, only if middle-class blacks are bused into predominantly white schools was expressed by 15 percent (31) of those interviewed. Some expressing the necessity for black students to stem from middle class families take the *standpoint of both black and white students.* An approximate equivalence in social class levels of blacks and whites in any given school facilitates "real" integration. If there were less social class cleavage among students, there would be more opportunity for development of positive forms of social interaction. One person states,

> You have a better chance of success with busing if the classes are kept parallel. Lower-class blacks should be with lower-class whites, and middle-class blacks should be with middle-class whites. There would be more similarity in values if blacks and whites were from the same social class level. The children would be more comfortable.

Others in supporting the condition that black children should be from middle-class families in order to be selected for busing to predominantly white schools take the *standpoint of the white students* to justify their position. White children will be negatively affected—socially, emotionally, and intellectually—if lower-class blacks are brought into their schools. One white liberal feels protective of white children,

> Only middle-class blacks should be brought in, because it would be better for the welfare of the white children. They won't be terrorized. There would be less trouble, because the main problems are among those blacks from the lower-class homes.

Another condition is that busing should be only *one-way busing,* with black children coming to predominantly white schools. The primary reason underpinning this view is that children from inferior schools will benefit by attendance at superior schools, and not vice versa. *Two-way busing* forces white children to attend ghetto schools not "up to par" with schools in white residential areas. It is unfair to force white or black students to attend schools outside their immediate neighborhoods. They express the view that "you can't force integration." Others believe that busing is an acceptable plan, only if it is a *temporary measure*—until there is full practice of integrated housing and employment in the community.

Ambivalent Attitudes

Most respondents are ambivalent about school busing. On the one hand, busing brings children of different races and ethnic groups into contact providing the basis for societal integration. On the other hand, busing creates more friction than presently exists between the races. Disclosing this type of ambivalence, one person states,

> Busing will be good for racial integration. It will bring together children of all races. But it will not really solve anything, because children will go back to their own communities and own families. Economic disparities will be accentuated. Conflict within the family will be increased. I really don't know how I feel about busing!

The main perceived role conflict concerns the incompatible expectations in roles as integrationists and roles as parents. As liberal integrationists, they believe that any procedure expediting integration of racial and ethnic groups should be wholeheartedly supported. As concerned parents, they express fears that their own children will be negatively affected by busing, because there will be physical danger caused by the mixture of races, the quality of education will go down, and the time spent on the bus will be detrimental to their children's health and welfare. One parent confirms these fears,

> Theoretically, I'm for busing. But it might hurt my kids. They would be a target of animosity by blacks who were racists. The general atmosphere in all black schools is bad. There is low morale and low educational level in ghetto schools. But intellectually, I would cooperate.

Others express the belief that too much of an issue is being made over school busing. Busing is really an unimportant feature in any legitimate discussion of racial integration. However, in their interaction with the interviewer, these respondents act *as if* they should be favorable toward busing. One person displays this type of ambivalence,

Busing isn't the real issue. Housing, fair employment practices, court decisions. . .these are real factors. You understand that I'm not against anything that would help the Negro or integration. After all, I'm a member of. . . . Maybe busing would help. I'm just not sure.

Unfavorable Attitudes

Clear antibusing sentiments reveal that it is an "artificial solution," it will be very costly for school districts already in deep financial straits, and money spent on busing could be better spent on improvement of educational facilities already in existence.

The fear that busing will bring physical danger for children was stated by 60 percent (122) of the respondents. Some specifically refer to the physical danger involved in the possible long bus rides required by a school busing program. Accidents might occur; freeways are dangerous; drivers are inattentive; pollution in the community is increased. More frequently, however, physical danger is envisioned as caused by the interaction of black and white students. Most expressing fears of physical danger take the *standpoint of the white children:*

Blacks are taught to fight it out. Blacks gang up on white children for nickels and dimes. They grow up in an area of violence. Blacks are prejudiced against whites. We are in the process of revolution, and I'd be afraid to go to Watts.

Some take the *standpoint of black and white children.* One person states the viewpoint of a "concerned third party,"

New conflict relations would be introduced. Whites are taught to hate blacks, and blacks are taught at an early age they are inferior. Mixed schools have more crime.

A few take the *standpoint of the black children* and say that "whites would not tolerate the Negro. Whites resent busing."

The negative consequence that the quality of education will be lowered if busing were instituted was expressed by 50 percent (102) of those interviewed. The level of educational material presented to children will be simplified. One parent expresses this view indicating the effects this lowered quality of education will have on white children:

Teaching is pitched to the "C" student. The level of education is lowered for the brighter child. If predominantly Negro, the quality will be lowered at all levels. It might even lower the IQs of the white children. Of course, in racially mixed schools, the quality of education is lowered, because the smart ones are held back so Negroes could catch up. After all, the cultural background of the Negro child is not educationally oriented.

Others think the quality of education will be lowered because of the problems created for teachers when racial groups are brought together. One teacher confirms this point of view,

Teachers would have to pay more attention to behavior problems. They would not have time to prepare lessons and to teach, due to constant interruptions. Fights and hostility between white and black children would affect the quality of teaching. The best teachers are driven out.

The fear that busing forcibly brings together students who might otherwise not socialize was expressed by 12 percent (24) of the respondents. Most expressing this view take the *standpoint of the white children:*

Blacks are angry, and I would not want my child physically hurt or called names.

Negroes do not have the character training of my children. Kids "down there" have problems which are internalized and will hurt my children. There is a higher level of antisocial behavior in the ghetto, and it will "rub off" on whites.

THE OCCUPATION SITUATION

How do you feel about Negroes (blacks) starting to work in *(the respondent's occupational field)?*[2]

Favorable Attitudes

Favorable views toward the entrance of blacks into various occupational fields incorporate the notion that "the color of one's skin does not make any difference" and the "blacks are considered as any other colleague, irrespective of race." Some articulate the belief that a mosaic of peoples in occupational settings makes the world a more interesting place and observe that "differences in cultural and racial backgrounds will make my field more attractive than it is now." Some say that because black people have personality qualities enabling them to more adequately perform the job, blacks will be better than whites in their fields. One person reports, "They have more patience than the whites already here." Others point to occupational qualifications and assert that because "they have to be twice as good to have gotten this far," blacks' qualifications are superior to those of whites. Others discuss the "plus value" of having blacks in their occupations. One states, "Hooray. We do have one! They should be given priority." Those favoring blacks entering their predominantly white occupations reason that the visibility of blacks serves as a positive symbol, indicating to other occupational areas and sectors of American society that racial integration is possible. A final positive consequence of favorable attitudes is that when their fields become racially integrated, white liberals need no longer feel defensive about involvement in a segregated and discriminatory occupation.

Conditional Attitudes

The opinion that blacks should enter the occupational fields under consideration, only if they have the necessary qualifications was expressed by 67 percent (137) of the respondents. The qualifications factor is the main condition the interviewees mention throughout the occupation situation. They invoke the principle that the same standards should be applied to all individuals in their occupational fields, irrespective of color. Standards should not be lowered for black people, because of their race. The concern with qualifications is usually expressed in connection with fear that qualifications will be lowered if blacks were to enter occupations where positions are primarily filled by whites. An accountant states,

> I'm favorable toward blacks coming into my field, only if the same board certifications and standards are met. Otherwise, standards will be lowered, and the quality of the work would not be as good. If blacks were here, it might seem like standards were lowered.

The condition that blacks should enter the occupational fields under consideration, only if they were middle class was endorsed by 56 percent (115) of those interviewed. Some stressing the importance of class status take what they perceive as the standpoint of the blacks. The job requirements are such that only middle-class people could engage in them successfully, and blacks will be unsuccessful if they are not from middle-class backgrounds. A lawyer contends,

> It's fine with me, as long as they are middle-class blacks. Because of the job requirements, they would have a better chance to succeed in this type of work if they were middle-class people. They wouldn't feel a sense of failure. Lower-class blacks couldn't be in this field.

Others are protective of blacks and reason that middle-class status will assure blacks of better treatment from those with whom they will come into contact. One person states, "You'd have to be more careful in selecting blacks in my field than whites, because there are so many prejudiced whites already."

Another group takes the standpoint of whites with whom the black person will be interacting. A businessman asserts, "They would have to be middle class in order to get along with the customers. The image of the company must be protected!" Others with whom blacks will be interacting are patients, clients, neighbors, and others within the occupational fields, such as other lawyers, doctors, administrators, teachers, and salespersons. These people will react negatively to blacks, unless they are from the middle class.

Ambivalent Attitudes

One attitudinal response includes conflict between dedication to the general principle of wanting blacks to enter new occupational fields for the purpose of racial integration, and the perceived reality concerns for problems they will meet in the particular fields under consideration. Two white liberals report,

> It's fine if blacks come into clerical work, but they aren't going to be decision-makers in this type of job. They would be overworked and underpaid. They'd have limited opportunities.

> I'm for integration; it would be fine. But as a medical technician, you need a "servant personality"! I can't see a black militant accepting orders and dealing with sick, cranky patients.

Another attitudinal dilemma takes the form of the *standpoint of a concerned party.* A head of an accounting firm states,

> I want to help blacks gain equal occupational opportunities, but I feel doubtful about the resentment of the whites the black will encounter in accounting.

Other respondents are ambivalent, because, on the one hand, they support the principle of "equal opportunities in occupations for all," and, on the other, entrance of blacks into their fields will be a "matter of whether you're willing to lower standards."

Some are ambivalent because they desire to implement racial integration in their occupational fields, but expect that blacks will have personality problems. A physical therapist reports, "Even when competent colored people are picked, they have a chip on their shoulders."

A typical role conflict is one in which the respondents as liberal integrationists are in favor of blacks entering their occupations because "color does not make any difference"; yet as businesspersons they might lose customers, patients, or clients. A realtor suggests,

> It would be wonderful for blacks to be in this business. We need to open up more avenues for blacks. But, in my type of work, I don't know. Business considerations lead me to not want blacks here.

Unfavorable Attitudes

The major reason respondents report when they express a clearly unfavorable attitude toward the entrance of blacks into their occupational fields is the negative consequence that standards will be lowered. The presence of blacks in their occupations will be a "reflection that qualifications are not up to standards." A doctor expresses this view,

> Standards have been lowered across the board for blacks to enter medicine. They're not qualified for medicine. They don't have the educational backgrounds.

Some underpin their unfavorable beliefs by citing the negative consequences of blacks interacting with clients, patients, customers, and others in the various occupational fields under consideration. In the sample 23 percent (45) support this view and are decidedly unfavorable toward blacks entering their fields for this reason.

Others cite the resentments of whites already working in their fields. This reason for unfavorable attitudes was invoked by 13 percent (26) of those interviewed. A lab technician states,

> It would scare the whites. My office would fall apart. Problems would be created which don't exist now. They'd never get along, and I'm unwilling to start trouble.

The view that "problems" will be caused by blacks is expressed by 9 percent (19) of the respondents, with one indicating that "Since Watts, I won't deal with blacks. They're militant, nervy."

Another group including 31 percent (63) expresses the feeling that there will be trouble in occupational fields other than their own. One respondent reports,

> It is so unlikely for blacks to enter the occupation. Even if they did, there wouldn't be any trouble. But there would be plenty of problems created

in other types of work, with other workers, with other professionals.
And the lowering of qualifications would be a great problem.

The fear that competition will be increased for whites already in the fields under discussion is expressed by 20 percent (41) of the respondents. Some are apprehensive that "blacks will replace whites already having a career here." Others perceive that competition will be unfair. A young professor shows his concern,

> I'm envious. Lower standards are set for them. They wouldn't be under pressure to publish. They will achieve tenure even though they are not publishing and are not good teachers. Minorities get grants on the basis of their color. They have top priority for positions, too. It's unfair.

The concern that their occupations will have less prestige value should blacks enter is endorsed by 12 percent (24) of the respondents stating unfavorable attitudes toward the entrance of blacks into their occupational fields. The primary reason substantiating this view is that lowering of qualifications to allow blacks to gain admittance will automatically lower the reputational standing.

Of those interviewed, 15 percent (30) affirmed that they will not feel comfortable with a black in a position higher than their own, "especially if the Negro were not qualified," while 6 percent (12) will not feel comfortable if the black is working at the same level. The rationale for unfavorable attitudes is, once again, the "image that qualifications had been lowered."

THE RESIDENCE SITUATION

What would you do if Negroes (blacks) began to move into your neighborhood?

If black families already lived in the respondents' neighborhoods, they were asked,

What would you do if more Negroes (blacks) began to move into your neighborhood?

Favorable Attitudes

Many affirming attitudes favorable toward blacks moving into their neighborhoods reason that blacks "have the right to live where they want as well as I do." These white liberals say that "color doesn't make any difference to me, black, brown, green, red or purple!" Residential integration is the solution to racial problems, since people of all races will get to know each other on a "neighborhood basis." Stereotypes will be splintered. Children will learn and socialize in schools together, and racial and ethnic barriers will be broken down.

Some express the idea that there will be a "plus value" to blacks moving into their neighborhoods. One respondent states,

> If Negroes came in, I'd call on them. I usually don't know any of my neighbors, but I'd go out of my way for a Negro. I'd knock on the door and introduce myself.

Some suggest that black neighbors will be better than white neighbors, as blacks are more interesting than whites. One person captures this feeling, "Blacks will be better than the whites here now. Middle-class whites are so dull!"

The presence of black families will demonstrate to other neighborhoods that racial integration is realistically workable. Those stating favorable attitudes will help form a group, such as Crenshaw Neighbors, to help form a successfully integrated community.

Conditional Attitudes

The condition that blacks moving into their neighborhoods is acceptable, only if blacks were middle-class people was endorsed by 75 percent (152) of the white liberals interviewed. Similarity in class status is more important than similarity in race, ethnic, or religious identification. Several respondents' attitudes exemplify this reasoning,

> It would be fine, if they could afford to live here. They would be a certain calibre of people. Their values and goals would be like mine. Their social and intellectual character would be good. Their ways of raising children would be similar to my own.

> They'd be closer to me than lower-class whites. They should be middle class, because the neighborhood is middle class. They'd fit in better and have more in common with the other neighbors.

> Yes, no riff-raff in this neighborhood! This is a middle-class area. I would prefer no one of lower class, especially Negroes.

The condition that only a certain percent of blacks should move into their neighborhoods was stated by 38 percent (78) who reason that this limitation is the only route to obtaining racial balance in a neighborhood. However, others think lower class families, lowering the educational quality of neighborhood schools, deterioration of property, and fears that "white kids will be picked on by blacks." One way to prevent trouble is by blacks moving into a neighborhood "slowly, and not en masse, forcing their way in."

Ambivalent Attitudes

Most respondents confirm their belief in racial integration and concur that the essence of integration is the desirability of blacks moving into predominantly white residential areas. If the pattern of residential segregation could be broken up, school segregation will be dismantled. Integration in neighborhoods provides the opportunity for peoples of different racial and ethnic groups to interact, and this interaction reduces prejudice. However, a major dilemma exists when the respondents raise the question of how long they could continue to live in their neighborhoods if blacks were moving in and whites were progressively moving out. A respondent points to this dilemma,

> It's fine for blacks to move here. It's good for integration. But I would not like to live in a ghetto, anybody's ghetto! I don't know what I'd do.

One main role conflict the respondents manifest is the incompatibility between the liberal integrationist role and the neighborhood friend role. In playing their roles as liberal integrationists, they will be favorable toward any forms of integration; they will be "happy to have blacks in this neighborhood because blacks have the freedom of living where they want." As neighborhood friends, they will be "causing the neighbors all kinds of problems" by being favorable toward blacks moving into their neighborhoods. This role conflict is reflected in two replies,

> I'd welcome blacks, and did, but I've slowed down because of rebuffs from other neighbors. I couldn't take it anymore.

> It's the thing to do for integration, but if they turned out to be crackpots and threw bombs, I'd never forgive myself for the trouble I caused my neighbors.

Some also state the conflict they will experience if they sell their homes to black families fulfilling their own expectations of what a liberal integrationist should do and then move out of the neighborhoods and "leave all the neighbors with the problems." One man reports his experience when he was trying to sell his home. He wanted to "stand up for his principles if a black came looking, but none did, and was I glad!"

Some role conflicts occur because of a clash between liberal roles and economic roles. As integrationists, liberals will act in support of racial integration in residential areas; as economic individuals they want to gain all the monetary profit possible from the sale of their homes, and if blacks actually move into their neighborhoods, the value of the property will "without question go down."

Unfavorable Attitudes

Those expressing attitudes decidedly against blacks moving into their neighborhoods state their reasons in terms of the negative consequences they envision occurring if blacks were to reside in white residential areas. The belief that the reputational standing of the neighborhood will go down if blacks move in was expressed by 67 percent (136) of the respondents. Some place blame on prejudiced whites when they think the reputational standing will be lowered because "there are still a lot of bigoted people. We have a racist society. Whites are prejudiced." Others believe the reputational standing of their neighborhoods is high because no blacks live there. One respondent says, "This is a high-class neighborhood and part of that high class is because it's all white."

Another group affirming that the reputational standing of their neighborhoods will be lowered if blacks move in place blame on blacks. Loss of prestige happens because "standards of maintenance will deteriorate if blacks move in here." The class level of the neighborhoods will be lowered, thereby diminishing the reputational standing.

The opinion that there will be an economic loss for whites already living in the neighborhoods if blacks move in was confirmed by 32 percent (66) of the interviewees. Evidence is usually cited by those endorsing this position. One person explains what happened to her family:

> I moved from an area in. . .that was turning black. We definitely lost money, and it took so long to sell the house. It was so hard for us, especially since we had put so much money into the house remodeling. My kids had such troubles at the high school there. . .blacks starting fights, teaching problems. . . . They were picked on because they were Jewish. Can you imagine blacks being angry at Jews? Our former neighbors are having such a time selling their homes. They'll really take a loss!

A few respondents had their homes for sale at the time of the interviews. Selling because of fear that the school system was deteriorating, one man in

Pasadena was certain he will lose financially in the sale of his home. Another reports,

> I moved in when Negroes already lived here, but now there are over fifty percent, and my home is up for sale. I've redecorated the whole place and remodeled the bathrooms and kitchen. My house is one of the best on the block. I know I'll lose money.

Some use facts based on their friends' or relatives' experiences. One white liberal claims, "My cousin took a loss when they had to sell after blacks moved into their block." Others reason that "values won't go down, but they won't go up either, and in this day and age, that's like taking a loss."

The concern that there will be "danger," if blacks move into their neighborhoods was expressed by 49 percent (100) of the respondents. There are many definitions of "danger," including physical danger for whites, economic danger, danger because of "lower class" blacks, danger of maintenance deterioration, danger caused by the formation of another ghetto, danger from prejudice by blacks toward whites, and danger from the lowering of the educational quality of neighborhood schools.

THE QUOTA SITUATION

What do you think about colleges using a quota system, so that minorities will be represented according to their proportion in the population?

Favorable Attitudes

The use of a quota system as a means of selecting students for admission to colleges is an excellent procedure of overcoming the present inequities in educational opportunities of minority students and white students. One liberal contends,

> It's a good idea. It will make up for discrepancies between minorities and whites. Anything that will help minorities would be good. They have been systematically excluded, and now they need to be systematically included.

Some supporters of quotas reason that blacks and other minorities should be "overrepresented" and should be "included in the colleges and universities more than their proportion in the general population."

The primary reason for favorable attitudes toward the quota system is the belief that education is the means by which people will improve their occupational statuses and standard of living. Education will create equal opportunities for all individuals; education will provide opportunities for all individuals to attain high status.

In addition, quota systems in the colleges will facilitate racial integration on the campuses. This experience will make it possible for people to extend integration to other areas of social interaction—in recreational facilities, in organizations, in occupations, and in residential areas. In effect, the goal of racial integration will be reinforced by the implementation of quota systems as a basis for selecting students for college admission.

Conditional Attitudes

The major condition for college quotas is that they are a satisfactory basis for selecting students, only if qualifications were established and maintained. Underlying this condition is the possible negative consequence that standards will deteriorate. One concerned liberal expresses this view,

> A quota system is O.K., if the same standards are applied to all. Otherwise, academic deterioration would occur. I'm favorable towards the use of quotas, as long as qualifications are kept up.

Another condition is that college quota systems will be acceptable admission's procedures, only if qualified white students are not excluded. It will be "racism in reverse," if qualified whites were excluded in order to permit the entrance of blacks or other minorities on the basis of their racial or ethnic identities. One person states,

> Quotas are fine, if they are set up so they won't exclude qualified white students. It would be discriminatory against whites to accept blacks into college just because they were black. White students may have better grades or better scores on entrance exams than blacks. I'll go along with quotas, if qualified students are not kept out.

Some favor the use of college quotas only as temporary, stop-gap measures. Black students should be given opportunities to "catch up with white students" by the creation of special programs, tutoring, and extra classes at the junior college level. If there were improvements in the educational facilities at the primary and secondary school levels, minority students will increase their educational potential. After a period of time, black and other minority students could then be chosen for college admission on the basis of qualifications and not on the basis of racial or ethnic background.

Ambivalent Attitudes

The main dilemma crystallized is whether a quota provides for a *system of inclusion* or a *system of exclusion*. There is a desire to include more minority students on campuses, as this inclusion will be beneficial to the minority students and will aid campus integration. However, there is a pervasive feeling that a quota system will also be an exclusive factor, limiting the entrance of qualified whites. One respondent encapsulates this dilemma,

> Quota systems are fine, in that they let more minority students into the colleges. But if they are a limiting factor, keeping able students out, they're not good. I want to see more minorities on the campus, but how can we exclude others, just because we want to let more minorities in? I can't make up my mind. . .

This issue of whether a quota system is inclusive or exclusive sometimes takes the form of a role conflict. As liberal integrationists the respondents want more representation of minorities on the campuses. Yet, as parents, they are concerned about their own children's acceptance into college if places were "taken by blacks or Mexican-Americans which may otherwise go to my child." One father told about his daughter,

> My daughter was valedictorian of her high school class. Her achievement test scores are in the top percentiles. Yet she couldn't get accepted into a top university when obviously less qualified blacks were getting accepted. Yet, I'm in favor of making up for past discrimination for minorities and for evening up the scales. It's the only way to achieve social justice. But it's not fair for my child.

Another role conflict indicates the exclusion-inclusion dilemma. As Jews, some respondents had the life-experience of being kept out of colleges of their choice or out of medical schools, because of quotas designed to restrict the number of Jewish students. If they did not have direct experience, Jews are well aware of quotas used in American universities to keep Jewish enrollment within a certain percentage limit. At the same time, these Jews, as liberal integrationists, desire to assist other minorities increase their numbers on the campuses in order to make up for disparities in the education of whites and minority groups and to fight institutionalized inequities in American society.

Another conflict surfacing during the interviews on the college quota system is a clash between two principles: the principle of helping minorities improve their educational opportunities and their chances for high occupational statuses; and the principle of maintaining very high standards of academic achievement. One person reports,

> We should make up for the disadvantage to the individual minority person because of discrimination. Yet I hate to see the world full of unqualified doctors and educators.

Unfavorable Attitudes

The main rationale against the quota system in colleges is that it establishes an ascriptive basis for the selection of students for college entrance. Those against quotas assert that percentages of any kind are discriminatory. Summarizing this viewpoint, one respondent says,

> All should get a chance, regardless of background. Quotas make an issue of race. People should be judged as individuals. Quotas have worked to exclude minorities.

Ideally, an achievement basis of selection should be the guiding rule in the admittance of students to college. Students should be chosen on the basis of their merit and qualifications, not on the basis of racial, religious, ethnic, or social backgrounds. A major reason for opposition to quotas is that qualifications of students and standards of colleges will be lowered if quota systems were instituted. Of those interviewed, 83 percent (169) endorsed this opinion. One respondent explains,

> We should not lower the standards of the university. It would be like a high school, where just about anyone can get a diploma. It would be suggestive that people are qualified in certain areas when they really are not. It could carry the whole group down. It's like baby sitting.

A quota system will cause administrative problems since academic standards will be lowered to bring in minority students. One liberal indicates this concern,

> Quotas would make it too hard on the school system, the administration, and the teachers. They would be poor students and create problems. They'd be troublemakers.

Opposition to quotas is supported by the belief that there will be an increase in physical danger on the campuses. This attitude was stated by 45 percent (91) of the interviewees.

Taking the *standpoint of white students,* some fear there will be an increase in physical danger in colleges where minority students are permitted entrance based on their minority status. Two responses document this opinion,

> The experience of my friends has been that with an increase in the black population, there has been an increase in physical danger for whites.

> Young blacks are indoctrinated by their parents. There is greater militancy among black students compared to white students. Street knowledge, acting out. . . . There is more unrest among Negroes than among whites. It's a fact.

Taking the *standpoint of both minority and white students,* some express the belief that when different races are brought together, there is a tendency for polarization to occur, with a concomitant increase in the chances for racial tensions and physical danger for members of the racial groups. One respondent's reply demonstrates this belief,

> With quotas, there would be racial antagonisms. There is prejudice between the two groups. Negroes don't beat people up. It's a civil rights' matter, a sociological problem if they're militant. And they can get hurt by hostile whites.

Taking the *standpoint of the minority students,* some reason that the recent disturbances witnessed on the campuses are caused by white students. One person says, "White students get emotional about new things." Another reports that "the presence of police creates the danger."

Of those opposing quotas, 43 percent (87) incorporated the opinion that the relative standing of the educational quality of a college using a quota system will be lowered. Quotas will lower the academic qualifications of students admitted to college, because "minority students just don't have the academic abilities of whites," and the ratings of colleges using quotas will go down.

The opinion that there will be less value for a degree received from a college using quotas was held by 27 percent (55) of the respondents. Diminution of degree value is a consequence of lowering qualifications for minority students.

The feeling that quotas on the campuses will bring together students who should not socialize was expressed by 5 percent (11) of the integrationists. Some liberals say, "it is not good for students to mix because of the lower-class level of blacks." In contrast, a few think black students will reject white students, as "militant blacks exclude whites. They don't mix socially, and this is true of all public mass gatherings."

THE APARTMENT SITUATION

What would you do if a Negro (black) family wanted to rent one of your apartments, and you personally didn't mind renting to Negroes (blacks), but your tenants threatened to move out?[3]

Favorable Attitudes

Standing by their principles, some white liberals favor renting to blacks in predominantly white-occupied apartment buildings. They will rent to the black family as they believe in the principle of equal rights for all people and willingness to rent reveals consistency with general ideals of not discriminating against any individuals because of their race, religion, or ethnic group. If black families were to move into predominantly white-occupied apartment buildings, the goal of racial integration will become a reality. Those favorable toward renting to blacks state they "would let those white people who were threatened move out!"

Conditional Attitudes

The position that they will rent to the black family, if the family were from a middle-class level, was stated by 55 percent (112) of those interviewed. Middle-class black people will get along best with the white people already living in the apartment house. Class status should be the same for blacks and whites living near each other, otherwise there will be an accentuation of racial antagonism and conflict. Some hold that middle-class blacks will "get along with me. They'd be more like me in so many ways."

Related to the class factor was the opinion expressed by 21 percent (42) that they will rent to the black family, if the family can afford to pay the price necessary for rental. If blacks can afford to live in the building, they will by definition be "middle class people who wouldn't cause trouble and would have the same values as the white people already living there."

Associated with the class factor is the condition that the standards of maintenance will be kept up and the building will not deteriorate, if only middle-class blacks were to move in. This condition was acknowledged by 17 percent (35) of the sample.

The condition that they will rent to blacks, only if a certain percentage of blacks were to move into the building, was endorsed by 41 percent (83) of the liberals interviewed. The percentage limitation rests on two main reasons. First, if a large percentage of apartments were occupied by blacks, a new segregation pattern will emerge. One respondent contends, "I don't want a ghetto. That would be reverse prejudice. I'm for integration, net segregation." Second, many fear that their economic interest will be threatened, if many blacks were to rent in their building. One respondent articulates such fears,

> It's O.K. for blacks to move into the building, but I wouldn't want too many blacks. Whites would flee, and my economic interest would be threatened. Whatever reservations I would have would be economic. I would rent to the blacks, but only within a certain percent.

Ambivalent Attitudes

One main role conflict made clear in the attitudes toward this situation revolves around the incompatible expectations of the role of liberal integrationist and the role of economic individual. As integrationists, liberals believe in open housing, and stress the rights of every individual, regardless of color, to live where desired. As individuals concerned with the profits their investments bring, they are pressured to deny rental to blacks, because of the expectation of the negative economic consequences. One person discloses this role conflict,

> I think there ought to be open housing. Everybody can live wherever they want. Of course, I'm worried about the collection of rents. And how about the whites moving out? I could conceivably be false to my principles in a situation like this one, though I don't really know.

Some resolve conflict in roles by saying they will avoid this situation in real life. One respondent says, "That's why I won't own an apartment house!" Others delegate the rental procedures to managers or coowners. One person states, "I don't do the renting. I have the feeling the manager is prejudiced. I'm glad I'm not involved."

Another role conflict is described by those who, on the one hand, believe in the rights of all individuals to live wherever they choose, and, on the other, believe that tenants already living in an apartment building might have their own feelings about such a circumstance. As landlords stepping into the roles of their tenants, the respondents believe they must "protect the interests" of the tenants. As liberal integrationists, they want to promote racial integration. The feelings of one respondent reveal this role conflict,

> I'd want to rent. I do not believe in discriminating against any individual because of color. But tenants have rights, too! They might not want to

live near blacks. It might upset them. I'd try to get them together. Maybe that would help. But it may not work. I really don't know what to do in this case.

Unfavorable Attitudes

Decidedly unfavorable attitudes against renting to a black family in a predominantly white-occupied apartment building are expressed in terms of two negative consequences. First, economic loss is assumed to result from renting to blacks. Second, lowering of the reputation of the property is associated with the rental.

The belief that an economic loss will result from rentals to blacks was stressed by 72 percent (147) of the respondents. Most cite evidence to support their negative statements. One respondent indicates, "Experience has shown that property values go down when Negroes move in." Others tell of experiences of their friends or relatives, or they speak about their own discomforting experiences.

Some place blame on whites, stating that it is "because of whites who are prejudiced and who move out that economic problems arise." Others place blame on blacks, indicating that "blacks do not maintain the property." The class status of blacks will not be "parallel with the whites already living there, and problems will be created because lower-class blacks cause all kinds of trouble." One respondent reveals his fears, "If a Negro doesn't pay, I'd be afraid to ask for the rent!"

The belief that the reputation of the apartment building will be lowered, if the black family were to move in, was expressed by 64 percent (131) of the respondents. Some find rationale for their opinion by placing blame on the white middle class. One person states, "The whites who do the evaluating of reputation, middle-class. people who are status minded, they will say it is lower." Others believe that it is a fact that the reputation will go down. One liberal says, "I have yet to see where an area became a Park Avenue because Negroes moved in!"

THE HIRING SITUATION

How do you feel about hiring Negroes (blacks)?

Favorable Attitudes

Support for every effort to hire blacks for various positions incorporates the ideal that equal opportunities should exist for all people, regardless of their racial, religious, or ethnic backgrounds. There should be no discrimination against black persons because of the color of their skin. Blacks "should have every opportunity to be hired on the same levels as whites in all jobs." Some white liberals suggest that blacks will be better than whites for certain positions and state that blacks are more qualified in many instances. Visibility of blacks in a wide range of positions symbolizes a racially integrated society.

Conditional Attitudes

The major condition in the hiring situation is that hiring blacks is a favorable procedure, only if the qualifications and standards of the position are met, and this factor was endorsed by 97 percent (197) of those interviewed. Expressive of this condition is this statement,

> I believe in fair employment, as long as the job requirements are kept up. Race is not relevant. Business is business. I want the job well done.

Support for hiring blacks, as long as they are middle-class persons, was affirmed by 59 percent (120) of the respondents. Some endorsing this condition state that class status is important because of the type of professional positions they have in mind. For blacks to best meet the requirements of the jobs, they will, by necessity, have to come from middle-class backgrounds. One lawyer says, "They'd have to be middle class, or they couldn't fit into the position. Part of being a lawyer is being middle class." Others feel that middle-class status is necessary for blacks to have good interpersonal relationships with people with whom they would be dealing. Middle-class status will assure the best communication with clients, patients, co-workers, and customers.

The opinion that hiring blacks is a good procedure, only if there will be a percentage limit on the number of blacks hired, was stated by 12 percent (25) of those interviewed. Some support their reasoning for this conditional response by indicating that a percentage limitation is necessary to see a "mixture" of blacks and whites. One respondent says,

> If there were a large percentage of blacks, they would ban together. There would be a rift between the two groups. They wouldn't get along. They wouldn't mix.

Ambivalent Attitudes

One problem encountered by some white liberals is that they are impeded in their efforts to act out their roles as liberal integrationists. They make efforts to hire blacks, but they "cannot find any blacks qualifying for the job." While they value integration as a goal, these integrationists are also committed to certain standards of job performance. They do not want to "lower qualifications in order to hire a black person." One person states this role conflict,

> I want to hire blacks. I've tried to find blacks for the jobs, but I can't find any who are qualified. They can't speak English properly and this is essential to this job.

Another role conflict exists because the liberal integrationist role is not always consistent with the businessperson role. There is a desire to hire blacks in order to provide them with more occupational opportunities. However, there are pressures from significant others who imply that blacks have difficulty interacting with patients, clients, and customers because of a "a chip on their shoulders." Also stressed are the implications that the quality of work is not up to par when blacks hold jobs and that whites do not feel comfortable working with blacks.

Another dilemma exists in that there is favorableness toward hiring blacks, but there is also the expectation that blacks will not get along with the white liberal. One individual reports a personal experience,

> It's fine with me. I like the idea of hiring blacks. They need opportunities for occupational improvement. But when I hired a Negro architect, he was not friendly with me!

One major dilemma involved in hiring blacks emerges in a series of three questions dealing with white liberals' perceptions of the qualifications of blacks.

(1) Would you hire a Negro (black) person in preference to a white person even though the Negro (black) person were quite a bit less qualified than the white person?

(2) Would you hire a Negro (black) if he or she were just a little less qualified than a white person?

(3) If both a white person and a Negro (black) person were equally qualified, whom would you hire?

One-half of the sample will hire blacks where both blacks and whites appear equally qualified. However, 46 percent suggest that hiring on the basis of race is discriminatory. These white liberals are caught between the implications of two principles: the principle of increasing the occupational areas in which blacks are included, for reasons of "making up for past inequities," for the purpose of furthering the goal of integration, and for the purpose of eradicating the subordination of blacks; and the principle that race is irrelevant in the selection of any individual for occupational positions. On the one hand, liberals want to provide blacks with increased occupational opportunities, but on the other, they must "be careful not to reverse the prejudice," since they believe hiring blacks because of the race factor is a discriminatory act toward whites.

Unfavorable Attitudes

Opposition to hiring blacks is stated in terms of the perceived negative consequences. The expectation that hiring blacks will cause white people already working at a particular place to develop hostility toward them was expressed by 36 percent (73) of the respondents. One person asserts,

> It would stir up prejudice. The reaction of the people around them, other workers, would be prejudicial. There would be a white backlash.

Others mention that whites will be insecure about their jobs and will fear being fired, if blacks are hired. One opponent to the practice of hiring blacks confirms this view,

> It would appear to be a decision made on a racial basis. If white people were fired, it would create another minority problem among whites. Another ghetto would be created. It shakes up the security of the whites and disrupts work. Everyone would be out of a job. The work force—Mexicans and whites—would say, "If you're not black, you will not get a job!"

The belief that the reputation of the positions for which blacks are hired will be lowered was stated by 27 percent (54) of the sample. The basic causal factor is that qualifications "will appear to be lowered if blacks hold certain jobs." Many place blame for this lowering of reputational standing on the "white racists, the bigots who make the judgements."

Some interviewees do not want to hire blacks, because they perceive hostility from blacks. Two replies represent this feeling,

> I do not want to hire Negroes, because there is so much Negro hostility now. I don't want to be surrounded by people who don't like me.

> I'd rather not hire blacks. They are resentful to orders which are accepted by white people. My position requires giving orders, and I don't want to tell blacks what to do.

Another group does not want to be involved in hiring blacks, because if they interview them for jobs and do not hire them, there will be "pressures from authorities" and they will be required to fill out "all kinds of forms and would rather not be bothered." Others do not wish to hire blacks, because if they had to fire them because of poor job performance, they "could not do it, because it would appear to be discriminatory."

SUMMARY OF WHITE LIBERALS' MAJOR DILEMMAS IN THE SIX SITUATIONS

The middle-class status factor is important in all six interracial situations. It is confirmed by 75 percent (152) in the residence situation, 59 percent (120) in the hiring situation, 56 percent (115) in the occupation situation, and 55 percent (112) in the apartment situation. Although the middle-class condition is directly affirmed by only 15 percent (31) in the busing situation, it is implied in the two situations in the educational sector by responses to fears of physical danger. In the busing situation, 60 percent (122) fear physical danger, while 45 percent (91) express such fears in the quota situation. The primary reason underlying this negative consequence of busing and quotas is the stereotypical perception that blacks and other minorities will hurt white students. Especially noticeable in the quota situation are fears of black militants on campuses.

A large proportion of the sample contends that academic standards will be lowered when quotas in colleges or busing in primary and secondary schools are instituted. For the quota situation, 83 percent (169) and for the busing situation, 50 percent (102) confirm this position.

The two situations in the residential sector bring economic factors sharply into focus. In the apartment situation, 72 percent (147) fear they will suffer an economic loss, if they rent to a black family in a building occupied by whites, and in the residence situation 32 percent (66) agree with this consequence.

The two situations in the occupational sector bring the qualification's condition to the surface. In the hiring situation, 97 percent (197), and in the occupation situation, 67 percent (137) allege they will favor blacks entering positions, only if all job requirements are met.

FROM QUOTAS TO HIRING

Will white liberals show ambivalence about specific interracial situations, or will they reveal ambivalence in all situations on a comprehensive scale as they question their adherence to the American Creed? Will retreats in one interracial situation be related to retreats in others? Will there be a hierarchical ordering of situations with variations in the degree of favorableness among them?

According to one viewpoint, white liberals retreating from racial integration in one situation will retain their commitment in other situations. Those faced with the possibility that their children will be bused to achieve racial balance in schools will favor integration, except where their children are involved. They will favor integration in housing and employment, but oppose the implementation of a busing program in their communities. Similarly, liberal employers will support occupational integration, except when their clients are unwilling to deal with black staff members. They protect their liberalism by compartmentalizing their attitudes. Liberal apartment house owners favor housing desegregation, except where they fear economic loss in their own rentals.

According to a contrasting viewpoint, any threatening encounter with racial integration in one situation will have an effect upon one's general ideals. Consequently, when commitment to integration is intense, one is unlikely to oppose busing of one's children. But when hiring blacks becomes questionable, then one's commitment to racial integration is weakened in a universal way.

The technique of scalogram analysis provides an instrument which will confirm one thesis rather than the other. If the views of white liberals form an acceptable scale, the situational hypothesis is rejected in favor of the universal hypothesis. If the attitudes do not form an acceptable scale, then the thesis of situationally discrete attitudes toward integration receives support.

Figure 1 summarizes the respondents' attitudes toward each situation. Four types emerge:

(1) *Unconditional Liberals:* respondents expressing only favorable attitudes toward the situation; these respondents do not express any conditional, ambivalent, or unfavorable attitudes.

(2) *Conditional Liberals:* respondents expressing a mixture of favorable and conditional responses, but no ambivalent or unfavorable attitudes.

(3) *Liberals in Conflict:* respondents expressing a combination of favorable, conditional, and ambivalent responses, but no unfavorable attitudes.

(4) *Liberals in Retreat:* respondents expressing all four attitudinal forms—favorable, conditional, ambivalent, and unfavorable responses.

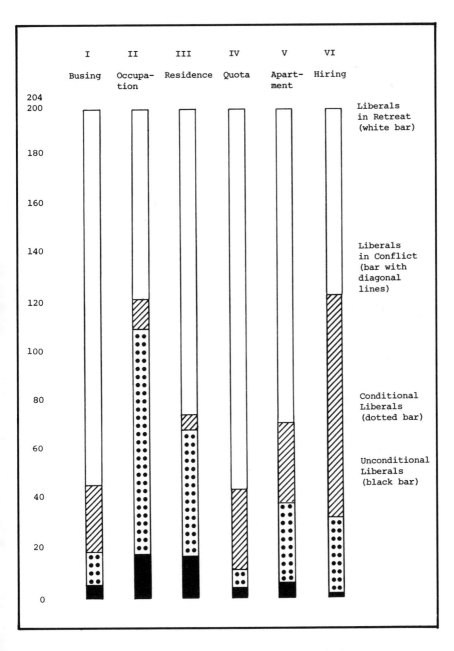

Fig. 1. Distribution of Respondents by Their Attitudinal Forms

TABLE IV

Marginals for Calculation of Minimal Marginal
Reproducibility

	more favorable		less favorable		Total
	%	N	%	N	
I. quota	18.2	37	81.8	167	204
II. busing	52.9	108	47.1	96	204
III. residence	61.7	126	38.3	78	204
IV. apartment	72.8	148	27.2	55	203*
V. hiring	78.4	160	21.6	44	204
VI. occupation	89.2	181	10.8	22	203*

*one case was missing from the occupation and apartment situations.

The quota and busing situations represent the largest percentages of *Liberals in Retreat,* with 79 percent (162) in the quota situation, and 73 percent (158) in the busing situation falling into this category. The residence and apartment situations are next in order, with 64 percent (130) in the residence situation, and 66 percent (134) in the apartment situation placing under the *Liberals in Retreat* category. The occupation and hiring situations are last in order, with 38 percent (79) in the occupation situation, and 39 percent (80) in the hiring situation falling in the *Liberals in Retreat* group. This analysis suggests that the situations most easily handled by the respondents are the occupation and hiring situations. Those producing the most difficulty and fears of negative consequences are the quota and busing situations. These situations evoke expressions of conditional attitudes, ambivalence, role conflicts, and unfavorableness. The residence and apartment situations fall between these two extremes.

Dichotomizing the respondents into two groups provides the basis for the scalogram. As seen in Table IV, those expressing a large proportion of favorable replies toward the initial, probing, and hypothetical action questions are placed in the "more favorable" group, while those expressing largely conditional, ambivalent, and unfavorable replies are placed in the "less favorable" group.[4]

Table V indicates that acceptable scalogram standards are met.[5] Respondents in Scale Type I are favorable toward all six interracial situations. Those classified as Scale Type II are favorable toward the busing, residence, apart-

TABLE V

Scalogram of the Respondents' Attitudes Toward
the Six Situations

N	Scale Type	Quota	Busing	Residence	Apartment	Hiring	Occupation
18	I	+	+	+	+	+	+
78	II	-	+	+	+	+	+
48	III	-	-	+	+	+	+
16	IV	-	-	-	+	+	+
20	V	-	-	-	-	+	+
17	VI	-	-	-	-	-	+
7	VII	-	-	-	-	-	-
204							

- signifies unfavorable attitudes
+ signifies favorable attitudes

Coefficient of Reproducibility	.90
Minimal Marginal Reproducibility	.73
Percent Improvement	.17
Coefficient of Scalability	.63

ment, hiring, and occupation situations, but they are not favorable toward
the quota situation. Those falling under Scale Type III express favorable
attitudes toward the residence, apartment, hiring, and occupation situations,
but demonstrate unfavorable attitudes toward the quota and busing situations.
The respondents classified as Scale Type IV express favorable attitudes
toward the apartment, hiring, and occupation situations, but state unfavorable attitudes toward the quota, busing, and residence situations. Those
classified as Scale Type V hold favorable attitudes toward the hiring and
occupation situations, but express unfavorable attitudes toward the quota,
busing, residence, and apartment situations. Those under Scale Type VI
reply favorably to the occupation situation, but hold unfavorable attitudes
toward the other five situations. Respondents falling under Scale Type VII
express attitudes not favorable toward any of the interracial situations
presented to them during their interviews.

Interpretation of the scalogram in terms of difficulty demonstrates that
the quota situation is the most difficult of the situations for the respondents.
If they do not express ambivalence, attitudinal dilemmas, role conflicts,
or attitudes unfavorable toward the quota situation, they do not express
difficulty in any of the other situations. However, if they express ambivalence

or attitudes unfavorable to the occupation situation, the least difficult of the situations, they likewise express dilemmas or attitudes unfavorable toward all the other situations.

The use of the scalogram technique furnishes a method of predicting white liberals' responses to six interracial situations with knowledge of their Scale Types alone. Without attention to any similarities or differences in the respondents' characteristics, such as their ethnicity or occupational mobility, there is demonstration of a systematic ordering of retreat or adherence to a belief in racial integration. Underlying this ordering is one universe of content, namely, the degree of attitudinal favorableness toward the situations. In addition, there is illustration of the degree of difficulty inherent in the situations, with the quota situation producing the most complexity and attitudinal unfavorableness for the whole sample of white liberals, and the occupation situation eliciting the least difficulty.

Favorableness is defined as endorsement of integration strategies for the explicit purpose of erasing institutional barriers which restrict blacks and other minorities in American society. Certainly, one primary attitude expressed by white liberals is a desire to make up for the inequities in education, occupation, housing, and income among blacks, other minorities, and whites. The integrationist position clearly holds that the implementation of college quota systems, school busing programs, the integration of residential areas, and the increase in the number of minorities in all levels of the occupational ladder will assist in the disappearance of social injustice evident in American society.

How shall one interpret the pattern of difficulty inherent in the situations? First, the ordering of attitudes does not support a situational direct threat thesis. If apartment house owners are directly threatened and retreat from their principles in the apartment situation, they will show ambivalence and retreats in their attitudes toward the residence, busing, and quota situations. In effect, white liberals may retreat in situations of direct threat, but only if they retreat in all those situations which are generally more difficult to the group as a whole. It is important to note that the white liberal not directly threatened by the apartment situation, but expressing unfavorableness nevertheless, will also retreat in the residence, busing, and quota situations. Likewise, if there are retreats from integrationist principles in the occupation situation, there will be unfavorable attitudes stated, in cumulative fashion, toward all the other situations. Should there be difficulty in the situation which is least problematical for the entire group, there will be ambivalent attitudes and retreats in all other situations, whether there is a situation of direct threat or not.

Second, the scale discloses that white liberals are confronted with the most difficulty in keeping their attitudes consistent with their principles in situations which involve their immediate families—situations such as quotas in the colleges and busing in the schools. The least difficult situations are those concerning interactions and possible confrontations outside the family circle, for example, the hiring and occupation situations. The residence situation is the setting for ambivalence between these two extremes. Insofar as the apartment situation elicits attitudes about integrated neighborhoods, it will parallel the residence situation in degree of difficulty.

Thus, the closer to the individual's family setting and primary responsibilities for significant others, the more difficult the situations are to resolve. As a consequence, many attitudinal dilemmas, role conflicts, and unfavorable attitudes will be expressed. Conversely, the further removed from the family setting and the white liberal's primary responsibilities for others, the less difficult the situations, and, accordingly, the less attitudinal dilemmas, role conflicts, and attitudes unfavorable to integration will be expressed.

This conclusion is consistent with Bogardus' findings in the analyses of social distance scales: "marry into a group" measures closeness to kinship settings; "have as next door neighbors" is analygous to the apartment and residence situations; and "work in the same office" parallels the hiring and occupation situations. Myrdal's ranks for Southern whites are also congruent with this interpretation: "bar against intermarriage" represents closeness to family relationships; "segregations and discriminations in use of public facilities such as schools" parallels the measures of attitudes toward quotas and busing; and "securing land, credit, jobs, or other means of earning a living" parallels the occupation and hiring situations. Unprejudiced people stating favorable attitudes toward interracial marriage will also express favorable attitudes toward neighborhood and work situations. Mildly prejudiced people may express unfavorable attitudes toward interracial marriage but favor other situations further from kinship involvement. Strongly prejudiced individuals affirming unfavorable attitudes toward interracial contact furthest removed from the family (Bogardus' "debar from my nation" and Myrdal's "discriminations in securing land") will be unfavorable toward all situations progressively closer to kinship settings.

A third implication is that white liberals experience the least difficulty in asserting attitudes consistent with integration in long standing situations which are clearly defined in the culture. The area of employment of minorities holds clear-cut "definitions of the situation" for those adopting integration as a solution to interracial inequities. White liberals are familiar with expected behaviors and ideological positions with respect to their roles. However, busing is a recent arrival on the integration scene; white liberals are thrust into attitudinal dilemmas about the perceived problems related to the implementation of busing programs in the schools. Their expected behaviors regarding busing are not clearly defined.

Quotas, too, currently produce ambiguity for the white liberal. What is new today is that the quota system provides a means of inclusion of minority students. The old definition of the situation held that minority students, including Jews, were excluded due to quotas. Most respondents repeatedly asserted negative statements about quotas in the colleges. The major dilemma centered around the belief that quotas provide for a system of inclusion as well as a system of exclusion. White liberals desire to include more minority students on the campuses, in order to increase minority occupational and educational statuses, make up for past inequities in educational opportunities, and help establish social integration on the campuses. At the same time, they are troubled because quotas institute the possible exclusion of qualified students who are not allowed into college because they are not members of a specific minority group. As liberal integrationists, the respondents want more representation of minorities on the campuses; their opposition is in terms of what they consider liberal grounds, the exclusion of qualified whites. Thus, the inclusion-exclusion dilemma, inherent in quotas, provides new ideological clashes on the interracial scene.

A fourth implication is that white liberals reject some interracial situations for reasons couched in liberal terms; but underlying these surface justifications are retreats from a prointegration standpoint. Observation of Table IV shows that 47 percent (96) of the respondents place in the "less favorable" group in the busing situation, while 82 percent (167) place in the "less favorable" group in the quota situation. This jump implies that many otherwise liberal whites oppose quotas. The issue is whether the people who reject quotas are more liberal or less liberal than those who accept quotas. If they are more liberal, then there should be an excess of errors in connection with the quota item, and one could accept the liberal reasons for rejecting quotas at face value. If they are less liberal than persons who accept quotas, then there should be no disproportionate error score, and doubt is cast on the liberal reasons they give.

The scalogram analysis gives assistance in deciding the answer to this question. Since the quota situation scales with the other items without producing a nonscale type, there is rejection of the seemingly liberal reasons stated in opposition to quotas. Rather, there is support for the existence of a substratum of unfavorableness and retreat from the ideology of integration common to white liberals' attitudes toward all six interracial situations.

The basic fact that these situations form an adequate scalogram suggests the importance of the cultural context within which white liberals exist. If they endorsed attitudes unfavorable toward only those situations with which they were personally faced, many differences among the respondents in their pattern of attitudes toward the six situations would be revealed. However, since the scalogram demonstrates the existence of an underlying principle common to all the situations and common to white liberals as a group, it can be concluded that the Scale Types are a result of the respondents' exposure to culture conflict, conflicts in values, cultural definitions of "threat," and new, sometimes ambiguous norms, irrespective of each white liberal's particular set of life experiences. Cultural definitions of the situations exist, or are in the process of becoming manifest and defined, whether or not individuals are confronted directly with them in real life.

Analogous to the mechanisms inherent in Ralph H. Turner's formulation of the emergent norm theory of collective behavior are the processes revealed here: existing norms relevant to integrationist strategies are becoming "inapplicable to the situations at hand" or are being "neutralized." Emergent norms are coming into existence—norms which redefine the attitudinal and behavioral components of the white liberal role. These redefinitions are of special political and social significance when black power advocates as well as traditional liberals are questioning the strategy of integration as a solution to interracial problems.

REFERENCES

1. For each of the six interracial situations, an ordinal rank scale was developed. The respondents' answers to the questions were weighted as follows: for every favorable reply, no points were given; for every conditional reply, two points; for every attitudinal dilemma or role conflict, three points; and for every unfavorable reply, four points. Thus, the respondents with the lowest scores express the most favorable, prointegration attitudes, while those with the highest scores express the least favorable, antiintegration attitudes. Thus, each respondent was placed along attitudinal continua from most favorable to least favorable in each of the six situations. This provides the basis for comparisons of respondents by using their ordinal ranks and calculating Mann Whitney U Tests.
2. Early in their interviews, the respondents showed preference for either "black" or "Negro" and the preferred term was used by the interviewer. For the retired, their occupation during the major years of work was used. For housewives who had never worked, their husband's occupations were used.
3. First, the respondents were asked if they owned any apartment buildings. If they did, they were asked if any blacks lived in the buildings, and if so, what percentage was occupied by blacks. If no apartment buildings were owned by the respondents, they were asked to imagine that they owned one and that it was occupied only by whites.
4. The differences in the percentage distributions between Figure 1 and Table IV exist because in the first instance, every reply to each question in a series for a situation was categorized as either favorable, conditional, ambivalent, or unfavorable; if there was one conditional reply, the respondent was classified in the "Conditional Liberal" category; likewise, if there was one ambivalent reply, the respon-

dent was placed in the "Liberals in Conflict" category. However, in dichotomizing for the Guttman scale procedure, the breaking points fell in a different place on the continuum for each of the six situations, in order to approximate the recommendation that at least some items exhibit close to 50%-50% marginals (Green, 1954: 356; Stouffer, et al., 1950: 119, 123, 129, 133, 151; Edwards, 1957: 192).

5. The Coefficient of Reproducibility was calculated following Guttman and Suchman:

$$\text{Rep.} = 1 - \frac{\text{Number of errors}}{\text{Number of items} \times \text{number of respondents}}$$

$$= 1 - \frac{127}{(6)(204)}$$

$$= .90$$

With respect to the item marginals, although Guttman (1950: 79) suggests that ten items should usually be used in a scalogram, he states that as long as several items display marginal frequencies of 30% to 70%, as low as four to five items are sufficient. Six items are used in this analysis based on attitudes toward six interracial situations.

The pattern of errors is random and does not display any particular clustering which might indicate a nonscale type. Further, each response category includes more non-error than error (as specified by Green, 1954: 356; Guttman, 1950: 78; Suchman, 1950: 122-177).

Response patterns which did not fit the perfect Scale Types were categorized into a Scale Type by the minimum error criterion. If the response patterns could fit two Scale Types by the minimum error criterion, they were assigned to the perfect Scale Type which had the greatest frequency of respondents. This method is suggested by Henry (1952: 94-106).

CHAPTER IV
Status Consciousness

Ambivalent white liberals often coin their opposition to interracial situations in terms of status concerns for themselves or their children. A considerable amount of ambivalence over the six interracial settings focuses on the middle-class status factor, the single most important reason liberals retreat from their general principles of equality for all and nondiscrimination in housing, education, and occupations. Fears of lower-class blacks residing in their neighborhoods, renting their apartments, joining their children in elementary school, appearing on college campuses, and entering their occupational fields become clearly apparent in white liberals' justifications for endorsing attitudinal dilemmas rather than a straightforward translation of the American Creed affirming equalitarianism.

Important to an understanding of status are the early writings of Max Weber who suggested that societies are stratified on a multi-dimensional basis. Rather than analyzing social structures in terms of an economic substratum only, he contended that there were several bases for people ranking higher or lower. He differentiated the dimensions of class, status, and party.

Whereas social classes rest on an economically determined direct relationship to the marketplace, status is rooted in consumption behavior or style of life. Members of society engage in the process of evaluating each others' prestige, what Weber terms "social estimation of honor." Education, occupation, and the social circles in which people interact determine their status. Persons in the same status group hold a sense of belonging and usually marry within the group. Status groups are often at the forefront of the emergence of ideologies which, in turn, affect the economic, political, legal, and educational institutions of society. Bendix explains, "Status groups may be—and frequently are—the fountainhead of moral ideas that shape the conduct and world view of the individuals belonging to them, and that may affect the self-interested actions of large numbers of others."[1]

Political parties stratify members of societies along authority lines, with some holding more influence than others. In sum, societies are comprised of many groups with different status rankings, each competing in a societal arena, each producing social change as they struggle to raise or maintain their power, privilege, and economic strength.

Status concern is revealed in white liberals' attitudes toward busing in schools and quotas in colleges. If academic standards are lowered by including minorities in predominantly white schools, then white children will not be as well prepared for occupational careers in the upper rungs of the prestige hierarchy. Fears that motivational levels will be lowered because minority students will "bring the whole group down" induce the perception that white liberals' children will not desire high educational and occupational status. Further, a status threat exists when quotas are used for college admissions, since places will be allotted to minority students rather than white students whose class of origin may be middle or upper middle class. The status attained by parents may not be maintained by their children. Quotas can obstruct efforts to retain an already won high status level.

Along with the lowering of educational standards is the lowering of the reputational standing of colleges using quotas to obtain a proportionate representation of minority students. Just as Eastern universities in the 1920s determined that the presence of a large percentage of Jews lowered their social prestige, academic institutions today are seen as losing prestige due to increases in minority enrollments. One way to prevent these negative prestige losses is by approving quotas or school busing, only if high potential, middle-class, or smart minority students are permitted admission to predominantly white educational settings.

White liberals' style of life is affected by economic losses predicted if blacks were to move into their predominantly white neighborhoods or rent apartments in their white-occupied buildings. Economic loss lowers one's standard of living and prestige ranking by others. If whites flee because blacks move into a neighborhood, white liberals will suffer monetary loss because of reduced property values. Ambivalent white liberals ascertain their neighborhoods as "high class, and part of that high class is because it's all white." Those revealing status concerns endorse blacks moving into their neighborhoods or apartments only if they are middle-class blacks. Then, there will be a common area of understanding of values, standards of maintaining property, and ways of raising children.

Concern with the prestige of their occupational fields is revealed by white liberals who endorse the merit system and declare that standards must be kept up and qualifications must be met if blacks obtain positions. Respondents working with blacks whom they perceived as "lower class" hold unfavorable attitudes toward the occupation situation. They feel the entrance of blacks into their occupation lowers the prestige and implies to others that the quality of the work is not high. A threat to job security when minorities compete for jobs will ensue.

Endogamous marriage is another feature of status discussed by Max Weber. The findings of this study confirm this view. Preference for marriage within the religious, ethnic, and racial group are indicators of maintenance of white liberals' prestige. Moreover, those revealing preference for marriage within their group demonstrate ambivalent and unfavorable attitudes toward blacks entering predominantly white educational, residential, and occupational settings. Respondents were asked,

> How important is it to you for (your children/people) to marry someone of the same race—is it very important, moderately important, somewhat important, or not important?

In all situations, those endorsing endogamous marriage within the same racial group expressed more ambivalent attitudes than the comparison group.[2]

For decades social scientists have tried to understand reasons people affirm prejudicial attitudes and engage in discriminatory behavior. Much social science literature supports the thesis that status-threatened people will exhibit prejudicial attitudes toward minorities. However, it should be pointed out that most studies focus on the lower-class, working-class, or blue-collar workers, and on those in the lower rungs of educational status.

Emory S. Bogardus pioneered in the field of social distance scales. Basing his measures on ideas consistent with those of Robert E. Park, Bogardus measured the interactional space people desired to maintain from members of various ethnic groups. The farthest distance on his scales is "would exclude from my country," and the closest "to close kinship by marriage." In between these two poles and indicating progressively closer social distance are "as visitors only to my country," "to citizenship in my country," "to employment in my occupation in my country," "to my street as neighbors," and "to my club as personal chums." Bogardus refined his techniques during the many years he spent on construction of social distance scales, though most measures are very similar to this one. Those ranking highest, with most persons desirous of close contact with them, include Americans (U.S. white), Canadians, English, Finns, French, Germans, Hollanders, Irish, and Scots. Those ranking lowest, with most persons desirous of avoiding interpersonal contact and maintaining great social distance, include Chinese, Filipinos, American Indians, Indians from India, Japanese, Japanese-Americans, Jews, Koreans, Mexicans, Mexican-Americans, Negroes, Russians, and Turks.

In explaining the justifications for selecting great social distance, Bogardus suggested that in certain geographical areas, persons in control feel that "it is in danger of losing status or control because of competition of any kind from the given race." In general, those fearing that the status quo is endangered, those whose own control and social position stand on unshaky grounds. or those fearing loss of status and power seek the greatest social distance from minority group members. Minorities are a status threat.

The "white man's rank order of discriminations," observed but not tested by Myrdal, is consistent with Bogardus' social distance scales. The farthest distance is shown by agreement with "discriminations in securing land, credit, jobs, or other means of earning a living, and discriminations in public relief and other social welfare activities." The closest interactions would be approval of intermarriage. In between are "barriers against dancing, bathing, eating, drinking together"; "segregations and discriminations in use of public facilities such as schools, churches and means of conveyance"; "political disfranchisement"; and "discrimination in law courts, by the police, and by other public servants."

The observation that there is decreased status threat when there is interaction among equal status blacks and whites was upheld by Deutsch and Collins in their study of interracial housing. In comparing integrated with segregated housing projects, they found that housewives in racially integrated contact situations showed more friendly relations with blacks than their counterparts in segregated projects. Concurrent with these findings were those of Wilner, Walkley, and Cook, who demonstrated further that proximity was important in decreasing prejudice. Whites living near blacks reported friendly neighborly contact, anticipated approval of their white friends, held blacks in the housing projects in high esteem, and believed the races were equal in cleanliness, manners, ambition, and intelligence.

Interracial contact in equal status circumstances does not always produce a decrease in status threat and a concomitant decrease in prejudice. Some conditions under which there will be greater status loss to dominant group persons in equal status contact with minorities are suggested by Hubert

Blalock. Important factors include visibility of the interaction, the degree that the average status of a minority group is lower in a community, the degree of anonymity in social situations, the extent that contact affects chances for upward mobility, the degree that the norms of occupations are "liberal," the degree of general prejudice within the community, and the extent of ethnic heterogeneity in the community.

Another question is whether there are differential prestige rankings for occupational positions when they are filled by women as compared with men. Peter Goldberg's experiment revealed that when groups of women students evaluated sets of articles, identical except for the name of the author, where one was female and the other was male, they evaluated the work by the male author more highly than that of the female author in values, persuasiveness, profundity, professional status, writing style, professional competence, and ability to persuade the reader. These findings are true for occupations strongly associated with women (elementary school teaching and dietetics), those associated with men (city planning and law), and neutral occupations (linguistics and art history). Goldberg concludes that the perception that men's articles are better than women's is a distortion and invokes processes similar to those involved in ethnic prejudices. Even in traditionally defined female fields, the perceived inferiority of women's work is apparent. In contrast, Christine E. Bose demonstrates that women are ranked higher in social standing than men, particularly in lower status type jobs. However, men rank highest in traditionally male-defined high status jobs. Investigating how the sex of an incumbent affects the prestige of a position, Linda B. Nilson found that women derive less prestige from a male-typed occupational position, and men derive less prestige from a female-typed occupational position. In fact, the prestige loss for males in female-typed occupations is greater than the loss for females in male-typed occupations.

Apparently, the highest occupational prestige results from high status, typically male-defined occupations filled by men. Women in male-defined occupations derive less status than men; women in traditionally female-defined occupations derive less status than men in male-defined positions; and men filling typically female-typed occupations suffer status loss greater than women filling male-defined positions.

Focus on the importance of family status is a character feature of those exhibiting the "authoritarian personality," where underlying personality dynamics are related to ethnocentrism, anti-Semitism, and tendencies to adopt fascistic attitudes. Challenging this study are the works of many social scientists who demonstrate that prejudice is more significantly associated with the degree of formal education than with the authoritarian personality syndrome. In general, those with a greater degree of formal education express less prejudicial attitudes and more favorable attitude toward desegregation than those with less formal education. For example, the Cornell Studies concluded that "educational level is significantly associated with degree of prejudice: the higher the educational level, the less frequent are high degrees of prejudice towards Negroes, Jews, and Mexican-Americans."[3] A consequence of formal education are abilities to see the world in all its complexities, rather than simplistically.

Working-class authoritarianism combines many features of the authoritarian personality with low formal education. According to Lipset, the working class is less likely to endorse civil liberties than those in a higher socioeconomic stratum. Further, working-class persons show support for radical right movements, view the world in simple and concrete terms, raise children in a power-oriented family milieu with rigid child rearing patterns, and adhere to fundamentalist type religious groups. Anxiety over economic status aids the working-class authoritarians' approval of welfare measures. Concern with others' judgement of their methods of child rearing manifests itself in strictness in toilet training, attention to table manners, and quickness of father's response to rule infractions. Reportedly, working-class persons are vehement opponents of busing in Boston and Louisville, and blue-collar workers endorse Governor George C. Wallace for president.

Further evidence of status as a key variable in understanding prejudice and discrimination are studies of intergenerational and intragenerational mobility. In an early study of Elmira, New York, Greenblum and Pearlin found that ethnic prejudice was associated with either upward or downward mobility, as compared to lack of prejudice among the nonmobile comparison group. Bettelheim and Janowitz discovered greatest prejudice among the downwardly mobile, less prejudice among the upwardly mobile, and the least prejudice among the stationary. Claiming lack of consistency in results among many studies, Lipset and Bendix affirmed that no decisive conclusions can be drawn about the relationship between mobility and manifestation of prejudice against minority groups. In *The Tenacity of Prejudice,* Selznick and Steinberg contend that occupational mobility has little relationship to endorsement of anti-Semitic beliefs. They state,

> ...The reason that upwardly mobile workers are higher in anti-Semitic prejudice than white-collar stationaries is that they have less education. Correspondingly, the reason that downwardly mobile workers are less anti-Semitic than blue-collar stationaries is that they have more education. ...[4]

In contrast, the study reported here, with its sample exhibiting a high level of formal education, clearly found that occupational mobility per se has a decided relationship woth variation in attitudes toward interracial situations. White liberals who were very upwardly mobile, downwardly mobile, or stationary compared with their parents, exhibited less favorable attitudes toward the six interracial situations than the somewhat mobile group.

Taking the total social structure into consideration is necessary in analysis of mobility. If the standard of living has been raised for many persons, then nonmobility could be experienced as downward mobility, except for those maintaining their parents' high ranks. Since the Depression of the late 1920s and 1930s, the somewhat mobile group represents the norm of expected mobility in American society. In any examination of the effects of mobility on prejudice and discrimination, it is also of value to determine the class of origin of those studied, aspirations for the class of destination of their children, the degree and type of unemployment in the country, the values and norms defining "success" in the society, and the social climate defining prejudice and discrimination.

In studying the "dispossessed," Daniel Bell contends that certain social groups in American society support movements of the radical right which often adopt ethnic prejudice in their ideologies. In describing the "generational dispossessed," he finds the old middle class, including the independent physician, farm owner, and small-town lawyer, most threatened by structural changes. The "managerial dispossessed" are those earning a living in the old family firm or those experiencing a discrepancy because they do not receive the same power and privilege in the society as a whole as they do in their managerial positions. Finally, the "military dispossessed" are traditionally trained military persons who lack the technical skills necessary in handling new problems of a nuclear era.

Similarly, Richard Hofstadter analyzes those gaining status and finds that immigrants engage in ethnic prejudice as they are attempting to rise in the social structure. Those losing status include old time Americans whose positions are challenged by structural changes. Because of status loss, these persons express prejudicial attitudes. Both groups provide sources of support for the radical right.

Status inconsistency offers another plausible explanation for the perpetuation of prejudice and discrimination. Resting on the early multi-dimensional view of stratification formulated by Weber and the elaboration of this view by Benoit Smullyan in his examination of status types and their interrelationships, Gerhard Lenski determined the degree of status crystallization by using objective indicators to measure four vertical hierarchies upon which one's status rests: occupation, based on the rank of the family head as classified by the National Opinion Research Center's study of occupational prestige; income, based on the annual income of the family head; education, based on the years of formal education of the family head; and ethnicity, based on a community evaluation scale, which determined that those from Northeast European origins were highest in rank and those from Southeast European origins were lowest in rank. This scale is consistent with the work of Bogardus.

A person's crystallization score is high if the four ranks are approximately the same, while a person's score is low if the ranks in the four areas do not match. For example, a businessperson high in income but low in years of formal education shows low status crystallization. A doctor high in education, occupational rank, and income whose family is from Northwest European origins would be high in crystallization. So, too, would be a black worker with little formal education and a commensurately low income.

Lenski found that individuals with low crystallization showed support for "liberal" views, such as favoring price controls, extension of government powers, and government health insurance. Further, particular profiles of status crystallization were related to political liberalism, measured by voting for the Democratic party rather than the Republican party. Persons high on income, occupation, or education, but low in ethnicity tended to be politically liberal.

In contrast, Gary Rush measuring status consistency by income, occupation, and education ranks, confirmed that low educational status was related to endorsement of radical right wing extremism.

Extending the areas of investigation of status inconsistency models, Donald Treiman not only measured one person's status on income and education ranks, but further examined discrepancy between the educational ranks of spouses. However, he concluded that there was no relationship between status discrepancy, presumed to lead to the experience of strain, and "pathologies," such as prejudice.

Examining the retired in terms of status discrepancy suggests an interpretation of the findings in the study reported here that the retired state ambivalent or unfavorable attitudes toward all six interracial situations, with four showing statistical significance.[5] Retired respondents disclosed more attitudinal ambivalence and unfavorableness toward the quota, residence, apartment, and occupation situations than the nonretired. Status loss is usually involved in retirement, so that persons are discrepant with their own former status. Components of retirement usually include loss of a previously held occupational status, economic loss, and a concomitant change in style of life. Often, there is a leveling of previous statuses when one becomes retired. Disaffiliation with prior statuses prevents others from assessing prestige in accordance with what retired persons feel they are entitled. One need only visit an "old folks home" to ascertain the common plight of those holding onto differentiating statuses before retirement. Status loss of the retired may produce aggression in the form of negative attitudes toward minorities. Retired white liberals reason that fair housing laws, integration in schools, nondiscrimination and equal job opportunities assist blacks who are visibly gaining status in jobs, housing, and education. For those not maintaining their former status, this new attainment of status by minorities seems threatening, especially when it is perceived as being won without "hard work and individual effort as we did in my day," but rather by governmental programs to insure higher status for blacks, minorities, and women. Indeed, in their younger years, these retirees supported such endeavors by the government.

Focusing on direct competition, other researchers examine instances where blacks and other minorities come into direct conflict with whites. In his work on East St. Louis, Elliott M. Rudwick showed that before the race riot in 1917, blacks were not considered a "serious problem." A series of factors laid the basis for racial violence. There was a large influx of blacks from the South, so that the black population of East St. Louis changed from 6,000 to 13,000 between 1910 and 1917. Unskilled white workers considered their jobs threatened by blacks. Democratic party leaders used prejudice to win a close election, charging the Republican party with "colonization of blacks," bringing them from the South to bolster the party's votes. Actually, this accusation was not implemented, because of a one-year's residency requirement before voting. But the implications of "colonization" were drawn by the community, nevertheless. Major employers in the area obtained a cheap labor supply and antiblack propaganda pervaded labor unions. Housing problems existed because of increases in the population and there was competition for improvement in status and style of life.

Hubert Blalock suggests that examination of coalitions is necessary to understand competition between black workers and white workers. Sometimes coalitions between white workers and management create powerlessness among black or minority workers. In other instances, coalitions among all workers produce greater bargaining power vis a vis management. The early work of Herbert Northrup finds evidence that craft unions are more discriminatory in their practices than industrial unions, such as those in the mining, steel, and auto industries. In times of demand, as during the two world wars, there was less competition between white workers and minorities than during times of decreased need for employees. The Philadelphia Plan and similar plans designed to include the proportion of minorities in industry as exist in the communities were readily opposed by whites in labor unions throughout the country during the late 1960s and early 1970s. Direct competition for jobs was at stake in these affirmative action plans, calling for "goals" and timetables to increase the percentage of minority workers in industries, particularly those holding federal government contracts.

Admittedly, the "frustration aggression thesis," well formulated by Dollard et al. in 1939, is applicable to this discussion. Briefly stated, frustration always leads to aggression of some form. Aggression may be aimed directly at the source of the frustration, or may be displaced onto another target, sometimes a scapegoat. Displacement of aggression occurs when the fear of punishment related to the direct source is strong. The expression of aggression provides for catharsis, or relief from feelings engendered by the frustration. Prejudice, discrimination, and genocide are forms of displaced aggression. Thus, when cotton prices fell in the South, whites suffering economically, displaced their aggression toward a convenient target. Blacks, already stereotypically defined in the culture as inferior, were the recipients of different treatment than whites and became the victims of lynchings. Similarly, when economic conditions were difficult in Germany, and after the country had suffered defeat in World War I and had failed in its efforts during the Weimar Republic, a convenient target for frustration expression was the Jews, already defined in a negatively stereotypical manner.

The frustration aggression thesis does not explain the origin of prejudice, discrimination, or genocide, nor does it explain the direction that aggression will take. Furthermore, it fails to explain how institutionalized forms of racism are perpetuated. However, it is useful in its examination of displaced forms of aggression and helps in understanding that prejudice may derive from forms of status threat unrelated to a direct source of frustration.

FINDINGS

Direct Threat

"Whites flee en masse" when blacks begin moving into their previously lily-white neighborhoods. Schools become resegregated, as whites send their children to private or parochial schools. White workers prevent blacks and other minorities from joining their labor unions. Protests or racial violence occur where blacks and whites are in direct competition for jobs. White professionals fear that black professionals will not maintain standards of the occupation, or fear that qualifications will be lowered to permit entrance of minorities where they were once excluded.

Will white liberals retreat from their general belief in racial integration only when they are in a position where a situationally-produced, direct threat occurs? If so, it is expected that generally liberal parents will retreat from commitment to integration when busing is imminent or being implemented in their school districts. Similarly, liberal apartment house owners will not support integration when there is the possibility that blacks will move into their apartments. Liberals in predominantly white filled occupational fields will adhere to their principles except when blacks begin to be hired. Homeowners who usually endorse racial integration will abandon their principles of fair housing when blacks move into their residential area.

Comparisons of the attitudes of homeowners with nonowners, parents with nonparents, apartment house owners with nonowners, and those working with blacks with those who do not, generate very few significant results. Indeed, the only significant findings relevant to this discussion are that parents are more ambivalent than nonparents. First, those with children in elementary or junior high schools express the least favorable attitudes toward busing.[6] Second, those whose children attend senior high and college affirm the least favorable attitudes toward quotas,[7] and third, parents whose children have completed their formal education express the least favorable attitudes toward the occupation situation.[8]

Homeowners and nonowners show no differences in attitudes toward the residence situation, apartment house owners and nonowners show no differences in attitudes toward the apartment situation, and those working or not working with blacks show no differences in attitudes toward the occupation situation. In effect, those in a position to be more directly threatened by the presence of blacks do not indicate any statistically significant differences in attitudes from those not in such a position, except for parents. A direct threat thesis has little support. Further, direct threat does not explain the differences between white liberals exhibiting attitudinal ambivalence, role conflicts, or retreating from their principles from those adhering to their principles. Other explanations must be sought.

Salience of Status Dimensions

Of importance is the examination of status dimensions and their relationship with attitudinal ambivalence or retreats from commitments to racial integration. Will white liberals retreat from their usual adherence to racial integration only when they perceive status dimensions per se to be important, whether or not they are in a situation of direct threat? Will the status conscious be more ambivalent than the nonstatus conscious when interracial situations unrelated to direct sources of threat become imminent?

If the importance of status is a reason white liberals retreat from their principles, it is expected that people perceiving education as a salient dimension of status will express ambivalence toward racial integration if quotas are suggested in the colleges or if busing is planned in the primary or secondary schools, whether or not they have children or are planning to attend college themselves. People believing their style of life to be a salient dimension of status will retreat when blacks move into predominantly white neighborhoods, whether or not they own homes or apartment buildings. Further, those acknowledging ethnicity as an important dimension of status will reveal attitudinal ambivalence in college quotas, busing, apartment rentals, blacks entering their occupational fields, or other interracial situations not directly related to a specific source of threat.

In concordance with Blalock and Kaufman, status consciousness refers to "the value placed on symbols of status and on the attainment of higher status." In this study, the dimensions of status explored include religion or ethnicity, social class, education, occupation and style of life.

The Interview Schedules contained the following questions to elicit the salience of these status dimensions:

> (1) *Religion.* How important is it to you for (your children/people) to marry someone of the same religion (as you/as they are)—is it very important, moderately important, somewhat important, or not important?
>
> (2) *Ethnicity.* Do you consider yourself a member of any particular nationality or ethnic group? (If "Yes") Which one? How important to you is your nationality or ethnic group—is it very important, moderately important, somewhat important, or not important?
>
> (3) *Social Class.* How important is it to you for (your children/people) to marry someone of the same general social standing (as you are/ as they are)—is it very important, moderately important, somewhat important, or not important?
>
> (4) *Education.* Which do you feel is the most important to you when other people estimate your position in life—your education, your occupation, your income, your standard of living, or your nationality or ethnic background? Which is next most important? Which next? Which next?
>
> (5) *Occupation.* What were your hopes for your children's occupations? (For respondents whose children had already begun their occupational careers.) Generally, what types of occupations do you hope your children will seek? (For respondents whose children are still in school, or whose children had not yet begun school.) For those without children, the question listed under "Education" was used to determine whether they placed occupation first in importance of the status dimensions.
>
> (6) *Style of Life.* How important to you is it to live in a (home/ apartment) which will be in keeping with your occupational position—is it very important, moderately important, somewhat important, or not important at all?

The results indicate that those viewing religion as a salient dimension of status express more attitudinal ambivalence, role conflicts and unfavorableness toward all situations than those not viewing religion as salient.[9] Those affirming the importance of their ethnic group exhibit more dilemmas toward busing, apartment rentals to blacks, and hiring blacks than the comparison group.[10] White liberals confirming the salience of social class endorse more attitudinal unfavorableness toward the quota, busing, residence, apartment, and hiring situations than those not concerned with social class status.[11] Those perceiving education as a salient dimension of status are more ambivalent about the busing and occupation situations than the comparison group.[12] Respondents stating the importance of occupational status exhibit more ambivalence toward the residence, apartment, and hiring situations than those not endorsing the salience of occupation.[13] Finally, those deeming style of life as a salient dimension of status express less favorable attitudes toward the residence and apartment situations than the comparison group.[14]

Status consciousness related to religious or ethnic identification is congruent with the notion of ethnocentrism, in which persons feel their own group is superior to other groups and consequently hold a high degree of group consciousness. Insulation of their group from other groups will be related to stress on intragroup interactions, rather than intergroup interactions. Consequently, it is expected that those committed to in-group solidarity will resist efforts to create interracial interactions.

These findings are concordant with the respondents' focus on middle-class status as a primary condition in the six interracial situations. In the residence situation, 75 percent of the respondents endorse the view that "it will be fine if blacks move into this neighborhood, as long as they are middle class." In the busing situation, 60 percent express this condition, in the apartment, hiring and occupation situations, over 55 percent of the respondents place importance on middle-class status, and in the quota situation, 45 percent affirm this view.

Occupational and Educational Mobility

In a society stratified by occupational and educational statuses, focusing on these two areas will shed light on the conditions associated with white liberals' attitudes toward interracial situations. Will upwardly mobile white liberals retreat from adherence to the American Creed? Will those who are recent arrivals in the middle and upper middle class rungs of the occupational ladder feel status threatened by imminent interracial situations? Or, alternately, will the stationary adhere to their belief in racial integration? Will women desiring to define their roles to incorporate occupational careers be concerned with their status when they feel impeded in mobility? What is the effect of educational mobility on attitudes toward interracial situations? Will those holding high aspirations for their children's occupational and educational status exhibit attitudinal ambivalence in situations where they customarily endorse racial integration?

In order to explore the relationship between both occupational and educational mobility and attitudes toward the six interracial situations, it was first necessary to compare the respondents according to their actual ranks on the occupation and education scales. It will be remembered that the average rank on Duncan's Index of Occupational Status for the group as a whole is the fifth highest rank, while the national United States population mean is rank thirteen. The average rank in years of formal education for the group is "some post graduate," while the national mean is between "two years high school" and "high school graduation." Even though the respondents' mean ranks are very high, they were placed into several categories and their attitudes toward the six situations were compared. Those whose ranks in occupation were between 1 and 6 (102) were compared with those ranking below rank 6 (96). For educational status, those whose education was "high school graduate" or lower (27) were compared with those whose education was "some college" or higher (177). In addition, several other comparison groups were devised. In all comparison groups, there were no significant differences in attitudes. Occupational ranks and educational ranks per se failed to separate the favorable from the ambivalent and unfavorable.

In contrast to this lack of findings are the significant differences among respondents categorized on the basis of intergenerational occupational mobility. Occupational mobility was determined by comparing the respondents' ranks with those of their parents. Those moving up six to fifteen steps were placed in the "very mobile" category. Those moving up one to five steps were placed in the "somewhat mobile" category. Respondents placing in the same category as their parents fell in the nonmobile group, while those whose status was below their parents placed in the "downwardly mobile" category. For example, a teacher (rank 5) whose father had been a textile worker (rank 18) is "very mobile," while a teacher (rank 5) whose father had been a self-employed proprietor in wholesale trade (rank 8) is "somewhat mobile." Table VI summarizes the intergenerational occupational mobility categories.[15]

Intensive analysis generated these results: respondents who were very mobile, downwardly mobile, or nonmobile in occupational status hold less favorable attitudes toward the interracial situations than the somewhat mobile comparison group.[16]

Looking at recency of high status demonstrated that the very mobile who also entered the highest occupational ranks (ranks 1 through 5 on Duncan's scale) affirm less favorable attitudes toward all interracial situations, and

TABLE VI

Intergenerational Occupational Mobility

	Women		Men	
	%	N	%	N
Very Mobile	32.3	30	49.0	50
Somewhat Mobile	34.3	32	27.5	28
Nonmobile	5.4	5	8.8	9
Downwardly Mobile	28.0	26	14.7	15
no answers		4		5
	100.0	97	100.0	107

particularly toward the quota, busing, and occupation situations.[17] Thus, the combination of the degree of upward occupational mobility and the recency of high status specifies some conditions leading to expressions of more favorable or less favorable attitudes: respondents who were somewhat mobile in occupation and maintained their parents' high occupational ranks or those who were somewhat mobile and had not attained the highest occupational ranks confirm the most favorable attitudes. At the same time, those who were very mobile and entered the highest occupational ranks exhibit the most attitudinal ambivalence, role conflicts, and unfavorable attitudes toward the situations.

The analysis of intergenerational educational mobility revealed different results than those obtained in the occupational mobility analysis. Table VII indicates the mobility categories. Educational mobility categories were created by comparing women's years of formal education to those of their mothers and men's years of formal education with those of their fathers. The "very mobile" group contains those moving up four to eight steps compared with their parents. The "somewhat mobile" group contains those moving up one to three steps, the nonmobile group includes those whose years of formal education were the same as their parents, and the downwardly mobile group contains those having less formal education than their parents.[18]

Contrasting with the results obtained in the occupational mobility analysis, those who were very mobile in educational status express the most favorable attitudes toward the situations, and those who were nonmobile, downwardly mobile, or somewhat mobile manifest the least favorable attitudes.[19] These findings afford support for the thesis that the higher the

TABLE VII

Intergenerational Educational Mobility

	Women		Men	
	%	N	%	N
Very Mobile	36.2	34	47.6	49
Somewhat Mobile	48.9	46	35.0	36
Nonmobile	10.6	10	8.7	9
Downwardly Mobile	4.3	4	8.7	9
no answers		3		4
	100.0	97	100.0	107

degree of formal education, the less the prejudice and the greater the endorsement of desegregation.

The fact that there were no significant differences between groups compared on the basis of their actual ranks in occupation and in education suggests that mobility per se, irrespective of the actual ranks, is associated with the degree of favorableness toward the six interracial situations.

Of interest is the finding that women hoping to be mobile in occupational status reveal less favorable attitudes toward the occupation situation than women having no such mobility hopes.[20] Similar to members of other minority groups, they view blacks as potentially obstructing their chances for occupational positions. A sense of competition with blacks is indicative of a potential status threat in the area of occupational mobility. Women perceiving the "plus value" in hiring blacks discern an impediment to their own chances for entering occupational careers, particularly where there are few positions available or when the unemployment rate is high. It is not so much status loss, but a blockage to status gain which is feared by these women.

In sum, the findings demonstrate that the following factors best differentiated the respondents' attitudes in each situation:

(1) For the quota situation, the best differentiator of attitudes was occupational mobility (very mobile) and recency of high status, with the very mobile moving into the highest occupational ranks confirming the most ambivalent and unfavorable attitudes.

(2) For the busing situation, the best differentiator of attitudes was

occupational mobility, with the very mobile, stationary, or downwardly mobile expressing the least favorable attitudes.

(3) For the residence situation, the clearest separation in attitudes was obtained in the combination of occupational and educational mobility, with the very mobile, stationary, or downwardly mobile in occupation and the somewhat mobile, stationary, or downwardly mobile in education expressing the least favorable attitudes.

(4) For the apartment and hiring situations, the best differentiator of attitudes was occupational aspirations, in terms of hopes for children's class of destination, with those holding the highest hopes affirming the least favorable attitudes.

(5) For the occupation situation, the clearest separation of attitudes was obtained in the occupational mobility analysis, with the very mobile, nonmobile, and downwardly mobile affirming the most unfavorableness.

Status Concern

As a consequence of these findings which show the importance of status dimensions in differentiating white liberals who retreat from their principles from those who do not, an inquiry into the degree of interrelatedness among various status dimensions was undertaken. Are status factors separate and isolated from one another, or are they overlapping, forming a unique sequence? If individuals feel social class is an important dimension of status, will they also feel religion is important? If they feel style of life is important, will they likewise feel occupational status is important?

The scalogram technique tests whether there is a unidimensional and cumulative scale.[21] The measures obtained produce a quasi-scale, in which the interpretation must be stated with caution, as factors other than a singular substratum of status consciousness may be operating. The order produced is as follows: respondents perceiving education as an important dimension of status also perceive all other dimensions as salient; style of life is next in order, then occupation, social class, and last, religion or ethnicity. Those perceiving religion or ethnicity as salient need not view any other dimensions as salient, but if they do not perceive religion or ethnicity as important, they will probably not feel any other dimensions are important.

The scalogram analysis suggests an additional interpretation, namely, the degree of pervasiveness, or potency, of the status dimensions. Analysis of the frequencies of each Scale Type shows that all but 34 respondents feel religion or ethnicity are important dimensions of status. All but 65 respondents perceive religion or ethnicity and social class as salient, while only 17 perceive all status dimensions as important. The differential importance of the dimensions is revealed, with religion and ethnicity most salient to the group as a whole, and education least salient.

Interestingly, there is a marked difference in the percentage of Jews considering religion or ethnicity as important (83 percent) and the percentage of non-Jews perceiving these factors as important (47 percent). Jews hold a sense of belonging with their ethnic group, while those from white Anglo-Saxon Protestant origins do not define themselves as belonging to any ethnic group.

CONCLUSIONS

The comparison of the attitudes of respondents in a position to be more directly threatened by the six interracial situations with the attitudes of those who are not shows some support for the direct threat thesis. Respondents with children in elementary and junior high school express the least favorable attitudes toward the busing situation, those with children in senior high school or college express the least favorable attitudes toward the quota situation, and those whose children have completed their formal schooling express the least favorable attitudes toward the occupation situation.

However, there is stronger support for the idea that status consciousness per se has an effect on white liberals' attitudes toward interracial situations. Specifically, the salience of religion, ethnicity, social class or education are more precisely associated with ambivalent attitudes toward the six situations than are factors such as parenthood, homeownership, apartment ownership, or whether one works with blacks.

The dimensions of status operationalized in this study are related to Weber's interpretation of status groups which rest upon prestige-related concepts, including style of life, education, and occupation. Further, status is discussed by Weber as rooted in ethnicity or religion, exemplified by his extensive discussions of Jews, castes, and Chinese literati. He also suggested the interrelatedness of the dimensions of class, status, and power. Concern with the prestige of one's status group, where there is a "sense of belonging" among the members, implies that when high status is threatened or persons are attempting to gain status, there will be conflict. The examination of groups attempting to gain status, maintain high status recently acquired by their parents' generation, or in positions where status threat will be perceived as leading to status loss, are areas of importance for sociological examination. Conflicts over prestige and status threat will challenge general principles supportive of egalitarian attitudes and practices when particular social situations emerge, such as quotas in the colleges or busing in the schools.

Of importance in this discussion of status is the issue of the scalability of several dimensions of status. Status factors tend to form an underlying interrelatedness, but further tests on different subpopulations are necessary to fruitfully examine the extent of status consciousness among various ethnic groups within American society.

The significance of the basic difference in findings among those in a position of more direct threat and those feeling threatened on the basis of status consciousness is more than a difference between the real and the hypothetical. As W.I. Thomas stated, "If men [and women] define situations as real, they are real in their consequences." Status consciousness, specifically the dimensions of religion, ethnicity, social class, education, occupation, and style of life, is a very real factor for many white liberals. Status dimensions are particularly pervasive when they apply to the lives of children, especially when viewed with a future perspective.

At their stage of life, many respondents are more apprehensive about their children's status than with their own. Support for this idea is demonstrated in the findings obtained in the comparison based on the desire for the occupational status of the respondent's children. These individuals are concerned with their children's future class status—with their children's class of destination. They are status threatened by situations which seem to block the potential avenues for status gain in their children's future mobility and status. Some respondents are uneasy about the maintenance of status ranks they have already attained. This finding is most apparent for those who have been very mobile and have entered the highest occupational rungs. Indeed, the clear association of these factors, as well as aspirations for high status for children, with attitudinal dilemmas, role conflicts, and attitudes unfavorable toward the situations is supported by the findings. The maintenance of high status for new arrivals in the highest rungs, as well as the attainment of high status for their children, may be particularly true of these respondents, since the educational, occupational, and income profiles show the means to be higher than those of the national United States Census figures.

In general, the more stable and status secure, the more likely white liberals will affirm favorable attitudes toward interracial social situations. Conversely, the more status insecure, the more status threatened white liberals will feel, and consequently, the more likely they will be to reveal attitudes unfavorable toward interracial situations.

Status consciousness provides the substructure upon which certain social situations make their impact. Where status factors are important, interracial situations will engender equivocal or unfavorable opinions toward integration or toward consistency with the principles of the American Creed. These attitudes not only affect the situation or its implementation, but have more general effects within the social structure, by obstructing the eradication of institutionalized inequities, by slowing the pace of racial integration, by a general questioning of the strategy of integration, or by electing governmental candidates uncertain in their action orientations toward the goals for which the civil rights and civil liberties movements stand.

REFERENCES

1. Reinhard Bendix, *Max Weber, An Intellectual Portrait,* 1962, p. 260.
2. In the comparisons of respondents considering race important (72) with those not considering race important (121), the former showed less favorable attitudes in all situations with statistical significance than the latter, as follows: for the quota situation, $z=4.17$, $p < .0001$; for the busing situation, $z=4.38$, $p < .00002$; for the residence situation, $z=4.58$, $p < .000001$; for the apartment situation, $z=4.34$, $p < .00002$; for the hiring situation, $z=2.89$, $p < .002$; and for the occupation situation, $z=252$, $p < .01$. One tailed Mann Whitney U Tests were calculated, and alpha was set at .05.
3. Robin Williams, *Strangers Next Door,* 1964, p. 65.
4. Gertrude J. Selznick and Stephen Steinberg, *The Tenacity of Prejudice,* 1969, p. 78.
5. The retired, or those planning to retire soon (55) showed less favorable attitudes than the nonretired (132), with four indicating statistical significance: for the quota situation, $z=3.05$, $p < .002$; for the residence situation, $z=1.75$, $p < .04$; for the apartment situation, $z=3.06$, $p < .002$; and for the occupation situation, $z=2.52$, $p < .01$. One tailed tests of significance were calculated, and alpha was set at .05.
6. $z=2.16$, $p < .02$.
7. $z=1.78$, $p < .05$.
8. $z=2.52$, $p < .01$.
9. Respondents perceiving religion important (83) expressed less favorable attitudes than those not perceiving religion important (109), as follows: for the quota situation, $z=1.88$, $p < .03$; for the busing situation, $z=3.12$, $p < .001$; for the apartment situation, $z=1.69$, $p < .05$; for the hiring situation, $z=2.35$, $p < .01$; for the occupation situation, $z=2.18$, $p < .02$. For the residence situation, the test was near statistical significance, $z=1.55$, $p < .06$. One tailed tests of significance were calculated, and alpha was set at .05.
10. Respondents stating the importance of their ethnic group (72) expressed less favorable attitudes than those not feeling their ethnic group to be important (121), as follows: for the busing situation, $z=2.68$, $p < .01$, for the apartment situation, $z=2.00$, $p < .03$; for the hiring situation, $z=2.79$, $p < .01$; for the quota, residence, and occupation situations, no statistical significance was obtained. One tailed tests of significance were calculated, and alpha was set at .05.
11. Respondents perceiving social class as important (71) stated less favorable attitudes than those not perceiving social class as important (118), as follows: for the quota

situation, z=2.34, p < .01; for the busing situation, z=2.20, p < .02; for the residence situation, z=3.14, p < .001; for the apartment situation, z=3.34, p < .001; for the hiring situation, z=2.10, p < .02; for the occupation situation, n.s. One tailed tests of significance were calculated, and alpha was set at .05.

12. Respondents placing education first (53) expressed less favorable attitudes than those not placing education first (144), as follows: for the busing situation, z=3.11, p < .001; and for the occupation situation, z=1.91, p < .03. The other situations are not statistically significant. One tailed tests were calculated, and alpha was set at .05.

13. Respondents holding high aspirations for their children's occupational status (60) expressed less favorable attitudes than those not holding high aspirations (70), as follows; for the residence situation, z=2.45, p < .01; for the apartment situation, z=2.98, p < .001; for the hiring situation, z=2.81, p < .002. The other situations show the same direction of response but are not statistically significant. One tailed tests were calculated, and alpha was set at .05.

14. Respondents placing importance on style of life (58) express less favorable attitudes in four situations than those not placing importance on style of life (145), as follows: for the residence situation, z=2.57, p < .01; for the apartment situation, z=2.89, p < .002. The hiring and occupation situations show the same direction of response but are not statistically significant. The quota and busing situations do not show enough difference between the two comparison groups to indicate any direction of response. One tailed tests were calculated, and alpha was set at .05.

15. The possibility of a "ceiling," as well as a "floor," exists in any analysis of this type. However, examination of the ranks of this group revealed that there was only one case where a respondent and his father placed in rank one, since both were doctors. For women respondents, the following classificatory scheme was used: for married women, their husbands' ranks were classified; for single working women, their occupational ranks were used; for a retired single woman (one case), her former occupational rank was used; for widows who were working, their occupational ranks were used; for widows who were not working (three cases), their husbands' ranks were used; for divorcees who were working, their ranks were used; for a divorcee who was not working (one case), her former husband's occupational rank was used. For men respondents, their occupational ranks were used. See Judith Caditz, "Dilemmas of the White Liberal," p. 170, for a discussion of the problems of classifying occupational ranks for women.

16. For a report of the Mann Whitney U Tests comparing various occupational mobility categories, see Judith Caditz, "Dilemmas of the White Liberal," Tables 9.4 - 9.6, pp. 172-178.

17. See Judith Caditz, "Dilemmas of the White Liberal," Tables 9.18 and 9.19, pp. 209-210.

18. The "ceiling-floor" problem affected the classification of several persons whose education was the highest rank (rank 8) and whose parents also placed in that category. They were placed in the nonmobile category. There were no respondents placing in the "0" category.

19. Statistical tests comparing various educational mobility categories and an exploration of the differential effects of occupational and educational mobility are found in Judith Caditz, "Dilemmas of the White Liberal," Tables 9.10 - 9.17, pp. 180-208.

20. $z=1.85$, $p < .05$. A one tailed test of significance was calculated, and alpha was set at .05.

21. These measures were obtained: Coefficient of Reproducibility, .88; Minimal Marginal Reproducibility, .66; Percent Improvement, .22; and Coefficient of Scalability, .61. See Judith Caditz, "Dilemmas Over Racial Integration: Status Consciousness vs. Direct Threat," *Sociological Inquiry,* (Winter, 1975), for the scalogram.

CHAPTER V
Ethnic Identification and Interethnic Conflict

Involvement in an ethnic community is related to white liberal's ambivalence toward racial integration. An inquiry into this social phenomenon begins with an understanding of some key ideas of social scientists in the field of ethnic relations. Since much of this analysis rests upon the theory of status groups formulated by Max Weber, it is necessary to examine his contributions. Weber's conceptions of status groups, including ethnic and religious groups, as well as other communities, demonstrate that members of such groups hold a "sense of belonging," a subjective feeling of solidarity among those identifying with the group. This commonality, from which a unique style of life emerges, rests upon a shared historical past, common culture, kinship patterns, religion, language, art, music, achievements, nationality, physical contiguity, or any combination of these features. In his discussion of status groups, Weber cites hierarchially arranged castes in India, with their particular laws, conventions, occupations, rituals, and stigmas; the Chinese literari, with their status linked to scholarly interpretations of Chinese traditions; the Jews, with their prophets' ideas of Talmudic law applied to everyday life; and, in the United States, the wealthy First Families of Virginia, engaging in privileged social circles inaccessible to others. Conflict between ethnic groups will be created by the impact of social situations developing within a societal arena, where the relative status and privilege of two or more minority groups are at stake. These groups are in relations of conflict, not only while pursuing economic goals, but also while endeavoring to attain or maintain high status, or a high ranking by "social estimation of honor."

In examining that unity and conflict are indissoluble, Georg Simmel predicted that intergroup conflict often increased the solidarity of groups and their degree of centralization. Although he proposed ideas similar to those of Weber, he more specifically stressed that definitions of a group's boundaries, increase in-group identifications, decrease in inner antagonisms, and concentration on the survival of the group all are enhanced by relations of conflict and hostility with out-groups.

Looking at the social structures of societies with small elites and peasant masses, Hubert Blalock surveys the literature on "middleman minorities," where visible minorities are perpetuated primarily by their highly adaptive skills. The history of Jews, the Chinese in Southeast Asia, East Indians in Burma and South Africa, and other minorities reveals the features of such perpetual minorities. These ethnic groups do not occupy the lowest rungs of societies, but fill occupational positions with middle range status. They serve as a buffer between the privileged elite and the powerless masses. In times of societal stability and prosperity, these minority groups rise in status, though never to the highest corporate positions. During times of stress, middleman minorities become the target of displaced aggression, the scapegoats, and consequently their prestige is lowered. Serving to perpetuate its existence is the visibility of the group by its maintenance of occupational skills and high degree of ethnocentrism with preservation of cultural traditions. Blalock contends, "we might call attention to the apparent paradox that although it may be to the minority *individual's* interest to preserve a cultural heritage which gives a competitive advantage to his children, this very practice may work to the long-run disadvantage of the *group* as a whole."[1]

Consistent with the notion of ethnic groups competing for high prestige, economic status, and power is the research on ethnocentrism, in which perceptions of in-group superiority and out-group inferiority are central. As early as 1906, Sumner cited numerous illustrations of ethnocentrism, where various societies viewed their own group positively and other groups negatively. Indeed, positive adulation of a group and negative hostility toward other groups could coexist. The Human Relations Area files also contain analyses of ethnocentrism existing in many tribes and societies around the world.

The formation and perpetuation of stereotypes are congruent with the processes of ethnocentrism. Most stereotypes of outsiders are negative, showing traits of aggression, uncleanliness, immorality, clannishness, laziness, ambitiousness, snobbery, egotism, hostility, and expansionism. If members of ethnic groups engage in stereotyping others, the groundwork for intergroup hostility is formed. Some researchers derive their hypotheses from the psychoanalytic school and contend that stereotyped imagery consists of projections to rationalize hostility toward other groups. For example, Bettelheim and Janowitz indicate that "id projections," such as uncleanliness, laziness, and immorality, will be visualized as belonging to people with the darkest hair and skin, while "super-ego projections," such as desire to work hard, ambitiousness and covetousness, will be seen as residing in persons with the lightest physical features. T.W. Adorno et al., in studying the roots of political conservatism, anti-Semitism, and fascistic attitudes among those with the "authoritarian personality" syndrome attribute the development of ethnocentrism to early socialization. Among the processes underlying high ethnocentric scorers is the tendency to project blame onto others when certain undesirable impulses are felt within the self.

Social distance measures, as developed primarily by Emory S. Bogardus, incorporate the degree to which people evaluate others in negative stereotypical ways. Those from Northwest European socieites are typically viewed more positively than those from Southeast European origins, with blacks even lower on the scale. A desire to maintain close personal contact or far interactional distances is concordant with this array of preferences.

Stereotypes undergo change, and sometimes this occurrence justifies negative behavior toward minority group members. By content analysis, Turner and Surace showed the symbolic context of the "zoot suit riots" in Los Angeles and the surrounding environs during World War II. Previous to the confrontations between Anglo Navy men and Los Angeles Mexicans, there were positive traits of Mexican-Americans in the newspapers stressing the romantic qualities of Mexican-American history, Mexican temperament in terms of "bravery" and "gaiety," Mexican culture, dance, arts, and music, and the devout religious values of Mexicans. During the conflicts, the imagery changed to clearly negative traits, such as the style of clothing and hair styles of the zooters, and the portrayal of Mexicans as law violators, engaging in gang violence, and needing government relief funds. The consequence of these changing stereotypes, from positively valued qualities to negative traits, was clarification of norms supporting the conflict. The researchers state, "A necessary condition for both uniform group action and unrestricted hostile behavior is the presence of a symbol which arouses uniformly and exclusively unfavorable feelings of the group toward the object under attack."[2]

Ethnocentrism and stereotyping serve as mechanisms of social comparison, and function to heighten positive self-perceptions and self-esteem by downgrading those in another ethnic group. The further the distance between the two groups, the more one's own group will seem positively valued in its history, values, religion, traditions, life style, or other cultural symbols. Insularity of one group from another will protect group boundaries by preventing intermarriages and retaining ethnic pride. It is in this way that castes in traditional Indian society showed highly segregated and hierarchically arranged positions with each engaging in a particular occupation, having its own customs, and each perceiving the others with mutual repulsion.

Sometimes, ethnic solidarity and ethnic pride help perpetuate the social, economic, and political subordination of certain groups. In South Africa, a minority of whites hold political, economic, and social control over a majority of blacks identified with different Bantu tribes. According to Leo Kuper in *An African Bourgeoisie, Race, Class, and Politics in South Africa,* the system of apartheid, along with the inculcation of ethnic pride, are some main reasons for the continuance of this plural social structure. The fragmentation of the majority of peoples by the system of Bantu education stressing tribalism rather than nationalism is a major factor upholding the lack of egalitarianism in the country. Nonwhite relegation to an apolitical unit, economic lines drawn along racial lines, and the system of apartheid could be challenged if "racialization" maintained by ethnic pride and exclusiveness were minimized. However, Kuper discerns that countering these institutionalized structures are factors which may encourage breakdown of inequality. Industrialization, urbanization, increase in the division of labor, the emergence of new independent states in Africa, and the influence of English speaking churches all contribute to growing forces reacting against the preservation of South Africa's segregated and unequal social structure.

Similarly, although Japan declared the caste system illegal in 1871, the approximately 3,000,000 burakumin or eta ("filthy ones") are still considered inferior in Japanese society and still engage in traditional "lowly" occupations. Although they are mainly farmers, fishermen, and unskilled laborers, they still engage in slaughtering and skinning animals to produce leather, burying the dead, and selling rags. Moreover, custom dictates that they step aside when other higher status Japanese pass. John Donoghue's analysis demonstrates that these outcastes are not racially distinct, yet they remain in residentially segregated areas. Not only do other Japanese consider the burakumin in negative stereotypes, but the burakumin also think of themselves as dirty, engaging in disgusting occupations, and other self-degrading traits which are counter to Japanese emphasis on purity, lineage, and health. In-group solidarity facilitates the lowly status of the burakumin. Common ancestors, kinship unity, religious identity, town meetings, and exclusiveness operate to maintain the system of low caste status. However, Donoghue points out that most burakumin regard the lifting of the whole group to higher status within Japanese society, rather than particular individuals within it, as a major political goal.

Conflict between ethnic groups struggling to exist in a multi-ethnic society also generates self-hatred, self-doubt, and negative images of others in the group. In Kenneth B. Clark and Mamie P. Clark's study of "Racial Identification and Preference in Negro Children," the experiment revealed that black children preferred the white doll rather than the black doll. Self-hatred among Jews results from experiences of discrimination. Comparing Jews and non-Jews who were emotionally disturbed, Ackerman and Jahoda discovered that non-Jews tended to direct prejudice against several groups, including Jews, while Jews directed hatred against Jews only. A study of Benjamin Ringer revealed that long time Jewish residents viewed Jewish newcomers as ethnocentric, lacking in social proprieties, and too concerned with possessions exhibiting wealth. Documentation of Jewish achievements in science, music, medicine, art, academic endeavors, and other areas of life often account for success as a response to discrimination and the Jews' history of persecution.

Everett Stonequist's early formulation of the concept of the "marginal man" was modelled after the Jew trying to leave the Southeast European ghetto and assimilating to the dominant society. Marginal persons are torn, having been socialized in one culture and thus deeply immersed in its values and traditions, and then trying to be accepted by another culture. The person cannot gain acceptance as an equal in the new culture, since remnants of the former, less prestigious style of life remain. Concomitantly, the person cannot return to the original culture because of the group's rejection due to the knowledge of attempts to leave and adoption of the dominant group's style of life. Consequently, the marginal person develops inferiority complexes, sometimes accompanied by over-compensation in the form of superiority complexes, fluctuations of moods, irrationality and "temperamental" behavior. The marginal person is caught between two identifications, and accepted by neither.

Self-perceptions among members of minority groups should be analyzed not only in terms of the negative images caused by prejudice, discrimination, racism and sexism, but also in terms of the positive evaluations saturating the ideology of social movements countering discrimination. Positive efforts to instill members of minority groups with preferred self-evaluations are part of the ideology of the black power movement, where themes such as "black is beautiful" are the central focus.

In *The Politics of Protest,* Jerome H. Skolnick discusses the current emphasis on inclusion of black history in school curricula and indicates that young militants and leaders of the black power movement affirm black values, provide positive self-identity and self-appreciation and by these means create dignity and self-confidence for black people. In-group pride is related to the drive toward cultural autonomy and community control of schools. These efforts demonstrate a major difference between the civil rights movement with its goal of racial integration and the strategy of the new militancy.

Today, attempts are being made to change TV commercials and other forms of advertisement to depict minority group members and women in roles other than those which represent negative stereotypes. Included are the banning of the "frito bandito" ads and current efforts of women's groups to portray women in roles other than home cleaning, grocery store shopping, driving children here and there in the newest station wagon, and "catching a man" by using the newest beautification processes.

In-group identification and positive evaluation of one's group are not only beneficial to the self-concept, but provide a precondition to positive attitudes and interactions with members of other groups. The view of Kurt Lewin is that positive in-group identification generates positive attitudes toward members of other groups. The more ethnic identifiers deem their group as desirable, the more they are likely to positively evaluate others' ethnicity, and the greater will be the interaction between members of different ethnic groups.

This is the essence of cultural pluralism as developed by Louis Wirth, in "The Problem of Minority Groups," and later Milton Gordan, in "Assimilation in America: Myth and Reality." Pluralistic minorities, according to Wirth, retain their unique cultural heritage and coexist socially, economically, and politically with other groups. Although they do not occupy the highest power positions in society, pluralistic minorities' goals include the maintenance of traditions along with "toleration" of their differences by the dominant groups. Intermarriage is discouraged in order to perpetuate the existence of the ethnic group. In contrast, an "assimilationist minority" attempts to gain access into the dominant group's style of life and positions of power and prestige. The dominant group must be willing to permit entrance into its ranks of the minority group, so that a "two-way process" is underway. Examining the sequences of strategies in which minority groups engage, Wirth proposes that if minorities are denied existence as a pluralistic group, or are not permitted entrance into the power structure by assimilation, they will adopt militant or secessionist tactics.

Conceptualizing the processes by which many immigrant groups were absorbed in American society, Milton Gordon suggests that cultural pluralism took into account the fact that many immigrants positively valued their traditions and desired to retain their cultural institutions, religion, or language. America could be viewed as containing cultural differences among diverse groups each cooperating with others. This type of accomodation of immigrants to the "host society" was different than "Anglo conformity," where adoption of the norms of the new society occurred while disidentifying with traditional cultures. It also differs from the melting pot idea, where each immigrant group contributed along with others to a "new blend" for a new American society. Gordan points out that social class levels often divide ethnic groups. Further, he affirms that behavioral assimilation, or acculturation, has occurred in American society, while structural assimilation has not, because immigrants are often barred from entrance into social cliques, organizations, or institutional activities.

Individuals holding strong affective commitment to an ethnic group will be interested in their group's relative prestige. Avenues for increment in prestige are higher occupational positions, increase in the quality of formal education, living in better neighborhoods, and increase in economic and political power. If ethnic group members view a social situation as threatening to their status or value interests, there will be an increase in the salience and intensity of the problems presented by that situation. The quota system in colleges provides an example. Some members of certain ethnic groups view quotas as an avenue for status improvement, while others view quotas as obstructing status gains or the maintenance of high status. Quotas implemented for minority students benefit primarily blacks, Mexican-Americans or those with Spanish surnames, and secondarily Asian-Americans, and Indian-Americans. Power struggles revolve around issues of whether to institute quotas, definitions of what constitutes a "minority group," and the percentage of students in a category qualifying for admission on the basis of quotas. All these issues involve competition, conflict, and power struggles not only between the decision-making administrators and the interested groups, but also between members of different minority groups.

In the fall of 1971, busing in San Francisco's public schools brought vehement protests from the Chinese community. Busing to schools for purposes of ethnic integration was perceived as eroding to Chinese style of life and cultural interests. Because the hours children would spend on school buses interfered with after school educational programs, the Chinese felt that busing hindered their rights to retain a unique cultural identity. The consequence of integration was seen as assimilation and loss of opportunities to inculcate children in Chinese customs, language, and other distinctive features of their heritage. Essentially, busing was perceived as threatening to the desires of the Chinese community to identify with their group and remain separate from other groups, rather than to integrate.

If those identifying with an ethnic group fear a loss in their relative power position or fear obstruction in the routes to potential gains of their group caused by the attempts of another ethnic group to improve its power position, they will develop attitudes which exhibit conflict and hostility. Sometimes these attitudes are inconsistent with principles of equality for all, irrespective of race, color, or creed. For example, several articles by Ruben Salazar point out the conflict between Mexican-Americans and blacks. With reference to the Head Start Program, he reported that "Mexican-American delegates to the Head Start and Child Development Conference Tuesday complained to the national director that the project is black and Anglo oriented and not relevant to the Chicano child. . . ."[3] Salazar also reported on black-chicano conflicts on California campuses, indicating that a conference at UC Santa Barbara brought into the open "underlying hostilities between the Chicano and black participants," where a chicano caucus charged "Blacks say that blacks and browns are fighting over the white man's bone, but that isn't so. The black man has the white man's bone and is fighting to keep the Chicano away from it."[4] In addition, he reported that a rift between the black and brown communities can only retard the civil rights struggle, but, at the same time, "it is becoming more difficult to hide the resentment building up between the two groups in their scramble for better jobs, housing and education."[5] Thus, the Mexican-American and black conflicts may be analyzed within the framework of ethnic group members' concern with their status interests and power relative to other groups within the social structure.

Further complexities in ethnic group conflict are brought out by the interplay between black anti-Semitism, its perceived causes, and Jewish "backlash." Jews detect a clash between traditional values of Jewish liberalism and feelings of resentment toward blacks for anti-Semitic statements. Many feel because they have been especially helpful to blacks in the Civil Rights Movement, blacks are unjustified in their negative attitude toward Jews. Others feel that although they have helped blacks in struggles for better housing, education, and jobs, blacks' hostilities toward Jews are justified. Of current interest is friction between the Hasidic Jewish community in the Williamsburgh neighborhood of Brooklyn and blacks caused by the New York Legislature's reapportioning of Assembly and Senate districts to increase black voting power. Redistricting divided the Hasidic community of 35,000 into two districts. In *United Jewish Organizations v. Carey,* the U.S. Supreme Court will decide the constitutionality of the redistricting insofar as its effect is discriminatory against whites.

Generational analyses of immigrants indicate tendencies among second and third generations to assimilate into American culture. Herberg suggests that second generation Jews' efforts to assimilate facilitated their upward mobility, which, in turn, increased assimilation. A demonstration of the association of maintenance of ethnic differences among immigrants with ambivalence or retreats from integration will be concordant with the general theoretical orientation of this analysis. When members of immigrant groups perceive status interests as salient, they will express attitudes favoring their groups' rankings in the social milieu, and simultaneously will express negative attitudes toward other groups.

Assuming the centrality of ethnic groups as status groups in the Weberian sense, it is proposed that when prestige or values are threatened by interracial situations, ethnic group members will respond by involing strategies protective of their group boundaries. Consequently, it is hypothesized that ethnic identifiers will express more role conflicts and attitudinal dilemmas toward a general belief in integration than nonidentifiers. Further, it is hypothesized that the closer to foreign birth, the more likely attitudinal dilemmas will be expressed in status threatening interracial situations.

INTERETHNIC CONTACT

Many studies on interracial contact concur that the greater the interaction between members of different ethnic groups, the greater the reduction in intergroup prejudice and hostility. Emphasizing that many variables enter into analysis of contact situations, Gordon Allport places importance on the degree of status differential between interacting members of different ethnic groups. Equal status provides the basis for less conflict than unequal status between interacting peoples. Blalock examines equal status contacts and focuses upon particular conditional variables, such as the degree of visibility of those interacting, the liberalism of one's occupational norms, the level of prejudice within the community, and the degree of ethnic heterogeneity of the community.

In further exploration of interracial contact, it is hypothesized that individuals engaging in *associational relationships* will adhere to their usual beliefs in integration, while those engaging in *communal relationships* will exhibit attitudinal ambivalence or will retreat.

Associational relationships subsume those in which the interacting individuals are involved with different sets of persons. They have many sets of relationships with different individuals in each set. When applied to members of ethnic, religious, or racial groups, this concept refers to heterogeneous interactions: with respect to ethnicity, individuals interact with many members of different ethnic groups; with reference to religious affiliation, interacting individuals belong to different religious groups; with respect to race, interacting individuals stem from different racial backgrounds. In effect, these heterogeneous interactions involve different individuals in many sets of relationships in a wide variety of social settings.

Communal relationships subsume those in which the same individuals interact in a wide variety of social situations. When the concept is applied to ethnic, religious, or racial groups, it implies homogeneity among interacting individuals: those belonging to a particular ethnic group interact primarily with others in the same ethnic group; individuals of a particular religious affiliation interact with others in the same religious group; individuals of a particular racial group interact with others in the same racial group. These homogeneous interactions involve the same individuals in many sets of relationships in a wide spectrum of social settings.

These definitions are an elaboration of Lenski's use of the terms "associational involvement" and "communal involvement" in his study of socio-religious groups in Detroit. Associational involvement is typical of individuals attending "worship services every week, plus those who attended services two to three times a month and also some church-related group at least once a month."[6] Communal involvement is typical of "those who were married to someone of the same socio-religious group, and who also reported that all or nearly all of their close friends and relatives were of the same group."[7] Associational ties reflect interactions to attain limited, specific goals, while the affective character is not a prime focus; communal ties, on the other hand, are indicative of interactions in which the social relationships are goals in themselves and not just the means of attaining other goals.

Although he quite skillfully uses these operational definitions in his study, Lenski excludes from analysis several types of relationships. First, individuals may interact associationally or communally on bases other than a socio-religious one; for example, ethnically based interactions may or may not contain a religious component. Second, people often marry within their socio-religious group and yet lack involvement in any other way. Third, people may attend religious services several times a month not as ends in themselves but because of communal involvement with others. Fourth, individuals may be communally involved with the same web of people in nonreligious functions taking place at a church or temple.

Taking into consideration the affective nature of social relationships, the concepts reported here primarily stress the extent of homogeneity or heterogeneity in social interactions. Though not operationalized in this study, variation in the degree of interpersonal psychological warmth exhibited (affective or impersonal) and the depth of involvement of the interacting individuals (strong or weak) are important in understanding the effects of interactions on attitude formation. Depth of involvement varies according to the amount of time individuals spend in various activities, the number of functions attended, the degree of commitment to the social relationships, and the purposes for which the functions are instituted. The social setting, location, or organization supporting the social relationships are elements to consider; this dimension enables inclusion of interactions not rooted in a socio-religious substratum.

FINDINGS

Subjective and Objective Ethnic Identification

Comparisons were calculated between the attitudes of ethnic identifiers and those of nonidentifiers. The classification is based on respondents' answers to the ethnic identification questions:

Do you consider yourself a member of any particular nationality or ethnic group?

(If "yes") Which one?

How important to you is your nationality or ethnic group—is it very important, moderately important, somewhat important, or not important?

Of those subjectively identifying with ethnic groups, 91 percent are Jews and 9 percent are non-Jews. Of those not identifying with ethnic groups, 36 percent are Jews and 66 percent are non-Jews. Respondents subjectively identifying with ethnic groups express attitudes less favorable toward all situations than nonidentifiers. Differences are particularly pronounced in the quota, hiring, and occupation situations.[8]

In the control for whether respondents are Jews or not, it was discovered that identified Jews express less favorable attitudes than nonidentified Jews toward three situations showing statistical significance: the busing, apartment, and hiring situations. When subjective identification was held constant, it was found that there are no significant differences between nonidentifiers, whether they are Jews or non-Jews.

In all tests, the direction of response is as predicted, with ethnic identifiers expressing less favorable attitudes toward the situations than nonidentifiers. Statistical significance is reached in 50 percent of the tests.

Another series of four questions measured the extent of Jewish respondents' identification with the Jewish group. The questions are as follows:

(1) Do you belong to a Temple? (If "yes") What kind—orthodox, conservative, reform, or another type?

(2) Do you observe most of the Jewish holidays, some of them, or none?

(3) Do you belong to any Jewish organizations? (If "yes") Which ones?

(4) Do you believe the Jews should identify culturally with the Jewish group, religiously with the Jewish group, or should assimilate into the American culture and not maintain their identity as Jews? How strongly do you feel about this—very strong, moderately strong, or not strong at all?

On the basis of the respondents' answers to these questions, four comparison groups were created. In addition, a fifth comparison group was formed: Jews answering "Jewish" on the religious affiliation question forming one group, and Jews answering "atheist" forming the second group. Except for one significant finding out of thirty Mann Whitney U Tests, the comparisons of respondents in these five series yield no results of significance.

Objectively the respondents were classified as either Jews or non-Jews according to their replies to three questions: some answered "Jewish" to the religious affiliation question (75); some answered "Jewish" to the ethnic identification question (63); and a few (3) stated "Jewish" to the question about their parents' religious affiliation.

Jews confirm more attitudinal dilemmas, role conflicts, and unfavorable attitudes than non-Jews in the busing, apartment, and hiring situations, and the direction of response is the same in the other situations.[9]

Jews are more likely than non-Jews to be in favor of busing, only if middle-class blacks were bused to predominantly white schools. Jews are more likely than non-Jews to view the "quality of education" as "going down" if busing were instituted. Further, Jews are more likely to perceive a conflict between their "liberal roles," in which they desire to make up for the inequities in education of blacks and whites, and their "parental roles," where they fear "physical harm" for their children from blacks in schools located in predominantly black neighborhoods.

In the apartment situation, Jews more than non-Jews fear potential economic losses by renting to blacks in predominantly white-occupied apartment buildings. Jews more frequently state they would rent to black tenants, conditional on their being from "middle-class backgrounds." They discern a conflict between their "liberal roles," where they desire racial integration in housing, and their "businessperson" roles, where they fear that "whites will run" or the "property will deteriorate."

In the hiring situation, Jews more readily express the view that hiring blacks is conditional upon their meeting the qualifications for the positions; many Jews feel middle-class status of blacks is necessary. They state a conflict between their "liberal roles," where they believe in equal job opportunities for all, and their roles as "professional or businesspersons," where they "must maintain high standards of work."

It is wise to note, however, in these situations, as well as in the others, many non-Jews affirm similar conditions, attitudinal ambivalences, and role conflicts. Furthermore, many Jews express decidedly favorable attitudes.

One surprising finding relates to the quota situation. In view of Jews' history of being excluded from colleges and professional schools by quotas, it was predicted that Jews would be less favorable toward quotas than non-Jews. But no significant differences were found when comparing the two groups. Most respondents in the sample (82 percent) oppose quotas as the basis for college admission, mainly because they produce "discrimination in reverse." However, when certain status dimensions are incorporated in the analysis, differences between Jews and non-Jews become apparent.

Stratification of Status Variables by Ethnic Identification

To further understand the effect of ethnic identification on attitudes toward the six interracial situations, seven variables were stratified by both objective and subjective ethnic identification. These include race, religion, social class, education, occupational status measured by aspirations for children's occupational status, intergenerational occupational mobility, and style of life. Also, objective and subjective ethnic identification were stratified. Thus, there were four comparison groups in each stratification procedure. For example, in the stratification of style of life by objective ethnic identification, the four groups include: Jews placing importance on style of life as a dimension of status; Jews not placing importance on style of life; non-Jews placing importance on style of life, and non-Jews not placing importance on style of life. Similarly, in the stratification of social class by objective ethnic identification, the four groups contain Jews perceiving social class as a salient dimension of status, Jews not perceiving social class as salient, non-Jews perceiving social class as salient, and non-Jews not perceiving social class as salient. Further, the stratification of objective and subjective ethnic identification produced four groups—Jews identifying with their ethnic group, Jews not identifying with their ethnic group, non-Jews identifying with an ethnic group, and non-Jews not identifying with any ethnic group.[10] In all cases, objective identification stratification yielded clearer differences among the attitudes of those in the comparison groups than did subjective ethnic identification. In other words, whether the respondents were Jews or not differentiated the attitudes more significantly than whether the respondents were subjectively identified with an ethnic group.

For the *quota situation,* the first comparison of Jews with non-Jews did not confirm any statistically significant differences. However, in the stratification procedures, important differences appear. Jews ascertaining the importance of religion, Jews who feel occupational status is important, and Jews who were very mobile in occupation affirm the least favorable attitudes.[11]

For the *busing situation,* Jews consistently elaborate the least favorable attitudes, not only in the first comparison based on objective ethnic identification, but also in all the comparisons in the eight stratification series. Jews who feel that race, religion, social class, or subjective ethnic identification are important dimensions of status show less favorable attitudes than both their non-Jewish counterparts and Jews not discerning these status dimensions as important. Likewise, Jews who were very mobile, nonmobile, or downwardly mobile in occupational status express less favorable attitudes than Jews who were somewhat mobile and both groups of non-Jews.

For the *residence situation,* the first comparison of Jews and non-Jews did not reveal any statistically significant differences. However, in the social class stratification series, Jews acknowledging the importance of class status express the least favorable attitudes. In the style of life stratification series, Jews ascertaining that style of life is important affirm the least favorable attitudes. In contrast, and not in accordance with the predictions, non-Jews holding high aspirations for their children's occupational status state the least favorable attitudes.

For the *apartment* and *hiring situations,* Jews display less favorable attitudes than non-Jews in the first comparison as well as in the eight stratification series.

For the *occupation situation,* there were no significant differences between Jews and non-Jews in the first comparison, but stratification demonstrates that Jews stressing the importance of either religion or style of life assert the least favorable attitudes. In contrast, stratification by the salience of race shows that non-Jews express the least favorable attitudes, and stratification by occupational mobility or education generates the findings that both Jews and non-Jews who are very mobile, nonmobile, or downwardly mobile or who stress the importance of education state the least favorable attitudes.

In conclusion, there is a clear association of ethnic identification, particularly objective ethnic identification, with attitudinal dilemmas, role conflicts, or attitudes unfavorable toward the situations. In some instances, ethnic identification alone is sufficient to separate those most favorable from those least favorable toward each situation. In other cases, the stratification of one of the seven variables by objective ethnic identification differentiated respondents affirming the most favorable attitudes from those stating the least favorable attitudes. Noticeably, there were some exceptions to this general pattern, e.g., in the residence situation, when the salience of occupational status was stratified by objective ethnic identification, those expressing the least favorable attitudes are non-Jews holding high status aspirations for their children.

The Jewish Response to Black Anti-Semitism

Jewish respondents replied to the following open ended question: How do you feel about black anti-Semitism? There are three major types of responses.

First, many respondents (59 percent) express the feeling that because Jews have been especially helpful to blacks in the Civil Rights Movement, blacks are unjustified in their negative attitudes toward Jews. For example,

> I'm against black anti-Semitism. It upsets me. It is uncalled for. The majority of Jews are good toward the blacks in their attitudes and actions.

> I'm deeply concerned because of the long history of Jewish help in the Civil Rights Movement. Look at the history of Jewish leadership in civil rights. I am of a generation of Jewish people who were considered a minority and potentially discriminated against. This kind of turn in cycle is a bitter irony.

Second, some Jewish respondents (36 percent) state that although Jews help blacks in their civil rights struggles, the blacks' hostilities toward Jews, are, in fact, warranted. One respondent states,

> I'm upset about it, but I can understand it. It's a serious problem. After all, look at all the Jews have done for the blacks. But the middle-class Jews are also antiblack. It's justified.

Third, a few Jewish respondents (4 percent) affirm a decidedly problack and anti-Jewish orientation. For example,

> I have seen in my lifetime too much of the patronizing housewife or businessman who honestly believe they are being good to the "schwartzas." ...The Jewish person came on the strongest and the loudest as to what he was doing for the Negro. They are very loud about it. They feel we two minorities who have been so persecuted shouldn't hate one another, and yet they never accepted a Negro as an equal.

The Newer Immigrants vs.
Third or Fourth Generation Americans

A comparison of respondents according to their generation of presence in the United States was based on the location of their birth, their parents' birth, and their grandparents' birth. In addition, the married were asked the location of their spouse's birth. First, the foreign born express less favorable attitudes toward four situations than those born in the United States—the quota, busing, apartment, and occupation situations. They also tend to show less favorableness toward the residence and hiring situations.[12] Second, foreign born respondents and/or whose spouse's are also foreign born state less favorable attitudes toward three situations—the busing, apartment, and hiring situations—than U.S. born respondents whose spouses are also born in the United States. The same tendency exists in the other three situations.[13] Third, the comparison of second generation Americans with third or fourth generation Americans indicates that the former express less favorable attitudes toward the busing and apartment situations than the latter, and the direction of response is the same in the other situations.[14] Fourth, the comparison of third generation Americans with the fourth generation yields no statistically significant differences.

Thus, the further removed from foreign origins, the more favorable are the respondents' attitudes toward the situations. Conversely, the closer to foreign birth, the more likely it is that individuals will express ambivalent or unfavorable attitudes toward situations involving black-white relationships, especially in the busing and apartment situations.

A further examination of the national origins data is necessary to determine whether the findings are duplications of those in the comparison of Jews with non-Jews. Of respondents born in the United States, 50 percent (86) are Jews, and 50 percent (86) are non-Jews. However, of those from Southeast European origins, 86 percent (103) are Jews and 14 percent (17) are non-Jews. Of those from Northwest European origins, 22 percent (8) are Jews and 78 percent (29) are non-Jews. Only one Jewish person's grandparents were born in the United States, in contrast to 41 non-Jewish respondents' grandparents.

The comparison of foreign born respondents with those born in the United States contains Jews and non-Jews in both groups. However, of the foreign born, 81 percent (26) are Jews, whereas of the U.S. born, 50 percent (86) are Jews. Thus, the tests calculated for the national origins analysis do not duplicate those in the analysis of objective identification; however, respondents from Southeast European origins are primarily Jews, those from Northwest European origins are primarily non-Jews, and fourth generation Americans are primarily non-Jews.

Communal and Associational Relationships

In the evaluation of the extent that the respondents' social interactions are homogeneous (communal relationships) or heterogeneous (associational relationships), all respondents (Jews and non-Jews) were asked,

About how many of your friends and other people you associate with in your various activities are of a different *nationality or ethnic group* than you—would you say less than one-third, between one-third and two-thirds, or more than two-thirds?

How about *religious affiliation*—about what percent would you say are different from you—less than one-third, between one-third and two-thirds, or more than two-thirds?

How about *race*—about what percent would you say are different from you—would you say less than one-third, between one-third and two-thirds, or more than two-thirds?

With respect to *ethnicity,* respondents stating that less than one-third of their friends and others with whom they associate are of a different nationality or ethnic group than they are express less favorable attitudes toward three situations—the busing, residence, and apartment situations—than those interacting with an ethnically more heterogeneous group. The same direction of response is indicated in the quota, hiring, and occupation situations.[15]

Regarding *religious affiliation,* respondents stating that less than one-third of their interactions involve people of different religious backgrounds affirm less favorable attitudes in four situations than those stating their interactions are with people of different religious affiliations. These situations are the quota, busing, apartment, and hiring settings. The residence and occupation situations show the same direction of attitudinal response.[16]

With consideration to *racial background,* respondents stating they interact with people of different racial groups in less than one-third of their relationships express less favorable attitudes toward the busing and hiring situations than those involved in more heterogeneous racial interactions. The direction of response is the same in the quota, residence, apartment, and occupation situations.[17]

In conclusion, respondents exhibiting communal interactions with respect to *ethnicity, religious affiliation,* and *racial background* affirm the least favorable attitudes toward most situations. Conversely, those exhibiting associational interactions express more favorable attitudes.

Interpretation of the results of these tests suggests support for the proposition that ethnocentrism is related to ambivalence toward racial integration. Respondents least ethnocentric—those not identified with an ethnic group and engaging in associational interactions—tend to support ethnic integration, while respondents most ethnocentric—those identifying with an ethnic group and engaging in communal interactions—find themselves in role conflicts or attitudinal ambivalence toward their usual beliefs in integration.

CONCLUSIONS

The general purpose in this inquiry is to examine some reasons that a portion of whites holding a strong and long term belief in racial integration are ambivalent about their principles when faced with the emergence of interethnic social situations. After a survey of the literature on ethnic relations and other areas of sociological inquiry, hypotheses rooted in two major theoretical perspectives were tested: the concept of ethnic identification and the concept of interethnic contact. In the first framework, it was predicted that respondents identifying with an ethnic group will experience the importance of their group identification, will maintain group boundaries, and will find attitudinal ambivalences in their belief in integration when they perceive situations as affecting the relative status of their group. There is considerable statistical support for the relationship between ethnic identification and ambivalence concerning integration. Similarly, respondents of foreign birth or whose parents were foreign born were expected to retreat from their belief in integration, while those coming from families living in the United States for several generations were expected to adhere to their general belief. Once again, there is support for these expectations. In the second framework, it was expected that respondents interacting within social circles comprised primarily of their own ethnic, religious, or racial group identities will be ambivalent about their general belief in integration when presented with the six interethnic situations. These expectations are supported by the statistical techniques applied.

In contrast to these significant findings, five additional measures of Jewish ethnic identification appear unrelated to ambivalence toward ethnic integration. Neither temple membership, holiday observation, organizational membership, expressed belief in "identification" or "assimilation," or religious identification as Jewish or atheist is significantly related to the dependent variables. One interpretation is that these factors fail to elicit the communal or associational dimension of social interactions; they do not separate Jewish respondents according to degree of homogeneity or heterogeneity in social relationships. These measures fail to be associated with adherence to or ambivalence toward integration beliefs, while contact patterns and other measures of ethnic identification are predictive. This suggests that ethnic involvement and ethnocentrism are the primary correlates.

The pervasive association of ethnic identification with attitudinal dilemmas, role conflicts, and attitudes decidedly unfavorable toward a situation is especially pronounced when either the status dimension or the situation is related to one's children. The salience of race, religion, social class, and occupational status directly related to their children, except where non-parents were questioned about "people" in general. Consistent with this observation is the order obtained in the scalogram presented in Chapter III, where the "more difficult" interracial situations are those relating to children. In addition, the findings generated in the occupational and educational mobility analysis demonstrate the high degree of upward mobility in status exhibited by most of those interviewed. Furthermore, it was demonstrated that status threat and occupational status are central in the respondents' lives. There is no doubt that those who are very mobile in occupation, stemming from the lower rungs on the occupational and educational ladders, and in addition, striving to overcome the barriers discrimination presented to their parents as well as themselves—primarily Jews—are very intense in their efforts for their children to maintain the status gains they achieved during their lifetimes.

The "time dimension" factor, stressed by Ralph H. Turner, is particularly essential to this discussion. Referring to youth culture, he states,

> Defining stratification exclusively according to origin or contemporary objective characteristics runs the danger of underestimating the importance and prospects of stratification in a future-oriented society such as high-school youth. . . . There is good reason to suppose that the cleavage and value differentiation are portents of the nature of the adult stratification into which the students are moving. The stratification of destination may provide a better clue to stratification in the larger society than the stratification of origin.[18]

White liberal respondents are viewing the time dimension—the class of destination—in terms of their children's futures. The centrality of high status in its various aspects must be interpreted within the context of this future orientation which is perceived as an attempt to retain for their children the status gained by respondents due to their efforts during their own lifetimes. Whereas Turner focuses on the ambition of youth in two generations and analyzes the time dimension by the framework of the class of origin and the class of destination, this analysis interprets the time dimension in a three generational perspective: the class of origin, the present status ranks of respondents, and the future class of destination of their children.

Any social situation seen as threatening to social status—occupational, educational, and style of life—will be responded to with trepidation. The importance of dimensions of status, the degree and direction of occupational and educational mobility, and the centrality of high status are best interpreted as resting on a fabric of concern for status maintenance in the class of destination of one's children.

Examination of the reasons for the different findings of this chapter reveals that Jewish respondents in the sample are primarily first and second generation Americans. Though they have assimilated into American culture, as Herberg demonstrates, many still maintain a communal identity with the Jewish group. They may state their religion as atheist, say they believe Jews should assimilate, and say they do not belong to any ethnic group; however, when asked whether their children should marry Jews, they say "yes." And when questioned on the extent of homogeneity or heterogeneity in their interactions with members of other religious, ethnic, or racial groups, many are likely to exhibit homogeneity.

In effect, the lack of support for certain measures of ethnic identification, such as organizational membership or holiday observation, and the evidence of support for other measures lead to an interpretation of the apparently conflicting results in terms of homogeneity or heterogeneity of interactional networks. Thus, "identification" may be defined in terms of communal relationships as well as by certain other objective and subjective measures of ethnic identification. In some instances, the measure of communal relation-ships is more closely associated with types of attitudinal responses than are objective measures, such as organizational membership.

The concepts of "assimilation" and "identification" are not, realistically, as mutually exclusive as they are commonly construed. Indeed, the lack of significant differences in the respondents' attitudes concerning belief that Jews "should assimilate" may demonstrate a response set, in which these two concepts are viewed as polarities and reified since they are long-standing beliefs in the popular culture and sociological literature. For example, one may "assimilate" into the American culture by adopting certain styles of life in consumption behavior, dress, social conventions, manners of speaking, and expressions of values and beliefs, and yet, at the same time, still "identify" with a particular ethnic group.

The framework of communal and associational relations—the degree of homogeneous or heterogeneous interactions—supplements the traditional concepts of "assimilation" and "identification." There are four possible groups emerging from combining the two sets of concepts. First, "assimilated-associationalists" are ethnic group members who assimilate to the majority group's values, beliefs, and customs while not maintaining communal sets of social relationships; this coalescence of assimilation and associational relation-ships represents the commonly used concept of "assimilation." Such indivi-duals will hold outer reference group orientations, stressing universalistic principles such as a belief in ethnic integration. Second, "identified-communalists" are ethnic group members not adopting the customs of the majority group but totally identifying with their group in a comprehensive way, such that their customs, manners, beliefs, and values are distinct from the majority group; this combination of identification and communal relationships indicates the commonly used concept of "identification." These persons will hold inner reference group orientations, stressing particularistic principles which will give priority to in-group status and identity. Third, "assimilated-communalists" are ethnic group members adopting many of the values, beliefs, and customs of the majority group and yet still maintaining a communal set of social relationships. Fourth, "identified-associationalists" are those identifying with their ethnic group and interacting associationally with other group members. Contact does not preclude identification with one's ethnic group. If, on the one hand, these individuals interact in an associational manner with members of their own group, Lenski's "associational involvement" is exemplified. If, on the other hand, individuals completely embrace their roles as members of an ethnic group, but nevertheless interact associationally with other ethnic group members, then there are the necessary conditions supportive of Lewin's proposition that only by acceptance of one's ethnicity can an individual express friendly, unprejudicial attitudes toward an out-group.

Merging several sociologically developed orientations—ethnic identification and ethnocentrism with interethnic contact—offers extended possibilities for future research in understanding attitudinal shifts among members of ethnic groups. Based on the evidence, it is predicted that "assimilated-associationalists" will adhere to principles of ethnic integration. In terms of the permeability or insularity of groups within a social structure, this group is expected to exhibit a high degree of permeability along with a lack of ethnocentrism and prejudicial attitudes, discriminatory behavior, and other social conflicts. Anchored in the findings is the prediction that "identified-communalists" will retreat from a prointegration position. This category will exhibit a high degree of insularity along with ethnocentric attitudes and social clashes to maintain group boundaries. The third and fourth categories offer possibilities for cross pressures by the impact of reference groups presenting different value perspectives and status concerns to members; manifestations of less stable attitudes by members of these groups and opinions varying according to the salience of a particular reference group in a specific interethnic social situation will exist. In the extreme categories—"assimilated-associationalists" and "identified-communalists"—it is suggested that there is consistency with Schermerhorn's thesis that the greater the degree of enclosure of an ethnic group, the greater the conflict.

Succinctly, when values clash with the value of social justice, when status interests conflict with principles of equal opportunity, many white liberals will opt for their salient values and status interests, and, in consequence, will retreat from their customary support for the American Creed.

A word of caution is necessary in interpreting the data presented here. The group studied exhibits bifurcation of its membership, with 44 percent primarily from Protestant origins and 55 percent primarily from Jewish origins. The hypotheses have not been tested on the interrelationships of other ethnic group members, or, specifically, on their adherence to ethnic integration in the face of social situations threatening to their salient values or status concerns. Other ethnics' degree of homogeneity or heterogeneity in social interactions has not been measured, nor has their degree of ethnocentrism. Supplementary research along these lines will enhance understanding of interethnic conflict, interethnic coalitions, and the extent of permeability or insularity of groups within a social structure.

REFERENCES

1. Hubert Blalock, *Toward a Theory of Minority Group Relations*, 1967, p. 84.
2. Ralph H. Turner and Samuel J. Surace, "Zoot-Suiters and Mexicans: Symbols in Crowd Behavior," in *Collective Behavior*, ed. by Ralph H. Turner and Lewis M. Killian, p. 50.
3. Ruben Salazar, "Head Start Fails Them, Chicano Group Says," *Los Angeles Times*, November 5, 1969.
4. Ruben Salazar, "Black and Chicano Ties Worsen After Walkout at Santa Barbara," *Los Angeles Times*, September 15, 1969.
5. Ruben Salazar, "Black-Brown Friction Growing," *Los Angeles Times*, October 26, 1969.
6. Gerhard Lenski, *The Religious Factor*, 1963, p. 23.
7. Ibid.
8. Those subjectively identifying with an ethnic group (73) expressed less favorable attitudes than nonidentifiers (131), as follows: for the quota situation, $z=2.68$, $p < .01$; for the hiring situation, $z=2.00$, $p < .03$; for the occupation situation, $z=2.79$, $p < .01$. The other situations showed the same direction of response, but the tests were not statistically significant. One tailed tests of significance were calculated, and alpha was set at .05.
9. Jews (112) expressed less favorable attitudes than non-Jews (92), as follows: for the busing situation, $z=3.54$, $p < .001$; for the apartment situation, $z=3.27$, $p < .01$; for the hiring situation, $z=2.08$, $p < .02$. The other situations showed the same direction of response, but the tests were not statistically significant. One tailed tests of significance were calculated, and alpha was set at .05.
10. Only 6 respondents identified with ethnic groups other than the Jewish group: 3 Italians, 1 Albanian, 1 Armenian, and 1 Irishman.
11. For comprehensive documentation of statistical tests and interpretation of their meaning, see Judith Caditz, "Dilemmas of the White Liberal," Tables 11.1 - 11.13, pp. 274-317.

12. The foreign born (32) expressed less favorable attitudes than those born in the United States (172), as follows: for the quota situation, $z=2.27$, $p < .02$; for the busing situation, $z=2.51$, $p < .01$; for the apartment situation, $z=2.34$, $p < .01$; for the occupation situation, $z=1.70$, $p < .05$. The other situations showed the same direction of response, but the tests were not statistically significant. One tailed tests were calculated, and alpha was set at .05.

13. The foreign born and/or those whose spouse's are foreign born (40) expressed less favorable attitudes than those born in the United States (130), as follows: for the busing situation, $z=2.10$, $p < .02$; for the apartment situation, $z=2.47$, $p < .01$; for the occupation situation, $z=1.78$, $p < .05$. The direction of response was the same in the other situations, but the tests were not statistically significant. One tailed tests were calculated, and alpha was set at .05.

14. Second generation Americans (82) expressed less favorable attitudes than third or fourth generation Americans (95), as follows: for the busing situation, $z=1.71$, $p < .05$; for the apartment situation, $z=2.31$, $p < .02$. The direction of response was the same in the other situations, but the tests were not statistically significant. One tailed tests were calculated, and alpha was set at .05.

15. The homogeneous (94) expressed less favorable attitudes than the heterogeneous (102), as follows: for the busing situation, $z=1.65$, $p < .05$; for the residence situation, $z=1.75$, $p < .05$; for the apartment situation, $z=2.26$; $p < .02$. The other situations indicated the same direction of response, but the tests were not statistically significant. One tailed tests were calculated, and alpha was set at .05.

16. The homogeneous (83) expressed less favorable attitudes than the heterogeneous (106), as follows: for the quota situation, $z=1.98$, $p < .03$; for the busing situation, $z=2.37$, $p < .01$; for the apartment situation, $z=1.70$, $p < .05$; for the hiring situation, $z=2.51$, $p < .01$. The direction of response was the same in the other situations, though the tests were not statistically significant. One tailed tests of significance were calculated, and alpha was set at .05.

17. The homogeneous (178) expressed less favorable attitudes than the heterogeneous (25), as follows: for the busing situation, $z=2.15$, $p < .02$; for the hiring situation, $z=1.73$, $p < .05$. The direction of response was the same in the other situations, but the tests were not statistically significant. One tailed tests of significance were calculated, and alpha was set at .05.

18. Ralph H. Turner, *The Social Context of Ambition*, 1964, p. 212.

CHAPTER VI

Dissonance Reduction

Will white liberals be ambivalent or retreat from their general principles with ease? Or will they experience dissonance and strain when they endorse attitudes contrary to the American Creed? Will a person committed to equality of opportunity in education experience discomfort when stating that bussing will lower the quality of education? Will those expressing opposition to quotas in the colleges because they exclude qualified persons feel uneasy when they also believe that society must make up for past inequities in which minorities were barred from a college education? How about the apartment house owner and the homeowner who support fair housing in principle but oppose blacks moving into their residential areas because of the fear of the economic loss they perceive is involved? What does the liberal integrationist do when blacks apply for jobs and there is pressure not to hire because of fear of clients, patients, customers, and coworkers hostilities? Will discomfort exist only when actions are discrepant with ideals, or will white liberals experience discomfort when their attitudes appear inconsistent? Then, what will those in states of dissonance do to resolve it?

Central to answering these questions is the work of Leon Festinger, whose contribution to the social sciences includes cognitive dissonance theory. Essentially, Festinger contends that when persons affirm inconsistent attitudes or behaviors lacking in congruency with their attitudes, they will engage in dissonance reducing mechanisms. Festinger states,

> Two elements are dissonant if, for one reason or another, they do not fit together. . . . Let us consider two elements which exist in a person's cognition and which are relevant to one another. The definition of dissonance will disregard the existence of all the other cognitive elements that are relevant to either or both of the two under consideration and simply deal with these two alone. These two elements are in a dissonant relation if, considering these two alone, the obverse of one element would follow from the other.[1]

> The presence of dissonance gives rise to pressures to reduce or eliminate the dissonance. The strength of the pressures to reduce the dissonance is a function of the magnitude of the dissonance.[2]

Although accepting Festinger's theoretical orientation, this analysis incorporates dissonance theory within a sociological framework, with emphasis on three aspects: the causal impetus to dissonance as rooted in a sociocultural substratum, the descriptive nature of experience as expressive of sociological content, and the sociological effects of dissonance and its reduction mechanisms.

TYPES OF DISSONANCE

Contradiction Between a General Belief and Specific Beliefs

With reference to the causal dimensions of cognitive dissonance, it is observed that many respondents express a contradiction between a general belief and specific beliefs. These specific beliefs become visible when interracial situations become imminent. For example, the members of the organization believe in general antidiscriminatory principles. They believe in racial integration. They believe in "fair treatment for minorities." They believe that "color makes no difference," that "people are people," and that "there should be one human race." However, when asked specific questions about specific interracial situations, many express attitudes which appear to be contradictory to these general principles. Specific questions on busing in the schools, blacks entering their occupational fields, blacks moving into their neighborhoods, the quota system in the colleges, the rental of apartments to blacks in white-occupied apartment buildings, and the hiring of blacks lead some respondents to affirm attitudes opposite those expected from an extension of a general frame of reference favoring the American Creed.

In addition, further probing questions about specific aspects of each situation brought out other specific attitudes, such as fears of economic loss in the apartment situation, fears of physical danger and the lowering of the quality of education in the busing situation, fears concerning the class status of blacks in the occupation situation, and fear of the loss of prestige and a decline of property values in the residence situation.

A conflict between general egalitarian principles and the status interests of some respondents' ethnic group created a juxtaposition of beliefs perceived as incompatible in specific situations. Jewish respondents recognize the difficulty in reconciling the existence of black anti-Semitism with their general principles of social justice for all.

Dissonance exists because many attitudes endorsed by the respondents seem to those expressing them to be attitudes which a discriminatory person, a "bigot," a "Bircher," a supporter of Wallace, or "someone from Orange County," would affirm. Often, the respondents act *as if* they should be in favor of busing, *as if* they should not fear any economic losses, *as if* they should favor quotas, *as if* they should not state a middle class condition, and *as if* they should not express many of the attitudes they do, in fact, express.

Conflict Between Two Salient Values

A conflict between two central values is apparent when the respondents are presented with the situations. For example, many place high priority on the quality of education. They also place high priority on favorable attitudes toward blacks and the eradication of institutionalized inequities in American society. These two values appear to be in a dissonant relation in certain specific interracial situations: busing in the schools; quotas in the colleges; hiring blacks, which is feared to produce "lowering of standards"; and the entrance of blacks into new occupational fields, which might cause "lowering of the reputational standing of the position."

An especially potent clash in central values is reported with respect to the conflict between the value of high status for the respondents' children and the value of facilitating the improvement of the status of blacks. Respondents who feel status dimensions are important, especially with reference to their children's class of destination, opt in favor of their children's status interests. This decision produces dissonance.

Conflict in the Interpretation of the Application of a General Principle

An unclarity in the meaning of a general principle is crystallized by people's responses to specific situations. There are two particularly significant areas in which this type of conflict is brought to the surface. First, in the respondents' attitudes toward the quota situation, the most prevalent question is whether support of a quota system excludes whites and thus constitutes "discrimination in reverse," or whether support of a quota system, by including more minorities on the campuses, facilitates an end to discrimination. Second, attitudes toward the hiring situation manifest a similar conflict. If blacks were hired, would this practice be interpreted as an elimination of whites who "were better qualified"? Or, alternately, would hiring blacks provide for racial integration, nondiscrimination, and the existence of equal opportunity for all, irrespective of race, color, or creed? Another dimension evidenced in the hiring situation concerns the conflict between the "plus value" derived by having blacks working at various places and the perceived "discrimination" against whites, if black persons were "favored over white people."

Conflict Between Two Roles Played by One Individual

Some spoke about the incompatible expectations they experience when exploring their attitudes and hypothetical actions in certain interracial situations. A typical role conflict is one in which the respondents desire to play the "liberal role," but when questioned about busing in the schools, they perceive the salience of their roles as parents. They fear the quality of education will be lowered and that there will be danger of physical harm from black children if busing were designed in their school districts. Yet, at the same time, they speak about their desires to help make up for the inequities in education between blacks and whites. In the apartment situation, the "liberal role" conflicts with the "economic role," with the respondents indicating their conflict between wanting to assist integration in apartment houses, and yet not wanting to lose any money in the process. In the hiring and occupation situations, the "liberal role" clashes with the "businessperson role" or "professional roles." Again, specific desires to implement racial and ethnic integration or to assist the entrance of blacks into a wider array of occupational fields at all levels of the occupational spectrum clash with specific desires to maintain high standards in work. Many respondents feel the "quality of work will go down" if blacks were to enter their fields or if they were to hire blacks. In the residence situation, some experience a conflict between the "liberal role," in which they want blacks to enter primarily "lily-white" neighborhoods, and the "neighborhood friend role," in which they do not want to move out and "leave their neighbors with all the problems and financial losses."

Conflict Crystallized During the Interviews

The type of conflict described here is a specific role conflict occurring with frequency during the course of the interviews. The interview situation itself brought role conflicts to the surface. Since the respondents knew that the organization supported the study, and because they had received a letter from the Executive Director endorsing the study, they perceived themselves as being selected by virtue of their genuine liberalism. When the respondents express attitudes which they perceive as contradictory, they experience discomfort in their interaction with the interviewers. The apparent disparities between what the respondents feel they ought to say and what they have actually said are often resolved by statements such as "You know how liberal I am!" (reaffirmation of liberalism) or "This study is biased against the Negro!" (derogation of the source of the conflict).

In sum, these attitudinal conflicts, belief dilemmas, conflicts in values, and role conflicts are sociological in origin. Specific social issues and social situations bring such conflicts into sharp relief. The conflicts described may take place in one's mind, with an experience of emotional difficulty. However, they are not isolated from the social situations and issues which give rise to them. Furthermore, the conflicts are often caused by a lack of accord in the definitions of the situations available in the culture. The interpretation of quotas and hiring of blacks as accelerating the cause of nondiscrimination, and the interpretation of the same situations as providing for "discrimination in reverse" are indicative of differential cultural perceptions for the same set of events. The perception of the positive value of high occupational and educational status, especially with reference to the class of destination of one's children, is socially determined. So, too, is the positive value attached to the principles of equal opportunities for all and racial integration as a means of achieving the goal of nondiscrimination.

Descriptively, the types of conflict illustrated here are of a sociological nature. The conflict between general antidiscriminatory principles and the specific fears related to busing, quotas, rentals to blacks, blacks in one's neighborhood, and blacks in one's place of work, are rooted in the interrelationships between people within specific social settings. The microsociological analysis of interview-situation role conflicts is descriptive of social interactions, rather than isolated, individual mental processes.

The effects of these ambivalences, attitudinal dilemmas, role conflicts, and consequent dissonances are interpreted within a sociological framework. Since attitudes affect behavior and attitudinal conflicts lead to lack of clarity as to what future attitudes or behaviors may be, the belief dilemmas may result in a withdrawal of support for the Civil Rights Movement, in an active opposition to specific programs designed to equalize the scales for all persons in a multi-ethnic society, or, alternately, may result in clearer support for efforts to achieve nondiscrimination in housing, jobs, and education.

It should be made clear that there is no denial of the individual causes of ambivalence, the individual experience of ambivalence, or the individual consequences of ambivalence. Social origins, social content, and social effects are, by definition, mediated through the persons composing society, social groups, and social interactions. Rather, it is important to emphasize the sociological aspects of the causes, content, and effects of cognitive dissonance and its resolution.

MECHANISMS OF COGNITIVE DISSONANCE RESOLUTION

Most respondents stating attitudinal dilemmas, role conflicts, or attitudes unfavorable toward one or more of the situations exhibit various modes of reducing the dissonance caused by their statements. A careful reading of all responses, which were taken down verbatim by the interviewers, produces twelve main categories of dissonance reduction. Each one will be defined and examples will be given for illustrative purposes.

Avoidance

By the mechanism of avoidance, respondents evade attitudinal expressions about specific situations or specific questions. This evasion functions to reduce the dissonance experienced by the posing of the question and the respondents' anticipated answers. An example from the busing situation illustrates the mechanism of avoidance:

> **Question**: Do you feel busing would lower the quality of education your children would get?
>
> **Answer**: I don't know.

There is always the possibility that people state "I don't know" to questions in which they really do not have an answer. The key element which differentiates those who are resolving dissonance from those who just "don't know" is to be found in the sequence of questions and answers. If the respondents have expressed ambivalence and doubts about busing and have especially mentioned the conflict between the "liberal role" and the "parental role," it may be assumed that "I don't know" is a mechanism of cognitive dissonance resolution.

Another form of avoidance occurs when individuals delegate certain role behaviors to others who then carry out the required behavioral expectations. William J. Goode suggests that delegation is one way individuals may "manipulate their role structures" and thereby reduce "role strain." For example,

Question: What would you do if a black family wanted to rent one of your apartments and you personally didn't mind renting to blacks but your tenants threatened to move out?

Answer: That's a rough situation. Theoretically, I'd rent, because I'm for fair housing and integration. That's why I won't own an apartment building. Or if I did, I'd let someone else do the renting.

Answer: I'm in favor of renting to blacks. They have the right to live wherever they want. The manager runs my building. He is instructed to rent to any good tenant. (Quietly, the respondent continues) I think the manager is prejudiced.

The avoidance mode is used most frequently in responses to the busing situation, where 8 percent of the dissonance reducing replies demonstrate this technique. However, a comparison of the frequencies of all the types of dissonance reduction shows that avoidance is only moderately utilized.

Derogation of the Perceived Source of the Dissonance

The respondents reduce the dissonance produced by the question or situation by asserting a negative attitude toward the specific question, the manner in which the question is worded, or the study in general. For example,

Question: How do you feel about blacks starting to work in *(the respondent's occupational field)*?

Answer: What kind of a question is this? Why do we even have to ask a question like this?

Question: What would you do if blacks began to move into your neighborhood?

Answer: What a strange question.

Question: Do you feel there might be less value connected with the B.A., M.A., Ph.D., or other degrees if more blacks were in the colleges?

Answer: This study is biased against the Negro. This is a bigoted question. White middle-class terminology.

This mode is most prevalent in the responses toward the residence situation, where of all dissonance reduction responses, 8 percent are of this type. The hiring situation also evokes a moderate percentage of replies demonstrating this mode (6 percent).

Denial

The respondents state that a particular conflict producing situation is nonexistent. They may simply state that it is not real, that it does not exist. For example,

> **Question:** How do you feel about black anti-Semitism?

> **Answer:** It doesn't exist. There is no anti-Semitism among blacks. It is a real problem, the blacks shouldn't hate the Jews. But it doesn't really exist.

Denial is infrequently used, with 2 percent of the dissonance reducing responses toward the occupation situation and 1 percent of those in the quota situation showing this form.

Minimization

Respondents reduce the impact of the problem raised or the significance of the attitudes expressed by reducing their importance. For example,

> **Question:** Do you feel the educational rating of the college would go down if more blacks attended?

> **Answer:** Yes. It lowers the qualifications of the graduates. They are less apt to fill job requirements. But it would be minimal.

> **Question:** How do you feel about black anti-Semitism?

> **Answer:** It's a terrible problem. The Jews have helped the blacks more than anybody else. The blacks say terrible things about the Jews. But it's exaggerated. It's not that much of a problem.

> **Question:** Do you feel the increase in the number of blacks on the campuses increases the possibilities of physical danger to students?

> **Answer:** Yes, it does. Whites can get hurt. But it's minimal. The majority are peaceful. It's only rumor.

This mode is most frequently used in dissonance reducing expressions in the quota situation, with 4 percent of the responses of this type. However, this form is not prevalent.

Reference to the Temporary Nature of the Problem

Respondents reduce the impact of the problem raised, or the effect of their expression of ambivalence or unfavorableness toward a situation, by stating the short duration of the problem. For example,

> **Question**: Do you feel renting to blacks might involve you in an economic loss?

> **Answer**: Yes. The whites would run, and I'd lose the rent. There would be vacancies. However, it would only be temporary.

> **Question**: How do you feel about blacks entering *(the respondent's occupational field)?*

> **Answer**: Great. But at first there would be all kinds of problems. They would have a chip on their shoulders. They would be resentful and defensive. Later, they'd be accepted as people.

This technique is most frequently used in responses toward the busing situation, with 8 percent of the dissonance reduction responses in this category. This form is used moderately as a method of dissonance resolution.

Categorization

Respondents enlarge the category to which their attitudes apply. For example,

> **Question**: Could you imagine that you owned an apartment building and that it was occupied only by whites. What would you do if a black family wanted to rent one of your apartments and you personally didn't mind renting to blacks but your tenants threatened to move out?

> **Answer**: That's a tough one. I wouldn't rent, if they were the loud mouth sloppy type. The same goes for whites, too.

> **Question**: Do you feel busing would bring your children into contact with children you'd rather they wouldn't socialize with?

Answer: Yes. They have a different set of moral values than we do. But this doesn't only apply to Negroes.

Question: Do you feel the hiring of blacks would affect the reputational standing of the position for which they were hired?

Answer: Yes. They are not as qualified and they'd have trouble dealing with the clientele. But that could go for low-class whites, too.

Question: How do you feel about blacks starting to work in *(the respondent's occupational field)?*

Answer: I'm in favor. I'm for the black gaining a better footing ("liberal role"). But I'm disappointed with the graduates from Southern segregated schools. They are not adequately prepared. Standards may go down ("professional role"). But the same goes for whites from Southern schools.

Categorization is exhibited in 16 percent of the dissonance-reducing responses toward the residence situation, 15 percent of those toward the apartment situation, and 12 percent of those toward the occupation situation. This form is moderately chosen as a method of dissonance reduction.

Differentiation

Respondents specify the group to which their responses apply or indicate the area to which their responses apply. Abelson defines differentiation as follows: "An element may be split into two parts with a strong dissociative relation between the parts."[3] For example,

Question: Do you think many problems would be created if blacks come into your occupational field rapidly?

Answer: Yes, there would be many problems. But actually not here. There would be problems in other schools.

Question: Do you feel the reputational standing of your neighborhood would go down if blacks were to move in?

Answer: Yes, it would. . .For people from Arkansas, not to those whose opinion I value.

Question: What would you do if a busing program were to be started in your school district?

Answer: I'm against busing. I don't want my kids on a bus for hours and hours every week. I want them close to home. I'm not against the concept of busing, though. In the South, in Orange County—that's where the people are against busing.

Differentiation is the most prevalent form of dissonance reduction used. In the occupation situation, respondents expressing modes of dissonance reduction use differentiation in 56 percent of the responses. The other situations are as follows: the hiring situation, 51 percent; the residence situation, 45 percent; the quota situation, 31 percent; the apartment situation, 30 percent; and the busing situation, 16 percent.

Reference to Facts

Respondents offer evidence that real facts support their unfavorable attitudes. For example,

Question: How do you feel about black anti-Semitism?

Answer: it exists. It's a fact. Christians have told me about it. My relatives in New York told me that blacks are favored over whites.

Question: Do you feel busing would bring any possibilities of physical danger for your children?

Answer: Yes, it's a fact. I have read about it recently. Mixed schools have more crime.

Question: Do you feel the reputational standing of your neighborhood would go down if blacks were to move in?

Answer: Yes, a ghetto would form. They let things go and the houses deteriorate. It's a historical fact.

This mode is most frequently used in the residence situation, with 6 percent of the dissonance reduction responses falling into this category. However, the other situations indicate only a small percentage of use of this technique.

Citing the Causes of the Problem

Respondents offer their interpretations of the causes of the problematical nature of the issues. By a process of intellectualization, they point out the reasons the problems exist.

Question: How do you feel about blacks entering *(the respondent's occupational field)?*

Answer: I feel uneasy about it. I'm ambivalent. Black clients don't want their own telling them what to do.

Question: Do you feel you have to be more careful in picking a black person for a position in your type of work than a white person?

Answer: Yes. You do have to be more careful. You never know what you're getting into. But it's because of race problems. There are so many prejudiced whites already.

Question: How do you feel about black anti-Semitism?

Answer: I'm against it. It upsets me and angers me—look at all the Jewish organizations that have helped blacks, like ADL. Jews have given so much money to support the cause of the blacks in this country. Blacks are anti-Semitic because it's hate for a particular white person. Militant black leaders manipulate blacks so that they will hate Jews.

Citing the causes of a problem can be done in terms of placing blame: whites are prejudiced, blacks "are taught to fight it out," society is at fault, realtors cause block busting, and "authorities must learn better methods of handling violence."

This mode appears most frequently in attitudes toward the busing situation, with 32 percent of the replies of this type. The other situations indicate frequent use of this mechanism, as follows: 22 percent of the dissonance reducing replies in the hiring situation; 20 percent in the apartment situation; 17 percent in the residence and the occupation situations; and 11 percent in the quota situation.

Offering a Solution to the Problem

Respondents suggest ways of solving the problems raised by the questions and their expression of unfavorable attitudes. This technique may involve the process of intellectualization. For example,

Question: What do you think about colleges using a quota system so that minorities will be represented according to their proportion in the population?

Answer: I feel ambivalent. I don't believe in quotas, but if it is the only way to get Negroes in, it's O.K. But that's not the solution. Minorities should be given special help and assistance.

Question: How do you personally feel about busing as a solution to de facto segregation in the schools?

Answer: I'm against busing. Of course I'm for integration. I really feel ambivalent, can't make up my mind. We need fair housing and desegregation in communities. That's the real solution.

Question: What would you do if blacks began to move into your neighborhood?

Answer: I don't know. I might not live up to my principles. It would be alright if it's done slowly. It must be done slowly for assimilation.

Solutions for perceived problems are offered most frequently as a mode of dissonance reduction for attitudes toward busing, with 11 percent of such replies of this type. Respondents' attitudes toward other situations indicate moderate use.

Reaffirmation of General Principles

Respondents restate their commitment to egalitarian principles after making statements seemingly contradictory to those principles. For example,

Question: Would you hire only middle-class blacks?

Answer: Yes, you can't have disrespectful characters. Since Watts, I won't deal with blacks. But this applies to the individual, not his color.

Question: Do you feel only the smarter black children, or those with the highest academic potential, should be bused into predominantly white schools?

Answer: Yes, because duller ones will feel frustrated and defeated among white students who have had better academic facilities. But I only am thinking in terms of the individual. People are people.

Question: Do you feel only those black children from middle-class families should be bused into white schools?

Answer: There are no problems with the wealthy ones. I do not want my kids terrorized. But all children should have the opportunity for a sound education. I believe in equal opportunity for all.

Question: How do you feel about black anti-Semitism?

Answer: It's a terrible thing. Blacks shouldn't be against the Jews. The Jews worked and fought for blacks in the Civil Rights Movement more than anyone else. Blacks are wrong. It makes me angry. There should be a common feeling of sympathy between the two minority groups. After all, color makes no difference. We are one human race.

Question: What would you do if blacks began to move into your neighborhood?

Answer: I'm not prejudiced, but I wouldn't like to be standing on Central Avenue. They have different standards, but I think in terms of the individual. I don't care if they're blue, green, or orange.

The appeal of general beliefs is used frequently in attitudes toward the quota situation (36 percent) and moderately in the apartment situation (19 percent) and the busing situation (16 percent). The other situations show some adoption of this mode among the dissonance reducing replies.

Transcendence

Respondents state a higher purpose which will be served, in spite of the problems created by the situation. Abelson defines transcendence as follows: "Elements, instead of being split down, are built up and combined into larger units organized on a superordinate level."[4] For example,

Question: Do you feel busing would lower the quality of education your children would get?

Answer: Yes, it may, but that's the risk you have to take.

Question: Do you feel the entrance of blacks into your occupational field would lower the quality of work?

Answer: Yes, they don't have the qualifications of whites. They don't have the training. But that's the price we have to pay for integration.

Question: Would you favor blacks moving into your neighborhood only if they were middle-class people?

Answer: Yes, I could only live with middle-class people. The lower class doesn't have the values I do. They might be loud and not maintain the property. That's the risk you have to take. We'd have to take that risk for integration.

This type is infrequently used, with only 2 percent of the dissonance-reducing responses toward the busing situation exemplifying this type.

In sum, this analysis reveals that "reaffirmation of general principles" is the most frequent mode of dissonance resolution in the responses to the quota situation, with "differentiation" next. "Citing the causes of the problem" is most often used to reduce dissonance in the busing situation. "Differentiation" is the most prevalent in the residence, apartment, hiring and occupation situations. In contrast, "transcendence" is the least frequently used mode, with its application primarily in the busing situation.

THE DETERMINATION OF THE EXISTENCE OF
COGNITIVE DISSONANCE

A question arises throughout this analysis of cognitive dissonance and mechanisms of dissonance reduction: are these really examples of dissonance? How does one know whether or not an attitudinal response expresses dissonance?

It is not definite that certain responses evidence dissonance and that the form of the responses exhibit cognitive dissonance-reduction mechanisms. One can only apply techniques of analysis which assist in determining what is construed as dissonant, rather than consonant, and as dissonance reducing rather than not dissonance reducing.

One of the differentiating factors between dissonance and lack of dissonance is the initial manner in which respondents answer the question under consideration. For example, the first question in the examples of minimization is "Do you feel the educational rating of the college would go down if more blacks attended?" If the respondent had answered, "No, race is irrelevant," dissonance would not be expected. Indeed, many answers throughout the interviews simply express the view that "color makes no difference."

But if respondents initially say "yes" in response to a question which they then perceive as indication that they have deviated from the ideology of the white liberal, they will proceed to perceive a dissonant relation between general equalitarian principles and their response to the question.

Another differentiating factor to be taken into account in the analysis of the presence or absence of dissonance is the sequence of attitudinal responses. If people have been ambivalent about busing in the schools, they may resolve their dissonance at various points during their discussion on busing. If they have expressed doubts about blacks moving into their neighborhoods, perhaps they will resolve the dissonance at the close of the sequence of questions on the residence situation by stating they are decidedly in favor of blacks moving into their neighborhoods.

The respondents may experience dissonance in the series of question on one situation and then reduce their dissonance in their responses to the next situation. For example, many express doubts about school busing. However, the next situation—the occupation situation—produces less dissonance since there are clearer definitions available in the culture to this long-standing situation. Thus, positive answers in a less complex situation may reduce the dissonance experienced in a more complex situation.

Finally, the respondents were given an opportunity to reduce the dissonance experienced because the interview itself "put them on the spot." Their final evaluation of the study by a follow-up mailed questionnaire allowed the expression of criticisms, suggestions, and further remarks; in addition, they were given a chance to state which situations produce the most dilemmas.

In sum, the interpretation of the degree of dissonance experienced by the respondents and the analysis of dissonance reduction mechanisms rests not only on attention to content-specific answers to content-specific questions, but also on the comparison of responses indicating no evidence of dissonance with those that do, the sequence of answers to a given situation, the sequence of answers to the series of situations, and the reaction to the study in general.

SUPPORT FOR THE DISSONANCE REDUCTION THESIS

A comparison of the percentages of unfavorable attitudinal expressions containing mechanisms of dissonance reduction with unfavorable attitudes not containing such mechanisms supports the thesis that role conflicts and dissonance producing statements will compel individuals to mitigate or resolve them.

Of those expressing unfavorable attitudes toward the initial question on the quota situation, 85 percent (173) utilize a mechanism of dissonance reduction and less than 1 percent do not. Attitudes favorable toward quotas are expressed by 15 percent (30) of the respondents; no dissonance reduction mechanisms are associated with these attitudes. Of those affirming the view that only middle-class blacks should be bused, 29 percent (50) show a mechanism of dissonance reduction, while only 3 percent (5) do not. Respondents not expressing the condition of middle-class status do not adopt a mode of dissonance reduction when asked about the class factor. Of respondents endorsing the opinion that the reputational standing of their neighborhoods will go down if blacks move in, 67 percent (137) state a mode of dissonance reduction, while only 4 percent (8) do not. Those not stating that the reputational standing will go down do not express any dissonance reduction. Examination of the statistical results reveals that in a majority of cases where ambivalent or unfavorable attitudes are stated by white liberals, there is a resolution of the dissonance by one of the modes of dissonance reduction.

ROLE THEORY AND COGNITIVE DISSONANCE THEORY

Role theories place emphasis on the *interactional* nature of role playing, role-taking, and the strategies individuals adopt in their tactics of coping with their own roles in relation to the roles of significant others. Cognitive dissonance theories place emphasis on the *intrapersonal* nature of dissonance and its reduction. Dissonance theorists focus on mental elements and their interrelationships with an eye to the degree of consistency, balance, or congruity between the various elements.

Both theoretical approaches subsume similar phenomena. For example, role theory analyzes the self concept as does dissonance theory. But each theoretical model emphasizes somewhat different aspects of the self concept. An integral part of role theory, stemming from Meadian perspectives, is the notion that "minds, selves, and self-consciousness" develop by virtue of "an ongoing social process of experience and behavior in which any given group of human individuals is involved." Role theory places more emphasis than does dissonance theory on the development of the self concept within a social-cultural context, the ways in which the self concept may be changed by various role enactments, and the manner in which role performance is either congruent or incongruent with people's self concepts. Dissonance theory places more emphasis than does role theory on the effects of the self concept on dissonance reduction and the effects of dissonance on the self concept. Dissonance theory may focus on individuals' intrapsychic experiences. For example, Dana Bramel states, ". . .a person's expectations about

his own behvior should be aroused most clearly when he perceives his behavior as emanating primarily from himself rather than from environmental
pressure."[5]

The areas of role conflict or role strain and cognitive dissonance clearly
overlap. There is an agreement not only in the idea that individuals
experience stress and anxiety in situations of role conflict or cognitive dissonance, but also there is a parallel development of theoretical concepts
concerning some of the mechanisms of the resolution of role conflicts and
those of the reduction of cognitive dissonance. For example, the "avoidance"
technique is developed in the literature of both theoretical orientations.
One avoids the relation of dissonance between two cognitive elements by
simply not observing one or both of them, or the dissonant relation between
the elements. Similarly, one avoids role conflict by simply not engaging,
in the behavioral expectations of one role, another role, or both roles. The
mental processes involved in "differentiation" are analogous to the role
tactic of "compartmentalization." In "differentiation" one splits apart a
mental element so that there is no relationship between the two parts thus
created; dissonance reduction will follow. In "compartmentalization," one
provides for "role segmentation," so that role demands are separately allo-
cated to different roles the individual plays. "Differentiation" is also similar
to the mechanism of "role distance" especially as this concept is defined by
Erving Goffman. He demonstrates that role distance is an important dimension
of the meeting of a role and the individual person. Role distance is a phenomenon which is an expression of the degree role players desire to be identified, or
disidentified, with the "virtual self" available in the role. Goffman indicates that
the "virtual self" is that image individuals have of themselves and others have of
them if they fully identify with the "formal status and identity" associated
institutionally or normatively with their roles. Role distance is an attempt on
the part of role performers to cope, strategically, with the situations at hand.
It is their attempt to alter the definition of the situation. Goffman suggests
that role distance provides for a "margin of reservation" between the persons
and their "putative" roles; it is in this discrepancy that people reveal their
own styles. The persons engaging in role distance strategies attempt to affect
the social milieu, so that they can convey the impressions they want to convey, and so that others will have a particular impression of them. Role distance provides a means of putting ego defense mechanisms into operation.
Thus, by disidentifying with some of the behaviors, values, and attitudes of
a role, one can engage in the mechanism of "differentiation."

Even though role theory and dissonance theory overlap, both of these
theories demonstrate their limitations when applied to this analysis. For the
nature of this study, for the interpretation of the role conflicts and disso-

nance the respondents express, and for the analysis of methods of role conflict resolution and cognitive dissonance resolution, both of these theories, if applied separately, limit the interpretative analysis.

Dissonance theory, though not excluding sociological aspects, is limited in its applications to socio-cultural analysis. As indicated in this chapter, the dissonance the respondents experience is rooted in their social experiences, values and exposure to differential norms. So, too, the dissonance they experience is brought into focus by their direct exposure to social situations presented during the interviews. The application of role theory to these aspects of the study permits a greater flexibility and a broader basis for understanding the processes involved than does dissonance theory.

However, the application of role theory evidences its limitations, too. The categories of role conflict resolution developed in the literature do not adequately explain the possibilities for role conflict resolution inherent in the six interracial situations presented to the respondents. Goode's development of the concepts of "compartmentalization," "delegation," "elimination of the role relationships," "extension," and "barriers against intrusion," will not apply when certain interracial situations become manifest. For example, how do people compartmentalize their "liberal roles" from their "neighborhood friend roles" or from their "economic roles" when blacks knock on their dorrs to look at their homes which are for sale? How do those who perceive conflict between their "liberal roles" and their roles as "businesspersons" resolve the dilemmas involved when they place ads in the paper for available positions and a black person comes for an interview? How do individuals delegate their "liberal roles" or their "parental roles" when they are questioned by an interviewer on what they would do if busing were instituted in their school districts? These situations and questions are direct; there is not time for compartmentalization or delegation; the situations and questions require a response; they create dissonance; the dissonance impels individuals to reduce the effects of the dissonance producing situations or questions.

In specific interracial situations, especially where the definitions of the situations are unclear, role conflicts become evident which are not resolved in the manner suggested by role conflict resolution categories. Dissonance theory offers extended possibilities for the interpretation of such role conflicts and the ways in which they may be reduced, especially when time factors do not permit the usual modes of resolution.

The effects of the conflicts raised during the interviews were not observed after the interview period; the behavioral effects were not measured; nor is it possible to predict the attitudinal and behavioral consequences of the actual confrontation of the individuals embracing the "liberal role" and other roles which they perceive to be in conflict. It is at these times that role theoretical approaches, rather than dissonance theoretical approaches, will be most fruitful in analysis. The effects of role conflict on voting behavior, the choices people will make if actually faced with these interracial situations, the role strategies they take—all these behaviors with their associated attitudes may be interpreted as means of role conflict resolution. Avoidance is demonstrated in nonvoting due to cross pressures. Compartmentalization is seen when individuals hire blacks meeting the role expectations of "true liberals," but, at the same time send their children to private schools meeting the role expectations of the "concerned parent." Delegation is demonstrated in cases where liberal businesspersons give the responsibility of hiring to their executive secretaries.

In sum, there is much to be gained in understanding the underlying principles of role conflicts and dissonance experiences by a coalescence of these two basic theoretical approaches. They are complementary, rather than mutually exclusive, theoretical orientations. Dissonance theory lends to role theory a framework for analysis where role theory fails: namely, where an interracial situation impinges upon people and generates conflicts otherwise avoided because the roles involved never come together; they are insulated from one another until the situation emerges. Role theory lends dissonance theory a framework where dissonance theory fails: namely, in conceiving of people in interaction, rooted in a culture, developing in social groups, and affecting social interactions and social groups by their sometimes dissonance producing life experiences.

REFERENCES

1. Leon Festinger, *A Theory of Cognitive Dissonance,* 1968, pp. 12-13.
2. Ibid., p. 18.
3. Robert P. Abelson, "Modes of Resolution of Belief Dilemmas," *Journal of Conflict Resolution,* 1959, p. 345.
4. Ibid., p. 346.
5. Dana Bramel, "Dissonance, Expectation, and the Self," in Abelson, et al., *Theories of Cognitive Consistency,* 1968, p. 365.

CHAPTER VII
Conclusions
and Implications

The social location of prejudicial attitudes, discriminatory behavior or racism has been shown to be the working class, blue-collar workers, and lower-class whites, as well as traditional Southern segregationists. Since the 1930s, social science research has supported these findings. While John Dollard et al. report that Southern white workers frustrated by economic conditions displace their aggression onto blacks, Seymour M. Lipset found lack of support for civil liberties among working-class authoritarians. Theodore W. Adorno et al. revealed that ethnocentrism, anti-Semitism, and fascistic attitudes are rooted in early childhood experiences and emerge in the authoritarian personality syndrome. Elliott M. Rudwick, through socio-historical analysis, found white workers in East St. Louis clashing violently with black workers in 1917, while Hubert Blalock summarized the history of union opposition to the membership of blacks. In the 1970s, opposition to school busing occurring among Boston and Louisville working-class people is reported in the newspapers.

What is the effect of formal education? Numerous social science studies consistently found that the higher the formal education, the lower the prejudicial attitudes and discriminatory behavior. Herbert H. Hyman and Paul B. Sheatsley report authoritarianism to be associated with low formal education rather than with personality factors showing in high scores on the Ethnocentrism, Fascism, and Anti-Semitism scales constructed by T.W. Adorno et al. Samuel A. Stouffer indicates more intolerance for communism and civil liberties among the poorly educated than among the well educated. Gertrude Selznick and Stephen Steinberg report greater acceptance of anti-Semitic beliefs among the less educated, and less endorsement among the more educated, although they indicate that education is not a "cure all" for the eradication of prejudice. Using information from the United States, England, Germany, Japan, India, Finland, Sweden, and elsewhere, Seymour M. Lipset shows that the poorly educated are most likely to comprise the working-class authoritarians who do not endorse civil liberties as readily as the well educated and well-to-do. Some research, such as that of Melvin Tumin et al., supports the thesis that the higher the formal education, the greater the support for desegregation. Thus, the strategy of racial integration is approved most strongly by the well educated.

The underlying rationale is that education leads to viewing the world in all its complexities, rather than simplistically and concretely. Education results in emphasis on the secular rather than the mystical. Education induces open mindedness, tolerance of differences between ethnic groups, and support for civil liberties. Education generates scientific experiment, hypothesis testing, and theory construction, rather than acceptance of myths, mysteries, and mysticisms.

White liberals in the study reported here rank high in degree of formal education, with an average education for the group as a whole in the "some post graduate" category, compared with a nationwide average of between "two years high school" and "high school graduate." The respondents rank high in occupation, the average rank for the group as a whole being the fifth highest on a scale from one to nineteen, while the national mean was the thirteenth rank. In terms of income, the average for the group as a whole was between $20,000 to $24,999, compared with a national average of between $8,000 and $8,999 in 1968. Yet, a large segment of this group was either caught in a web of attitudinal ambivalences and role conflicts, or retreated from its general commitment to equality for all, specifically as manifested in attitudes toward racial integration in education, housing, and employment.

This study clearly challenges the notion that the source of opposition to racial integration lies only in the working class or only among the poorly educated. Many white liberals are consistent with their lower-class and working-class counterparts in that status threats—including job security—threats to prestige and style of life and threats to their children's class of destination, affect their attitudes. Though they do not clearly and easily concur that they are oftentimes aligned with the lower class, many white liberals do, indeed, experience inconsistencies between their general commitments and their specific attitudes, do face role conflicts as integrationists and parents, and do feel discomfort in other dissonance producing clashes. Fears of lower-class blacks failure to maintain property, fears of blacks not conforming to white middle-class values and ways of raising children, fears that qualifications will be lowered in occupations, fears that the quality of education will be reduced if schools are integrated, and other fears manifest in specific interracial situations. The roots of prejudice and discrimination are exposed.

THE INTEGRATION ISSUE

Racial and ethnic integration as a method of eradicating institutionalized inequities in the United States is being questioned today by black power advocates as well as white liberals. Concurrently with an increase in the legal sanctions favoring integration, blacks and other minorities are becoming more militant than ever before in relation to white institutions. Black protest to economic, social, and political subordination has existed from the beginning of the slavery period. However, in recent years, there is an unprecedented development of a social movement of blacks actively seeking change or removal of oppressive institutions within American society. The 1960s were the scene of numerous urban racial confrontations; the 1970s are the scene of minority groups' pursuits for community control. separatism with power bases apart from the white institutional structures, and increasing awareness and sense of belonging among members of different third world liberation movements.

There is a seeming contradiction between the progress of the Civil Rights Movement and the abandonment by many of the strategy of integration. Although the 1954 Supreme Court decision in *Brown v. the Board of Education* ruled that separate schools are inherently unequal, blacks are vehement in desiring local control and a retention of power over school boards within the black community. The New York school crisis of 1967 and 1968, particularly in Ocean Hill-Brownsville, engendered a confrontation, with overtones of black anti-Semitism and Jewish backlash, between community school boards and the teachers union. At the same time, while school desegregation plans are being formed in many communities, white liberals are retreating from their general support for integration, preferring the "neighborhood school concept." Further manifestations of progress of the Civil Rights Movement's goals are the establishment of FEPC, laws against restrictive covenants in housing, the Civil Rights Acts of 1964 and 1968, and the Voting

Rights Act of 1965. While these acts cement the strategy of racial integration because they are written into law, white liberals applaud them as successes, but, concomitantly, retreat when a black family moves into their neighborhood or feel ambivalent about hiring minority group members because they are perceived as "unqualified."

Why is it that these long sought avenues to racial integration, fulfilling the values implicit in the American Creed, are being questioned today? Why are black, Chicano, Asian, and Indian-Americans becoming vociferous and visible in their relations with white society? David O. Sears and John B. McConahay found that the Northern "new urban black man" is different from his Southern counterpart. Socialized in a different context, young Northern blacks accept more aggressive norms toward white authority than Southern blacks. Racial socialization is a key factor in determining the political strategies adopted by segments of the black population. W. Brink and L. Harris report that Southern Negroes are more accepting than Northern Negroes of existing housing, school, and transportation patterns, attitudes toward police and white business. In his accounting for the Black Revolution, Lewis M. Killian reports that integration is viewed by many blacks as "the token integration of a minority of qualified Negroes into what remained a white man's society."[1] Analyzing the ghetto riots and rise in importance of black militants, Robert Blauner sees their occurrence as springing from the social structure of the United States, viewed as a form of internal colonialism. He discerns that control of the ghetto by blacks is necessary to change the oppression and division of American society. Jerome Skolnick also describes urban unrest as rooted in the colonial structure of American society; he suggests that black power and protest have changed from an emphasis on "equality to liberation, from integration to separatism, from dependency to power."[2]

Why is it that white liberals retreat from their usual support for racial integration? The primary intent in this study is to understand the conditions differentiating white liberals who maintain their integrationist principles from those who do not. Paul B. Sheatsley reports that "nationwide, support for integration was now characteristic of about half the white population, while in the North it had clearly become the majority view."[3] Further, his findings are consistent with the contact theories, since more whites in the South tend to support integration where it is practiced. In contrast, the study reported here found a major portion of a group of white liberals expressing attitudinal dilemmas, role conflicts, or retreats from their general support for integration when they replied to questions on six interracial situations.

The search for reasons for this shift away from a belief in integration reveals that part of the answer lies in an analysis of two central areas in a social science inquiry on race and ethnic relations: status consciousness and ethnic identification.

SUMMARY OF MAJOR FINDINGS

Originating in two unique social-historical roots but basically committed to antidiscriminatory principles are persons from white Anglo Saxon Protestant origins who have maintained the high economic, educational, and social status of their parents, and persons from Jewish origins who have attained high status in education, occupation, and income, and aspire for their children to maintain this high status. The commitment of those from Protestant origins is traced to their historical involvement in the mainstream of American democratic ideals and values, as manifested in the Bill of Rights, Jeffersonian and Jacksonian democratic philosophy, and the Fourteenth Amendment to the United States Constitution. The basis for the commitment of those individuals from Jewish origins is found in their religious-cultural values of social justice (Zedakeh) and humanitariansim, and in their experiences of genocide and anti-Semitism, particularly in the countries of their origin.

First, by use of the Guttman Scale technique, it was demonstrated that the attitudes expressed by the respondents toward the six interracial situations, are scalable. The "most difficult" situation is the quota situation, and the "least difficult" is the occupation situation. Thus, it can be predicted that if individuals affirm attitudinal dilemmas, role conflicts, or attitudes unfavorable toward the quota situation, they will not necessarily express ambivalence toward the other situations. However, if they express attitudinal dilemmas, role conflicts, or attitudes unfavorable toward the occupation situation, they will express ambivalence toward the other five situations. The order of the situations obtained in the scalogram, from "most difficult" to "least difficult," is as follows: the quota situation, the busing situation, the residence situation, the apartment situation, the hiring situation, and the occupation situation. Noticeable is the finding that the "most difficult" situations are those involving persons for whom the respondents are most responsible, namely, members of their family circles. The "least difficult" situations are those in which the respondents' family members are least involved and in which the respondents assume the least family responsibility. The quota and busing situations hold implications for white liberals' children's class of destination, while the hiring and occupation situations are most applicable to their own interactions and status.

Second, certain status dimensions form a quasi-scale. Once again, the use of the Guttman Scale procedure demonstrated that the "most difficult" status dimensions are religion or ethnicity, while the "least difficult" status dimension is style of life. "Difficulty" is interpreted as follows: respondents who feel religion or ethnicity are salient do not perceive the other status dimensions as salient. However, those who feel style of life to be salient also feel the other dimensions as salient. The order of the status dimensions from "most difficult" to "least difficult" is as follows: religion or ethnicity, social class, education, occupation, and style of life. Once again, the "most difficult" dimensions are those which the respondents perceive as applicable to their children's future status, particularly with respect to religion or ethnicity and social class.

Third, disclosed in this analysis is the association of particular variables with the expression of attitudinal dilemmas, role conflicts, and attitudes clearly unfavorable toward the six interracial situations.

Respondents who consider certain status dimensions important affirm the least favorable attitudes toward the six situations. These factors include the salience of religion, ethnicity, social class, education, occupation, and style of life. Conversely, those who do not feel status dimensions important generally adhere to their commitment to racial integration. Moreover, status consciousness per se is more clearly associated with attitudinal ambivalence than are direct threats.

The very mobile, stationary, and downwardly mobile in intergenerational occupational mobility endorse more ambivalent and unfavorable attitudes than does the somewhat mobile group. In addition, those recently attaining the highest occupational ranks, measured in terms of intergenerational mobility, express less favorable attitudes than those maintaining the high status ranks attained by their parents. However, in educational mobility, those affirming the most favorable attitudes toward the six situations are the very mobile.

The investigation into the association of ethnic identification with the attitudes expressed toward the six situations reveals that those identifying with an ethnic group, either objectively or subjectively, affirm less favorable attitudes than those who do not identify. Since the sample contains 55 percent (112) respondents from Jewish origins and 44 percent (90) respondents from Protestant origins, the ethnic identification hypothesis was tested upon Jews compared with non-Jews, and not on other ethnic group members adherence to or retreat from the principles of ethnic integration.

As a corollary to this finding, it was also determined that respondents closest to foreign birth are most likely to state attitudinal dilemmas or attitudes unfavorable toward the six interracial situations. Conversely, those furthest removed from foreign origins are most likely to express attitudes favorable toward the situations.

The distinction between communal relationships and associational relationships is of particular importance in its application to the concept of ethnic identification. Communal relationships are those in which the participating individuals engage in a wide range of activities with others of the same ethnic group identification; a homogeneity in social interactions is evidenced. Associational relationships, in contrast, are those in which the participating individuals belong to many different social groups, involving interactions with people of varied ethnic, religious, or racial groups; a heterogeneity of social interactions is evidenced. Respondents engaging in communal relationships express attitudes less favorable toward the six situations than those engaging in associational relationships.

In most cases, the combination of ethnic identification with other important variables increases the statistical significance of the findings in the comparison of respondents' attitudes toward the situations. For example, status conscious Jewish respondents express the least favorable attitudes, while non-Jewish respondents who are not status conscious affirm the most favorable attitudes. Jewish respondents who were very mobile, nonmobile or downwardly mobile in intergenerational occupational status state the least favorable attitudes, while non-Jewish respondents who were somewhat mobile express the most favorable attitudes toward the situations.

Because of their commitments to the ideology of the white liberal, most of those revealing attitudinal conflicts, role conflicts, or attitudes unfavorable toward any of the six interracial situations were thrust into a cognitive dissonance producing experience. The ideology of the white liberal places central value on the principles of social justice, equal opportunities for all, and nondiscrimination in employment, housing, and education. Confrontation with the problems inherent in the six situations produces belief dilemmas and ambivalence for white liberals because of the juxtaposition of their ideology and their attitudinal expressions which they perceive as incongruent. Based on the conclusions of both role theory and cognitive dissonance theory is the description of mechanisms by which respondents displaying belief dilemmas attempt to resolve their experienced dissonance.

RIGIDIFICATION OF THE IDEOLOGY
OF THE WHITE LIBERAL

White liberals holding strong beliefs in the principles embodied in their ideology sometimes evidence a calcification of their ideas. Rigidity of ideas causes an automatic recital of the elements inherent in the ideology, whether or not such elements are applicable to the situation at hand. Issues and alternatives are obscured, and the ideology becomes a "theme without variations."

Karl Mannheim noted this possibility in the development of ideologies when he stated, "There is implicit in the word 'ideology' the insight that in certain situations the collective unconscious of certain groups obscures the real condition of society both to itself and to others and thereby stabilizes it."[4] In essence, an ideology may become separated from the reality of a current social situation; it may become a method by which individuals blind themselves to the real issues and alternatives brought to the surface by a situation and may become the justification for avoidance of the problems inherent in a situation and the beliefs of other group members within the social structure. It may become a rationalization for behaving in one way, while espousing the principles and values impelling one to behave in another.

A few examples of the rigid application of some elements in the "ideology of the white liberal" are stated here:

> **Question**: Do you feel only a certain percent of black children should be bused into white schools?

> **Answer**: No! There should be no limits. Percent is another discriminatory basis.

The same question elicited the following type of response:

> **Answer**: Yes, because that's the only way to obtain a mixture. Otherwise, you could get a complete reversal. Whites would run, and then what would you have accomplished? Resegregation. But I don't know what's fair. How could you set a limit?

The "percent" questions in each of the six situations brought the same types of responses: first, those indicating that percent is another discriminatory basis; second, those indicating that percent limits are the only way to bring about integration. The first type of rsponse exemplifies a rigidity in the application of a rule without an adequate understanding of the implications of such a rule.

Another example of the calcification of ideological principles is demonstrated by those answering "color makes no difference" to the questions in an entire series on one situation, or to most questions in the entire series of six situations. There is no other comment, just a carbon copy of the same statement throughout the interview. Further, some respondents say "no" consistently when probed on their attitudes toward the situations. There is no recognition of the problems involved or of the alternatives and issues applicable to the definition of the situation. It appears as though these persons do not want to get involved in any discussion, lest it lead them to stating their attitudes which might contradict their ideal principles. In this sense, these carbon copy respondents may have been reducing anticipated dissonance by means of avoidance tactics. In effect, the carbon copy respondents espouse a rigid assertion of certain themes available in the "ideology of the white liberal." Often lacking in specific information, they state their dedicated beliefs in the ideology, obscuring an intellectual awareness of new situations, such as school busing, or blinding themselves to new alternatives to older, more common situations, such as the hiring and occupation situations.

A further example of carbon copy responses is represented by expressed attitudes indicating a "plus value" toward blacks. For example,

> **Question**: How do you feel about blacks starting to work in *(the respondent's occupational field)*?

> **Answer**: Differences in cultural backgrounds make it more interesting. We need all races in the various occupations. They have to be better than whites to have gone this far, and blacks should be given priority.

> **Question**: Do you feel the reputational standing of your neighborhood would go down if blacks were to move in?

> **Answer**: No, it may be better because it would show that Negroes live here. It would be enhanced.

> **Question**: Do you feel the educational rating of the college would go down if more blacks attended?

> **Answer**: No, the rating goes up. It's an "in thing" to have blacks.

> **Question**: Would you rent only to middle-class blacks?

> **Answer**: No, it is a good thing to experience all types of people. Sometimes they are better than the white element here now.

> **Question**: How do you feel about hiring blacks?

> **Answer**: I make a special effort to hire them. It is the thing to do. I'm prejudiced in favor of blacks.

These attitudes reflect that portion of the ideology of the white liberal which asserts the positive value of the visibility of blacks within various interactional spheres. Blacks at one's place of work, at schools which one's children attend, or in one's neighborhood are proof of the dedication of the white liberal to the principles of the ideology.

THE POSITIVE STEREOTYPE OF THE WHITE LIBERAL

Stereotypes are generally defined as rigidified views of individuals which are simple and serve to obscure differences. Stereotypes are pervasive; they attribute to individuals traits assumed to characterize the social groups to which they belong. Stereotypes tend to prevent people from reality testing. They freeze the judgments of those holding the stereotypes. Walter Lippmann's classic definition of stereotypes indicates that "the trickle of messages from the outside is affected by the stored-up images, the preconceptions, and the prejudices which interpret, fill them out, and in their turn powerfully direct the play of our attention, and our vision itself. . . . In the individual person, the limited messages from outside, formed into a pattern of stereotypes, are identified with his own interests as he feels and conceives them."[5]

In general, stereotypes convey negative images. The Negro is seen as lazy, fearsome, dull, and lacking in motivation. The Mexican is viewed as careless, prone to siesta-taking, and sloppy. The Jew is perceived as mercenary, shrewd and clannish. In his discussion of the portrayal of the enemy in radio and film propaganda, Robert K. Merton states, "The use of simplified personalized stereotypes presents the enemy as consisting essentially of a small band of evil men and implies that once these men are destroyed, all will be well."[6] Analyzing the stereotypes of the lower caste in paternalistic societies, Pierre L. Van den Berghe says these stereotypes exist: "childish, immature, exuberant, uninhibited, lazy, impulsive, fun-loving, good-humored, and inferior but lovable." In competitive societies, the lower caste is depicted as "aggressive, uppity, insolent, oversexed, dirty, and inferior, despicable, and dangerous."[7]

Stereotypes have primarily been studied by researchers in the field of inter-group prejudice, its causes and its persistence. One main aspect of such studies is the finding that the greater the contact between people of various groups, the greater the breaking down of stereotypical patterns of thinking with the consequent reduction of prejudice.

According to Roger W. Brown and Eric H. Lenneberg, stereotypical thinking also applies to all individuals, not only those engaging in prejudice or discrimination. They state,

> Everyone wants to predict what other people will do but we have no general consensus on the categories that are most useful for discovering general uniformities of behavior. Some people operate with ethnic categories: Negroes are expected to be superstitious and Turks to be cruel.

Some people operate with physiognomic categories: nice faces go with nice behavior but look out for the evil eye. The behavioral sciences have not originated the interest in predicting human behavior; they have rather professionalized a prior general concern. The cognitive business of these sciences is essentially continuous with the business of the whole community: to find the categories in terms of which reliable important expectancies may be formed.[8]

Many respondents adopting the ideology of the white liberal are engaging in stereotypical thinking–rigidified, categorical thinking which simplifies and obscures the issues of the six interracial situations under consideration.

However, in contrast to the stereotypes studied by most researchers, these elements of stereotypical thinking are positive in tone. They elevate white liberals, indicating their lack of prejudice; they stress the white liberal's unwillingness to be discriminatory and point out the color blindness of the white liberal. The themes that "color makes no difference," that "I don't care if he is black, brown, yellow, orange, or purple," and that "I will not discriminate"–all these statements may be used as expressions of white liberal stereotypical thinking. Reality is concealed and sometimes distorted, issues and discussion about alternatives are avoided, and blindness to new information becomes evident. But in this process, the individuals may glorify the white liberals with whom they identify. These white liberals are the upholders of freedom and justice, the "true believers" in the American Creed. The discriminators are the Birchers, Wallaceites, McCarthyites, "hard hats," people in Orange County, Arkansas, or the South. Thus, in a process of creating distance between the roles of the white liberals and the Birchers, these individuals further raise the worth of their own values and principles. However, in this process, rigidification of portions of the ideology often prevents an examination of the real issues.

Another difference between the negative stereotypes and the positive stereotypes of the white liberal is that in the former, the stereotype typically refers to members of other groups as objects. The prejudiced individuals point to the Jew, the Negro, the Japanese, or some other ethnic, racial, or religious group members. The white liberals point to themselves as objects, or to others whom they perceive as ideal white liberals with whom they identify. In a process of maintaining their self concepts as "true believers" in their own liberalism, and of defining and reaffirming their roles as white liberals, they stereotype themselves by asserting elements of principles which may have become detached from the social origins in which they were originally anchored.

In sum, the ideology of the white liberal can be interpreted in terms of the positive stereotypical qualities it produces. Whether for the purpose of reaffirming individuals' self concepts as truly liberal, avoiding conflict producing situations, or blinding and screening individuals from reality testing and further inquiry into the nature of the issues and problems inherent in new interracial social situations, these positive stereotypical statements and images are quite standardized, quite simple, and quite prevalent among the sample of white liberals.

A TYPOLOGY OF THE WHITE LIBERAL

In view of the preceding discussion and the descriptive analysis presented in Chapter III, a typology of six ideal-typical white liberals emerges.

First, there is the *color-blind white liberal,* who absolutely, emphatically and unmistakenly affirms a belief in nondiscrimination. Saying "color makes no difference," this person will not deviate from an antidiscriminatory position. Racial integration in housing, education, and employment, as well as interethnic interactions in all social situations, is based on the value "I don't care if they're black, brown, green, yellow, red, or purple!"

Second, there is the *white liberal plus,* who perceives an extra "plus value" to accepting blacks anywhere—in the schools, in occupations, and in neighborhoods. These liberals desire to make up for the past inequities blacks have suffered. They believe that the more contact between various types of people, the less prejudice there will be in American society. Further, they believe it is the "in thing" to have blacks visible in their children's schools, in their places of work, and in their neighborhoods. Blacks become a "status symbol" for the "true believer."

Third, there is the *conditional white liberal.* These liberals are willing to integrate blacks and other minorities into social settings, as long as certain conditions, qualifications, or limitations are attached. They favor busing in the schools, as long as white students are not bused into predominantly black schools. They favor quotas in the colleges, as long as the quality of education does not go down. They favor renting to blacks, as long as there is no economic loss involved. Thet favor hiring blacks, as long as customers, clients, patients, and other workers will not object.

Fourth, there is the *compartmentalized white liberal,* who will segmentalize roles so adherence to the "liberal role" is undertaken in certain situations, but deviation is the style in other situations. For example, these liberals may be against busing in the schools and quotas in the colleges because they perceive these situations as detrimental to their children's status attainments; but, at the same time, they might hire blacks and take pride in the visibility of blacks at their places of work.

Fifth, there is the *white liberal in conflict*—a liberal in the throes of belief dilemmas or role conflicts. On the one hand, these liberals maintain their belief in antidiscriminatory principles; on the other hand, they perceive a clash between their principles and other values and beliefs. They view the implementation of busing as advantageous for integration, but they are fearful of sending their children to ghetto areas. They see the benefits derived from blacks working with them, but they fear the lowering of standards and qualifications in their occupations or places of work. They want blacks to integrate all residential areas, but they are not willing to take a predicted economic loss or do not want to antagonize their neighbors. They want to express attitudes concordant with their general equalitarian principles, but they hold values central to a high status attainment for their children.

Sixth, there is the *white liberal in retreat.* These liberals will depart from their original dedication to general antidiscriminatory principles. They are status threatened by blacks in educational, residential, and occupational sectors, since they observe blacks gaining visibility and status within American society. They disidentify with the traditional white liberal roles and withdraw support for measures implementing racial integration.

Seventh, there is the *reaffirmed white liberal.* Some white liberals will embrace their original commitment to ethnic integration. Though in conflict when particular situations arise on the interracial arena, they resolve their conflicts by dedicated endeavors to facilitate legal and social measures to attain integration in American society.

Eighth, there is the *white liberal redefined.* In adopting a new characterization of racial liberalism, they perceive society as composed of separate and equal parts, a mosaic of peoples living together in segmental fashion, each with economic, political, and social power. The traditional concept of integrating various racial, ethnic, or religious groups is not essential to this newly defined liberal role. However, the principles of egalitarianism and nondiscrimination form the substratum of values, beliefs, and actions. This stance is consistent with the ideology of the black power movement.

CHALLENGE OF THE FUTURE

As new social situations involving interactions between blacks, whites, and other minorities are discernible, new conflict relationships will develop within American society. Paralleling the racial-economic conflicts existing between blue collar workers and blacks, conflicts will become apparent between minorities and white liberals generally supportive of their gaining entrance into higher educational, occupational, economic, and power hierarchies of the social structure. Especially when status threats for these white liberals or their children are perceived, either as obstructions to the maintenance of high status already gained or to the attainment of high status, they will express attitudinal ambivalence or will retreat from their traditional support for general antidiscriminatory principles. As blacks and other minorities gain visibility within the higher educational, occupational, and economic rungs of American society, they will present an increasing threat to the status of those generally committed to the principles of the American Creed.

Applicable to this analysis of conflicting interests is the "cross pressures" thesis. Basic to this conception is that people belong to many social groups in a complex society, such as religious and ethnic groups, occupational groups, socio-economic groups, regional groups, political parties, interest groups, social circles, and family circles. These groups convey differing definitions of the situation to their members, and, in consequence, create cross pressures.

In voting behavior analysis, the cross pressures thesis has been studied and developed by researchers in the field of political behavior and political socialization. In their secondary analysis of the 1952 presidential election, Janowitz and Marvick found where there were increased cross pressures, there was an increase in nonvoting. Berelson, Lazarsfeld, and McPhee demonstrated that people under attitudinal cross pressures decrease their interest in political affairs. Sometimes those in a cross pressured setting choose one reference group's definition of the situation over that of another. For example, Campbell and Converse showed that persons under cross pressures of occupation and class identification reflect the view of their occupational group more than the view of their class group.

It is predicted that white liberals traditionally supportive of racial integration, but who are challenged by situations such as busing in the schools or quotas in the colleges, will either be so cross pressured that they are unable to make decisions and thus refrain from voting, or will vote for candidates who oppose busing, quotas, or other white-minority interactional situations. The status conscious, those who are very mobile, stationary, or downwardly mobile in intergenerational occupational status, or those identifying with an ethnic group will fit in with these predictions. The political effect will be that certain white liberals are likely to align themselves with those they usually consider their ideological opponents: Wallaceites, Birchers, those from Orange County, "hard hats," Governor Reagan, or others defined as conservative with respect to the Civil Rights Movement. In doing so, they will experience cognitive dissonance and role conflicts. The means adopted by them for reducing such conflicts and dissonances are likely to be the mechanisms of role conflict or cognitive dissonance resolution described in Chapter VI.

One of the main impacts of this analysis is its support for the Weberian thesis that society is composed of competing and conflicting status groups. It is in this competing battleground that status groups formulate their views of the world and become the carriers of ideas which change the society in which the members of the competing groups live. The findings reported here indicate that the status conscious affirm the least favorable attitudes toward the six interracial situations. Particularly salient is the dimension of ethnicity. Jews, considered an ethnic status group, are expressive of more attitudinal dilemmas, role conflicts, and retreats from integrationist beliefs than non-Jews. For a more complete analysis and test of Weber's concepts, it is suggested that further studies must be made on the attitudes of ethnic groups other than Jews. Evaluations of such other group members attitudes toward new interracial situations will aid in understanding the processes underlying ethnic group conflicts. The primary question in such studies is whether members of ethnic groups other than Jews disclose attitudinal ambivalence and retreats from general equalitarian principles when asked about current interethnic situations involving education, occupation, and employment. Do other ethnic group members perceive status threats when certain social situations become manifest on the social scene?

Looking to the future, it is expected that when blacks and other minority groups support quotas in the colleges for the purpose of including members of their groups, many white liberals will oppose such plans. When busing in the schools becomes imminent or actually instituted, many will send their children to private or parochial schools, or move to another residential area. When blacks buy homes in their neighborhoods, many will move. When blacks desire to rent apartments in a predominantly white-occupied apartment building, many will not rent to them. Many white liberals will not hire blacks because of fears of losing clients, patients, or customers. Many will not approve of blacks entering their occupational fields. Many will object to other black-white situations. Many will vote against specific plans for lifting institutional barriers which obstruct the advancement of blacks and other minorities. Especially when new social situations arise in which these white liberals feel status threatened, either with respect to themselves or with respect to their children's future class status, they will withdraw their usual support for civil rights causes.

The essential question arising at this point is whether or not the findings imply a complete abandonment of antidiscriminatory principles and integration of the various minority groups and majority groups within American society. Does the evidence which supports the Weberian thesis that status distinctions characterize societies imply that ethnic identification, racial distinctions, and religious, economic, educational, and occupational differences will constantly plague societies and the individuals within them? Will such distinctions provide a seedbed for constant hostilities, prejudices, discriminations, conflicts, and subjugation? What are the implications of the cultural, religious, and racial differences among people?

Some adopt the view that differences among people should be reduced; that distinctions should be eradicated; that cultural variation should be minimized. This reduction in differences among peoples will mitigate prejudices, discrimination, and other forms of intergroup hostilities. Assimilation of the ethnic, religious, and other social groups will provide the basis for a truly equalitarian society.

The underlying assumption in this analysis is that cultural variation is existent and will be so for the foreseeable future. Further, cultural variation is desirable, in that it provides for new ideas, flexibility within the social structure, and social innovations which sometimes change the social structure.

It is expected that there will not be a complete abandonment of beliefs in antidiscrimination, beliefs in eradicating prejudice in American society, and beliefs in egalitarianism.

Based on Weberian theoretical orientations it is considered likely that there will be some groups dispossessed and also that there will be some groups attaining higher status. Further, the children of such dispossessed peoples will form new strata and differentiated groups within American society. Thus, although there will be a depletion of some liberals from the community of liberals, there will also exist an increment of new people within their ranks.

Political and civil rights interest groups dedicated to the advancement of egalitarianism, the protection of minority rights, and the eradication of discrimination and prejudice will continue to function. Such organizations will continue their efforts to affect legislation, court decisions, and the stimulation of belief in antidiscriminatory principles. Even if particular individuals retreat attitudinally from their general principles, they will not necessarily withdraw their membership from civil rights organizations. In addition, even though particular civil rights leaders send their children to private schools when busing programs are instituted, they will continue to fight for integration at the institutional level, in the legislatures and courts.

Of benefit to white liberals would be an awareness of their ambivalences, attitudinal dilemmas, and retreats from general principles supporting racial integration. In a process of intellectualization, traditional liberals should be able to look at the facts, not only about Birchers, Wallaceites, and Southerners, but also about themselves. A realistic appraisal of the attitudinal dilemmas revolving around such issues as busing in the schools, the quota system in the colleges, rentals to blacks and hiring blacks will make it possible for white liberals to be more reality oriented. There should be a lifting of the screens shielding white liberals from the attitudes expressed by their liberal friends.

The alternatives available, faced squarely and realistically, will uncover an entanglement of calcified phrases. In this way, stereotypical thinking will be lifted, so that the real social processes, the status threats, the existence of upward mobility, and the fact of ethnic identification will be studied in terms of their relationships to attitudes, dilemmas, and recognized retreats from a rigidified liberalism. In this process of intellectualization, white liberals will better cope with new interracial situations and will better understand new strategies on the part of blacks and other minority groups in American society. Rather than blinding themselves to the real issues, power struggles, and intergroup conflicts, white liberals will enable themselves to perceive new alternatives and issues created by new interracial situations. Rather than steadfastly reiterating that "color makes no difference," white liberals will make possible new evaluations of interethnic social encounters.

Liberalism will be perceived in innovative terms, as liberals permit themselves to perceive interethnic social situations in terms of new definitions. Indeed, rather than white liberals, liberals from many different ethnic groups will be found. Minority group members who become higher in their education, occupation, and standard of living will fight for equality. Due to their past experience of discrimination and prejudice, these people may become leaders in endeavors to attain egalitarianism.

Current issues are not resolved easily. Should school integration be accomplished by the merger of city-suburban units creating metropolitan area population bases which include several ethnic groups? Or should autonomy of local control with the rights of parents and ethnic communities to control their own districts be instituted? Should assignments to schools and affirmative action goals in employment be set on the basis of race, color, creed, or sex to insure racial, ethnic, and sex balance in the major institutions? Or, alternately, should school composition and employment be determined, irrespective of race, color, creed, or sex? Is the American Creed used to support principles of egalitarianism as well as to rectify institutionalized inequities? Do themes in the American Creed camouflage and shroud prejudicial attitudes and discriminatory behavior? Are separate schools inherently unequal? Do affirmative action plans provide for inclusion of those previously excluded or do they facilitate "reverse discrimination" and "preferential treatment"? How do these plans affect the degree of conflict between minority groups, and between minority groups and women? What will the courts decide?

New supporters of social justice, as well as traditional supporters, may define interethnic situations in terms other than the traditional definition of integration. In order to attain the goals of better opportunities for all, some may redefine political, economic, and social situations in a manner preserving their racial and ethnic differences. They may recognize the desirability of maintaining their "own turf." They might view traditional concepts of integration as outmoded and as representing only one method of attaining social justice. In effect, they will define the social scene by recognizing the differential cultural heritages of peoples and will find methods for the egalitarian diffusion of power and privilege with the recognition of these differences.

REFERENCES

1. Lewis M. Killian, *The Impossible Revolution?* 1968, p. 147.
2. Jerome Skolnick, *The Politics of Protest*, 1969, p. 171.
3. Paul B. Sheatsley, "White Attitudes Toward the Negro," *Daedalus*, (Winter, 1966), p. 220.
4. Karl Mannheim, *Ideology and Utopia*, p. 40.
5. Walter Lippmann, *Public Opinion*, 1922, p. 21.
6. Robert K. Merton, *Social Theory and Social Structure*, 1949, p. 513.
7. Pierre Van den Berghe, *Race and Racism*, 1967, p. 32.
8. Roger W. Brown and Eric H. Lenneberg, "Studies in Linguistic Relativity," in Proshansky and Seidenberg, editors, *Basic Studies in Social Psychology*, 1965, p. 252.

Bibliography

Abelson, Robert P. "Modes of Resolution of Belief Dilemmas." *Journal of Conflict Resolution* 3:343-352, Dec., 1959.

Abelson, Robert P.; Aronson, Elliot; McGuire, William J.; Newcomb, Theodore M., Rosenberg, Milton J.; and Tannenbaum, Percy H., editors. *Theories of Cognitive Consistency: A SourceBook.* Chicago:Rand McNally and Co., 1968.

Abramson, Joan. *The Invisible Woman: Discrimination in the Academic Profession.* San Francisco:Jossey-Bass Publishers, 1975.

Abramson, Rudy. "Ford Won't Visit Louisville Due to Busing Threat." *Los Angeles Times,* October 10, 1975.

Ackerman, Nathan W., and Jahoda, Marie. *Anti-Semitism and Emotional Disorder: A Psychoanalytic Interpretation.* New York:Harper & Row, 1950.

Adorno, T.W.; Frankel-Brunswik, E.; Levinson, D.J.; and Sanford, R.N. *The Authoritarian Personality.* New York:Harper & Row, 1950.

Allport, Gordon W. *The Nature of Prejudice.* Reading, Mass.:Addison-Wesley, 1954.

Alsop, Joseph. *Los Angeles Times,* editorial, January 6, 1970.

Austin, Lee. "Pasadena Tells Plan to Alter Integration Ordered by Court: Elimination of 'Forced' Busing Would be Accomplished by Returning District to Neighborhood School Concept." *Los Angeles Times,* December 19, 1973.

Banfield, Edward C. "Atlanta: Strange Bedfellows." *Big City Politics.* New York:Random House, 1965.

Banton, Michael. *Roles: An Introduction to the Study of Social Relations.* New York: Basic Books, 1965.

Bell, Daniel, ed. *The Radical Right.* Anchor Books. New York:Doubleday and Co., Inc., 1964.

Bell, Daniel. "The Dispossessed (1962)," in Daniel Bell, ed., *The Radical Right.* Anchor Books. New York:Doubleday and Co., 1964, pp. 1-45.

Bendix, Reinhard. *Max Weber: An Intellectual Portrait*. Anchor Books. New York: Doubleday and Co., Inc., 1962.

Bendix, Reinhard, and Lipset, Seymour Martin, eds. *Class, Status, and Power*. 2nd ed., New York:The Free Press, 1966.

Benoit-Smullyan, Emile. "Status, Status Types and Status Interrelationships." *American Sociological Review* 9:151-161, 1944.

Berelson, Bernard R.; Lazarsfeld, Paul F.; and McPhee, William N. *Voting*. Chicago: The University of Chicago Press, 1954.

Bergholz, Richard. "State GOP Calls for End to Forced Busing: Central Committee Urges Congress to Pass Amendment." *Los Angeles Times*, September 22, 1975.

Berson, Lenora E. *The Negroes and The Jews*. New York:Random House, 1971.

Berube, Maurice R., and Gittell, Marilyn, editors. *Confrontation at Ocean Hill-Brownsville.* New York:Praeger Publishers, 1969.

Bettelheim, Bruno, and Janowitz, Morris. *Dynamics of Prejudice*. New York: Harper and Brothers, 1950.

Blake, Gene. "Pasadena Schools Told to Integrate: Judge Rules That Racial Balance Must be Achieved by September." *Los Angeles Times*, January 21, 1970.

Blalock, Hubert M., Jr. "Status Consciousness." *Social Forces* 37:243-248, Mar., 1959. *Toward a Theory of Minority Group Relations*. New York:John Wiley & Sons, 1967.

Blau, Peter M., and Duncan, Otis Dudley. *The American Occupational Structure*. New York:John Wiley & Sons, 1967.

Blauner, Robert. "Internal Colonialism and Ghetto Revolt." *Social Problems* 16:393-408, Spring, 1969.

Bogardus, Emory S. "Racial Reactions by Regions." *Sociology and Social Research* 54:286-290, Mar.-Apr., 1959.

"Race Reactions by Sexes." *Sociology and Social Research* 43:439-442, July-Aug., 1959.

"Racial Distance Changes in the United States During the Past Thirty Years." *Sociology and Social Research* 43:127-135, Nov.-Dec., 1958.

"A Social Distance Scale." *Sociology and Social Research* 17:265-271, Jan., 1933.

"Measuring Social Distance." *Journal of Applied Sociology* 9:229-308, Mar.-Apr., 1925.

Bose, Christine E. *Jobs and Gender: Sex and Occupational Prestige*. Baltimore:Johns Hopkins University, Center for Metropolitan Planning and Research, 1973.

Bramel, Dana. "Dissonance, Expectation, and the Self." in Abelson, et al., eds. *Theories of Cognitive Consistency: A Sourcebook*. Chicago:Rand McNally and Co., 1968.

Brink, W., and Louis Harris. *Black and White*. New York:Simon and Schuster, 1966.

Bronz, S.H. *Roots of Negro Racial Consciousness*. New York:Libra, 1964.

Brown, Roger W., and Lenneberg, Eric H. "Studies in Linguistic Relativity." Harold Proshansky and Bernard Seidenberg, eds. *Basic Studies in Social Psychology*. New York:Holt, Rinehart and Winston, 1965.

Caditz, Judith. "Dilemmas of the White Liberal: A Study in the Application of Anti-Discriminatory Principles to Current Situations." Ph.D. dissertation, University of California, Los Angeles, 1972.

"Coping With the American Dilemma: Dissonance Reduction Among White Liberals." *Pacific Sociological Review*, 1977.

"Ethnic Identification, Interethnic Contact, and Belief in Integration Among White Liberals." *Social Forces*, Spring, 1976.

"Ambivalence Toward Integration: The Sequence of Response to Six Interracial Situations." *The Sociological Quarterly* 16:16-32, Winter, 1975.

"Dilemmas Over Racial Integration: Status Consciousness vs. Direct Threat." *Sociological Inquiry* 45:51-58, Winter, 1975.

"Jewish Liberals in Transition." *Sociology and Social Research* 59:274-287, April, 1975.

Campbell, Angus. *White Attitudes Toward Black People.* Ann Arbor, Michigan: Institute for Social Research, The University of Michigan, 1972.

Campbell, Angus; Converse, Philip E.; Miller, Warren E.; and Stokes, Donald E. *The American Voter.* 5th ed. New York:John Wiley & Sons, 1967.

Campbell, Donald T., and LeVine, Robert A. "A Proposal for Cooperative Cross-Cultural Research on Ethnocentrism." *The Journal of Conflict Resolution* 5:82-108, Mar., 1961.

Carmichael, Stokely, and Hamilton, Charles V. *Black Power: The Politics of Liberation in America.* Vintage Books. New York:Random House, Inc., 1967.

Clark, Kenneth B. *Dark Ghetto: Dilemmas of Social Power.* New York:Harper Torchbook, 1967.

Clark, Kenneth B., and Clark, Mamie P. "Racial Identification and Preference in Negro Children." in Eleanor Maccoby, Theodore M. Newcomb, and E.L. Hartley, eds., *Readings in Social Psychology,* 3rd ed., New York:Holt, Rinehart and Winston, 1958.

Cohen, Rabbi Henry. *Justice, Justice A Jewish View of the Negro Revolt.* New York: Union of American Hebrew Congregations, 1968.

Coleman, James S.; Campbell, Ernest Q.; Hobson, Carol J.; McPartland, James; Mood, Alexander M.; Weinfeld, Frederick D.; and York, Robert L. *Equality of Educational Opportunity.* U.S. Office of Education, 1966.

Coser, Lewis. *The Functions of Social Conflict.* New York:The Free Press, 1956.

DeFleur, Melvin L., and Westie, Frank R. "Verbal Attitudes and Overt Acts." *American Sociological Review* 23:667-673, Dec., 1958.

Deutsch, Morton, and Collins, Mary E. *Interracial Housing: A Psychological Evaluation of a Social Experiment.* Minneapolis:The University of Minnesota Press, 1951.

Donoghue, John. "The Social Persistence of an Outcaste Group." George DeVos and Hiroshi Wagatsuma, eds., *Japan's Invisible Race: Caste in Culture and Personality.* Berkeley:University of California Press, 1966.

Dollard, John; Doob, Leonard W.; Miller, Neal E.; Mowrer, Orval H.; and Sears, Robert R. *Frustration and Aggression.* New Haven:Yale University Press, 1939.

Edwards, Allen L. *Techniques of Attitude Scale Construction.* New York:Appleton-Century-Crofts, Inc., 1957.

Epstein, Benjamin R., and Forster, Arnold. *The Radical Right: Report on the John Birch Society and Its Allies.* Vintage Books. New York: Random House, Inc., 1967.

Fendrich, J.M. "A Study of the Association Among Verbal Attitudes, Commitment, and Overt Behavior in Different Experimental Situations." *Social Forces* 45:347-355, Mar., 1967.

Festinger, Leon. *A Theory of Cognitive Dissonance.* 6th ed. Stanford:Stanford University Press, 1968.

Fine, Morris, and Himmelfarb, Milton, eds. *American Jewish Yearbook 1969.* New York:The American Jewish Committee, 1969.

Fishel, L.H., Jr. and Quarles, B. *The Negro American: A Documentary History.* Glenview, Ill.:Scott Foresman, 1967.

Fuchs, Lawrence H., ed. *American Ethnic Politics.* Harper Torchbooks. New York: Harper & Row, 1968.

The Political Behavior of American Jews. Glencoe:The Free Press, 1956.

Gans, Herbert J. "Negro-Jewish Conflict in New York City: A Sociological Evaluation."

Midstream 15:3-15, Mar., 1969.

Geltman, Max. *The Confrontation: Black Power, Anti-Semitism, and the Myth of Integration.* Englewood Cliffs, New Jersey:Prentice-Hall, 1970.

Glazer, Nathan. *American Judaism.* Chicago:The University of Chicago Press, 1957.

"Blacks, Jews, and the Intellectuals." *Commentary* 47:33-39, April, 1969.

"Negroes and Jews: The New Challenge to Pluralism." *Commentary* 38:29-34, Dec., 1964.

Goffman, Erving. *Encounters.* Indianapolis:Bobbs-Merrill Co., Inc., 1961.

The Presentation of Self in Everyday Life. Anchor Books. New York:Doubleday & Co., Inc., 1959.

Goldberg, Peter. "Are Women Prejudiced Against Women?" *Transaction* 5:28-30, April, 1968.

Goldbloom, Maurice J. "The New York School Crisis." *Commentary* 47:43-58, Jan., 1969.

Goldschmid, Marcel L., ed. *Black Americans and White Racism.* New York:Holt, Rinehart and Winston, Inc., 1970.

Goldstein, Sidney, and Goldscheider, Calvin. *Jewish Americans: Three Generations in a Jewish Community.* Englewood Cliffs, New Jersey:Prentice-Hall, 1968.

Goode, William J. "A Theory of Role Strain." *American Sociological Review* 25:483-496, Aug., 1960.

Gordan, Milton M. *Assimilation in American Life.* New York:Oxford University Press, Inc., 1964.

"Assimilation in America: Theory and Reality." *Daedalus* 90:263-285, Spring, 1961.

Greeley, Andrew M. "Ethnicity and Racial Attitudes: The Case of the Jews and the Poles." *American Journal of Sociology* 80:909-933, Jan., 1975.

Green, Bert F., Jr. "Attitude Measurement," Gardner Lindzey, ed., *Handbook of Social Psychology.* Reading, Mass.:Addison-Wesley, pp. 335-369, 1954.

Greenblum, Joseph, and Pearlin, L.I. "Vertical Mobility and Prejudice," Reinhard Bendix, and Seymour Martin Lipset, eds., *Class, Status, and Power.* New York: Free Press, pp. 480-491, 1953.

Guttman, Louis. "The Basis for Scalogram Analysis," Samuel A. Stouffer; Louis Guttman; Edward A. Suchman; Paul F. Lazarsfeld; Shirley A. Star; and John A. Clausen, eds., *Studies in Social Psychology in World War II.* Vol. IV. *Measurement and Prediction.* Princeton:Princeton University Press, pp. 60-90, 1950.

Hager, Philip. " 'Quota Mentality' in Seeking Equality Rapped by Educator: Merit Still Should Be Determining Factor, San Jose State President Declares in Speech." *Los Angeles Times,* February 15, 1975.

Harris, Louis, and Swanson, Bert E. *Black-Jewish Relations in New York City.* New York:Praeger Publishers, 1970.

Henry, A.F. "A Method of Classifying Non-scale Response Patterns in a Guttman Scale." *Public Opinion Quarterly* 16:94-100, Spring, 1952.

Herberg, Will. *Protestant, Catholic, Jew.* Garden City, New York:Doubleday & Co., Inc., 1955.

Himmelfarb, Milton. "Is American Jewry in Crisis?" *Commentary* 47:33-42, Mar., 1969.

Hofstadter, Richard. "The Pseudo-Conservative Revolt (1955)," Daniel Bell, ed., *The Radical Right.* New York:Doubleday and Co., Inc., 1954, pp. 75-95.

Houston, Paul. "Rights Advocates Clash on Quotas Ban." *Los Angeles Times,* May 1, 1975.

Hyman, Herbert H., and Sheatsley, Paul B. "The Authoritarian Personality: A Methodological Critique," R. Christie, and Marie Jahoda, eds., *Studies in the Scope and Method of The Authoritarian Personality*. Glencoe, Ill.:Free Press, 1954.

Katz, Daniel, and Braly, Kenneth W. "Verbal Stereotypes and Racial Prejudice," Eleanor E. Maccoby; Theodore M. Newcomb; and Eugene L. Hartley, eds., *Readings in Social Psychology*. 3rd ed. New York:Holt, Rinehart and Winston, Inc., 1958.

Katz, Shlomo, ed. *Negro and Jew*. London:The Macmillan Co., 1967.

Kaufman, Walter C. "Status, Authoritarianism, and Anti-Semitism." *American Journal of Sociology* 62:379-382, Jan., 1957.

Killian, Lewis M. *The Impossible Revolution?* New York:Random House, 1968.

Korey, William. "Quotas and Soviet Jewry." *Commentary* 57:55-57, May, 1974.

Kornhauser, William. *The Politics of Mass Society*. New York:The Free Press, 1959.

Kuper, Leo. *An African Bourgeoisie: Race, Class, and Politics in South Africa*. New Haven:Yale University Press, 1965.

Kuper, Leo, and Smith, M.G., ed, *Pluralism in Africa*. Berkeley:University of California Press, 1969.

Kutner, B.; Wilkins, C.; and Yarrow, P. "Verbal Attitudes and Overt Behavior Involving Racial Prejudice." *Journal of Abnormal and Social Psychology*, 47:649-652, Oct., 1952.

LaPiere, R.T. "Attitudes vs. Action." *Social Forces* 13:230-237, Dec., 1934.

Leavy, Zad. Letter to The Regents of the University of California for the Pacific Southwest Regional Office, Anti-Defamation League of B'nai B'rith, July 12, 1972.

Letter to Trustees of the California State University and Colleges for the Pacific Southwest Regional Office, Anti-Defamation League of B'nai B'rith, July 14, 1972.

Lenski, Gerhard E. *The Religious Factor*. Anchor Books. New York:Doubleday & Co., Inc., 1963.

"Status Crystallization: A Non-Vertical Dimension of Social Status," *American Sociological Review*, 19:405-413, August, 1954.

Lewin, Kurt. *Resolving Social Conflicts*. New York:Harper & Row, 1948.

Linn, L.S. "Verbal Attitudes and Overt Behavior: A Study of Racial Discrimination." *Social Forces* 43:353-364, March, 1965.

Lippmann, Walter. *Public Opinion*. New York:The Macmillan Co., 1922.

Lipset, Seymour Martin. *Political Man: The Social Bases of Politics*. Anchor Books. New York:Doubleday and Co., Inc. 1963.

Lipset, Seymour Martin, and Bendix, Reinhard. *Social Mobility in Industrial Society*. Berkeley:University of California Press, 1959.

Litt, Edgar. *Ethnic Politics in America*. Glenview, Ill.:Scott, Foresman, 1970.

Lohman, J.D., and Reitzes, D.C. "Deliberately Organized Groups and Racial Behavior." *American Sociological Review*, 19:342-344, June, 1954.

Lubell, Samuel. *The Future of American Politics*. New York:Harper & Row, 1951.

Mannheim, Karl. *Ideology and Utopia*. Translated by Louis Wirth and Edward Shils. Harvest Book. New York:Harcourt, Brace & World, Inc., 1936.

Massey, Grace Carroll; Scott, Mona Vaughn; and Dornbusch, Sanford M. "Racism Without Racists: Institutional Racism in Urban Schools." *The Black Scholar* 3:2-11, Nov., 1975.

Mathews, Linda. "Supreme Court Declines to Rule on Reverse Discrimination Case." *Los Angeles Times*, April 24, 1974.

Mead, George Herbert. *Mind, Self and Society*. Chicago:University of Chicago Press, 1934.

Merton, Robert K. "Discrimination and the American Creed," Robert M. MacIver ed., *Discrimination and National Welfare.* New York:Institute for Religious and Social Studies, pp. 99-126, 1949.

    Social Theory and Social Structure. 11th ed. Glencoe: The Free Press, 1967.

Minard, R.D. "Race Relations in the Pocahontas Coal Fields." *Journal of Social Issues,* 8, No. 1:29-44, 1952.

Myrdal, Gunnar. *An American Dilemma.* New York:Harper & Row, 1944.

New York City Board of Education. "City-Wide Ethnic Census N.Y.C. Schools." October 31, 1973.

Nilson, Linda B. "The Occupational and Sex Related Components of Social Standing." *Sociology and Social Research,* 1976.

Northrup, Herbert R. *Organized Labor and the Negro.* New York:Harper & Row, 1944.

Park, Robert E. "The Concept of Social Distance," *Journal of Applied Sociology* 9:339-344, March-April, 1925.

Pasadena Unified School District. Department of Planning, Research and Development. "Racial and Ethnic Distribution of Enrollments." Research Report No. 75/76-02, November 6, 1975.

Pettigrew, Thomas F. *Racially Separate or Together?* New York:McGraw-Hill, 1971.

Photiadis, John D., and Biggar, Jeanne, "Religiosity, Education, and Ethnic Distance." *American Journal of Sociology* 67:666-672, May, 1962.

Powers, Charles T. "Troops, Police Ready for Violence: Boston Uneasy on Eve of School Year." *Los Angeles Times,* September 9, 1975.

Raab, Earl. "The Black Revolution and the Jewish Question." *Commentary* 47:23-33, January, 1969.

Rawitch, Robert and Austin, Lee. "Pasadena Board Enthusiastic: Officials See Chance to 'Expose' Busing." *Los Angeles Times,* November 12, 1975.

Reiss, Albert J., Jr. *Occupations and Social Status.* New York:The Free Press, 1961.

Rubin, Lillian B. *Busing & Backlash.* Berkeley:University of California Press, 1972.

Rudwick, Elliott M. *Race Riot at East St. Louis, July 2, 1917.* Carbondale, Ill.:Southern Illinois University Press, 1964.

Rush, Gary B. "Status Consistency and Right-Wing Extremism." *American Sociological Review* 32:86-92, February, 1967.

Salazar, Ruben. "Head Start Fails Them, Chicano Group Says." *Los Angeles Times,* November 5, 1969.

    "Black-Brown Friction Growing," *Los Angeles Times,* October 26, 1969.

    "Black and Chicano Ties Worsen After Walkout at Santa Barbara," *Los Angeles Times,* September 15, 1969.

Schermerhorn, R.A. *Comparative Ethnic Relations.* New York:Random House, 1970.

Schuman, Howard. "Attitudes vs. Actions versus Attitudes vs. Attitudes." *Public Opinion Quarterly* 36:347-354, May, 1972.

Sears, David O., and McConahay, John B. "Racial Socialization, Comparison Levels, and the Watts Riot." *Journal of Social Issues* 26:121-140, Jan., 1970.

Selznick, Gertrude J. and Steinberg, Stephen. *The Tenacity of Prejudice: Anti-Semitism in Contemporary America.* New York:Harper & Row, 1969.

Sheatsley, Paul B. "White Attitudes Toward the Negro," *Daedalus* 95:217-238, Winter, 1966.

Silberman, Charles E. *Crisis in Black and White.* Vintage Book. New York:Random House, 1964.

Simmel, Georg. *Conflict and the Web of Group-Affiliations.* Translated by Kurt Wolff and Reinhard Bendix. 2nd ed. Free Press Paperback, New York:Macmillan Co., 1966.

Simpson, George E., and Yinger, J. Milton. *Racial and Cultural Minorities.* New York: Harper & Row, 1972.

Sklare, Marshall. *American's Jews.* New York:Random House, 1971.

——— ed., *The Jews: Social Patterns of an American Group.* New York:Free Press, 1958

Skolnick, Jerome. *The Politics of Protest.* New York:Simon and Schuster, 1969.

Solomon, Judge Gus J. *The Jewish Role in the American Civil Rights Movement.* Jewish Topics of Today, No. 10. London: The World Jewish Congress, British Section, 1967.

Steinberg, Stephen. "How Jewish Quotas Began," *Commentary* 47:67-76, September, 1971.

Stonequist, Everett. *The Marginal Man.* New York:Charles Scribner's, 1937.

Stouffer, Samuel A. *Communism, Conformity and Civil Liberties.* New York:Doubleday & Co., Inc. 1955.

Sumner, William G. *Folkways.* Boston:Ginn, 1906.

Treiman, Donald J. "Status Discrepancy and Prejudice." *American Sociological Review* 34:651-664, May, 1966.

Turner, Ralph H. "The Public Perception of Protest." *American Sociological Review* 34:815-831, December, 1969.

——— "Role-Taking: Process Versus Conformity," in Arnold M. Rose, ed., *Human Behavior and Social Process.* Boston:Houghton Mifflin, 1962.

——— "Role-Taking, Role Standpoint, and Reference-Group Behavior," *American Journal of Sociology* 61:316-328, 1956.

——— *The Social Context of Ambition.* San Francisco:Chandler publishing Co., 1964.

Turner, Ralph H., and Killian, Lewis M. *Collective Behavior.* Englewood Cliffs, New Jersey:Prentice-Hall, Inc., 1972.

Turner, Ralph H., and Surace, Samuel J. "Zoot-Suiters and Mexicans: Symbols in Crowd Behavior." *The American Journal of Sociology* 62:14-20, July, 1956.

Tumin, Melvin M. *Desegregation: Resistance and Readiness.* Princeton:Princeton University Press, 1958.

Tumin, Melvin; Barton, Paul; and Burrus, Bernie. "Education, Prejudice and Discrimination: A Study in Readiness for Desegregation," *American Sociological Review* 23:41-49, Feb., 1958.

U.S. Bureau of the Census. "Educational Attainment, March, 1969." *Current Population Reports,* P-20, No. 194, February 19, 1970.

——— "Income in 1968 of Families and Persons in the U.S." *Current Population Reports,* P-60, No. 66, December 23, 1969.

U.S. Commission on Civil Rights. *Civil Rights, U.S.A., Racial Isolation in the Public Schools,* 1967.

——— *Higher Education Guidelines-Executive Order 11246.* October 1, 1972.

U.S. Department of Health, Education, and Welfare. Office for Civil Rights. *Directory of Public Elementary and Secondary Schools in Selected Districts. Enrollment and Staff by Racial/Ethnic Group,* 1968.

——— *Directory of Public Elementary and Secondary Schools in Selected Districts. Enrollment and Staff by Racial/Ethnic Group,* 1970.

——— *Directory of Public Elementary and Secondary Schools in Selected Districts. Enrollment and Staff by Racial/Ethnic Group,* 1972.

Van den Berghe, Pierre L. *Race and Racism.* New York:John Wiley & Sons, Inc. 1967.

Warner, Lyle G., and DeFleur, Melvin L. "Attitude as an Interactional Concept: Social Constraint and Social Distance as Intervening Variables Between Attitudes and Action." *American Sociological Review* 34:153-169, April, 1969.

Weber, Max. "Class, Status, Party," H.H. Gerth and C. Wright Mills, eds. and trans., *From Max Weber*. New York:Oxford University Press, Inc., pp. 180-195, 1946. *The Theory of Social and Economic Organization*. A.M. Henderson and Talcott Parsons, trans. New York:Oxford University Press, Inc., 1947.

Westie, Frank R. "The American Dilemma: An Empirical Test," *American Sociological Review* 30:527-538, August, 1965.

Westin, Alan F. "The John Birch Society," Daniel Bell. ed., *The Radical Right*, Anchor Books. New York:Doubleday and Co., 1964, pp. 239-268.

Will, George F. "Busing and the Frightening Prospect for '76." *Los Angeles Times*, June 4, 1974.

Williams, Robin M., Jr. *Strangers Next Door*. 2nd ed. Englewood Cliffs, New Jersey: Prentice-Hall, Inc., 1964.

Wilner, Daniel M.; Walkley, Rosabelle P.; and Cook, Stuart W. *Human Relations in Interracial Housing*. Minneapolis:University of Minnesota Press, 1955.

Wirth, Louis. "The Problem of Minority Groups," Ralph Linton, ed., *The Science of Man in the World Crisis*. New York:Columbia Press, 1945, pp. 347-372.

Wish, H. *The Negro Since Emancipation*. Englewood Cliffs, New Jersey:Prentice-Hall, Inc., 1964.

Subject Index

Affirmative action, *See also* Preferential treatment, Quotas, Reverse discrimination
  Chicago Plan, 25
  definition in Executive Order 11246, 21
  fear of, 1, 21, 24, 97
  issues around, 21-27
  Philadelphia Plan, 25, 97
  "reverse discrimination," 21, 26, 171
  Undergraduate Recruitment and Development Program, UCLA, 24
American Civil Liberties Union, 20
American Creed,
  can camouflage prejudice, 20, 32, 171
  ideology of, 1, 17, 20-21, 32-33, 45, 51, 158
  respondents' belief in six interracial situations, 38-42
  white liberals' ambivalence, 79-80, 89, 101, 135-136
  white liberals' belief in, 37-38
American Dilemma, 1-2, 32-33
Anti-Defamation League, 22, 29-31
Anti-Semitism, 6, 93, 94, 113, 155, 156 159
  black, 10, 118, 137

Apartment rental situations,
  respondents' ambivalence toward, 73-75, 79-87
  respondents' support for, 73
Assimilation, 115, 116, 118, 128-132
Authoritarian personality, 6, 93, 113, 155, 156

Bagley Act, in California, 19-20
Berkeley school district, 2
Black power movement,
  ideology of, 10-11, 16, 115, 157-158
Brown v. Board of Education, 2, 14, 157
Burakumin or eta, 114
Busing, school,
  Berkeley, 2-3
  Biden and Byrd amendments, 20
  Boston, 3, 4, 155
  California Republican Party, 20
  Chinese community in San Francisco, 11-12
  Detroit, 8
  Gallup Poll, 2
  Gary, Indiana, 5, 6
  Inglewood, 12
  Los Angeles, 3, 54
  Louisville, 4, 5, 155

Author Index